THE DEMISE AND REBIRTH OF AMERICAN THIRD PARTIES

Virtually all academic books on American third parties in the last half-century assume that they have largely disappeared. This book challenges that orthodoxy by explaining the (temporary) decline of third parties, demonstrating through the latest evidence that they are enjoying a resurgence, and arguing that they are likely to once again play a significant role in American politics. The book is based on a wealth of data, including district-level results from US House of Representatives elections and state-level election laws after the Civil War, and recent district-level election results from Australia, Canada, India, and the UK.

Bernard Tamas is Assistant Professor of Political Science at Valdosta State University. He was a Postdoctoral Fellow at Harvard University, Fulbright Scholar to Central European University in Budapest, Hungary, Visiting Research Scholar at Columbia University, and software developer at Princeton University. He has also taught at Williams College and Brandeis University. Tamas is the author or co-author of four books.

Praise for *The Demise and Rebirth of American Third Parties*

Backed by stunning scholarship, Bernard Tamas boldly encounters and deconstructs one of the prize shibboleths of political science: that the United States is a two-party system, full stop. Sensitive both to the reigning arguments that assume permanent major-party hegemony and to hangdog efforts to showcase third parties, Tamas focuses on two critical factors that herald a new era of third party growth: rising polarization and the media revolution that gives third parties hitherto shut out by the monopolistic major parties a strong voice that can be heard by millions of people. He makes a fresh and compelling case.

John Rensenbrink, *Bowdoin College;*
Co-founder, United States Green Party and Maine Green Independent Party

If you agree with the conventional wisdom that third parties are doomed to remain relegated to the margins, read this book. You will be in for a surprise. Bernard Tamas's highly innovative, mixed-method analysis makes a convincing case for the resurgence of third-party dynamics that is crucial for understanding American politics in the age of Trump.

Manfred B. Steger, *University of Hawai'i-Manoa and RMIT University*

Bernard Tamas skillfully challenges the conventional wisdom that American politics is doomed to an unchallengeable two-party system. Combining a deep grasp of the theoretical literature with sure-handed statistical analysis, this book persuasively argues that the time has arrived for innovation and disruption by new third parties. As the nation declines into the nadir of Trumpism, we must hope that Tamas provides one alternative path that leads us toward a revival of democracy in the United States.

Gerald Pomper, *Rutgers University*

With sound scholarship and a provocative argument, *The Demise and Rebirth of American Third Parties* addresses a question that many Americans will find compelling in the face of increasingly negative partisan attitudes.

Marjorie Randon Hershey, *Indiana University-Bloomington; Author of* Party
Politics in America

This book offers a fresh analysis of the American two-party system. Through impressive historical research and insightful observation of contemporary politics, Tamas persuasively argues that third parties will increasingly benefit from technological change and elite polarization. As in our past, third parties may significantly affect national party politics in our future.

Kenneth Janda, *Northwestern University*

An enlightening contribution on third parties, this book delivers a serious challenge to the conventional wisdom that minor parties are perpetually on the margins of the American political system. Scholars and students looking for a comprehensive understanding of the fluctuating performance of third parties in modern American history must read this book.

Brian Frederick, *Bridgewater State University*

We like to teach students that the two-party system flows neatly out of our voting rules. Bernard Tamas shows how third parties emerge, in spite of those, when the party system becomes unresponsive. Scholars of parties both major and minor have much to gain from Tamas' polarization thesis.

Jack Santucci, *Democracy Fund*

THE DEMISE AND REBIRTH OF AMERICAN THIRD PARTIES

Poised for Political Revival?

Bernard Tamas

NEW YORK AND LONDON

Published 2018
by Routledge
711 Third Avenue, New York, NY 10017

and by Routledge
2 Park Square, Milton Park, Abingdon, Oxon, OX14 4RN

Routledge is an imprint of the Taylor & Francis Group, an informa business

© 2018 Taylor & Francis

The right of Bernard Tamas to be identified as author of this work
has been asserted by him in accordance with sections 77 and 78 of the
Copyright, Designs and Patents Act 1988.

All rights reserved. No part of this book may be reprinted or
reproduced or utilised in any form or by any electronic, mechanical,
or other means, now known or hereafter invented, including
photocopying and recording, or in any information storage or retrieval
system, without permission in writing from the publishers.

Trademark notice: Product or corporate names may be trademarks
or registered trademarks, and are used only for identification and
explanation without intent to infringe.

Library of Congress Cataloging-in-Publication Data
A catalog record for this book has been requested

ISBN: 978-0-8153-5637-0 (hbk)
ISBN: 978-0-8153-5639-4 (pbk)
ISBN: 978-1-3511-2826-1 (ebk)

Typeset in Bembo
by codeMantra

To my wife and partner, Rie, with all my love

CONTENTS

List of Figures	*x*
List of Tables	*xii*
Acknowledgments	*xiii*

	Introduction: A Third-Party Revival?	1
1	Unraveling the Conundrum of Third-Party Decline	14
2	Duverger's Law and the American Electoral System	34
3	The Impact of Ballot Access Laws	57
4	The Prohibition of Fusion	76
5	Do Primaries Undermine Third Parties?	95
6	Co-optation and Third-Party Waves	114
7	The Decline and Rise of Political Polarization	129
8	The Evolution of Party Resources	146
	Conclusion: A Reemergence of Third Parties?	169

Bibliography	*185*
Index	*193*

FIGURES

I.1	Percent vote for third-party and independent House candidates, 1870–2016	4
I.2	Percent of House districts with third-party candidates by decade, 1870–2016	5
I.3	Median percent vote for third-party House candidates by decade, 1870–2016	6
2.1	Average percent seats won and votes received for two strongest parties in SMP and PR systems	41
2.2	Average percent votes for two strongest parties in four SMP countries, 1945–2015	47
2.3	Mean percent vote for third parties at district level	52
2.4	Percent of district-level elections that third-party candidate could have spoiled	54
3.1	Difficulty of ballot access laws, 1886–2016	63
3.2	Average percent of districts that have easier ballot access requirements	66
3.3	Percent third-party candidates on House ballot compared to signature requirements	67
3.4	Impact of ballot access laws on probability a district will have a third-party candidate	72
4.1	Percent of districts having different types of fusion candidacies, 1870–2016	80
4.2	Percent of House districts with third-party and fusion candidates by decade, 1870–2016	86
4.3	The percent of House districts with third-party candidates in fusion versus non-fusion states, 1870–2016	90

4.4	The percent vote for third-party candidates in fusion versus non-fusion states, 1870–2016	91
5.1	Rise of primaries and decline in third-party vote, 1870–2016	103
5.2	Impact of primaries on whether a House district had third-party candidates, 1904–1924	106
5.3	Percent of districts with primary elections and third-party candidates, 1880–2016	107
5.4	The impact of primary elections on third parties in Minnesota and Wisconsin, 1870–2016	109
6.1	Percent House vote for third parties and predicted co-optation years, 1870–2016	118
6.2	Percent potential third-party electoral subversion, 1870–2016	120
6.3	Shifting mean of percent House vote for third-party candidates and 1932 election	123
6.4	Percent vote for Progressive and Socialist party candidates, 1900–1940	124
7.1	Partisan polarization and third-party activity, 1880–2014	137
7.2	Ideological polarization and third-party activity	140
7.3	Impact of polarization on the vote for third-party candidates by decade, 1890–2014	142
8.1	Campaign spending by types of House candidates, 2014	153
8.2	Mean percent district-level vote and expenditures for third parties across SMD systems	161
C.1	Median percent vote for third-party House candidates, 1920–2016	177

TABLES

3.1	Impact of ballot access laws on third-party success in House elections, 1890–2014	70
4.1	Impact of fusion on third-party success in House elections, 1870–2014	89
5.1	Impact of primary elections on third-party success in House elections, 1904–1924	105
7.1	Impact of polarization on third-party success in House elections, 1870–2014	138
8.1	Regression of third-party vote on campaign expenditures and electoral system in Australia (2013), Canada (2009), the United Kingdom (2010), and United States (2010)	162

ACKNOWLEDGMENTS

I have far more people to thank for their help in the various stages in developing this book than I will be able to mention here. I especially wish to thank Kenneth Janda, Manfred Steger, Garrett Glasgow, Michael Baun, Gerald Pomper, and Marc Hetherington for their significant contributions to my thinking on this project as I developed it.

The research behind this book began as a study of the impact of ballot access laws on third parties with Matthew Dean Hindman, my graduate student at the time and currently Assistant Professor at University of Tulsa. We began with the assumption that ballot access laws had a significant, negative impact on American third parties, as had been argued throughout the third-party literature, and so our goal was to specify in more detail how these laws helped secure the overwhelming domination of the Democratic and Republican parties. Instead, after tracing the history of these laws through each state's session laws, which we found mostly on microfiche in the basement of the University of Illinois's College of Law library, we discovered to our surprise that there was little relationship between these election laws and third-party activity and voter support. Even more surprising, considering the state of the third-party literature, we also found significant evidence that third parties had not simply disappeared but had instead been gaining strength since 1968.

One of the great things about science is that it can often be more interesting to be wrong than right, and our initial failure spurred my determination to get to the bottom of what actually drives third parties in America. Like most research without clear answers, this one had periods of sputtering and stopping, but eventually I came to the conclusion that most of the widely held explanations for the long-term decline of third parties should be reevaluated. I have long believed that Walter Dean Burnham was right that American party

xiv Acknowledgments

politics evolves through periods, and the evidence I found convinced me that this applies to third parties as well. The middle of the twentieth century was not the end of American third parties but simply a period in which they were particularly weak.

Throughout this process, quite a few students, both graduate and undergraduate, helped me work through the vast range of data collected for this study. I am very thankful to Tami Stone for expertly organizing the mountain of ballot access law information we had gathered, for example, and to the graduate students in my Research Seminar in American Third Parties at Illinois State University (Jake Owen, Tanya Austin, Lindsay Barber, Kara Bavery, Anthony Bolton, Amanda Conley, Russell Godwin, Ali Grigoletto, James Keith, Sarah Lager, Tomas Malina, Adrienne Martin, Matt Mills, Vanda Rajcan, Nadejda Sledneva, Tami Stone, Tawnya Taylor, Emily Wittrig, and Zack Wolfe) for helping clean a century of House election data. I am also grateful to David Hanna at Valdosta State University for helping update the data on ballot access laws.

I am indebted to my colleagues at Valdosta State University who contributed to my thinking on third parties: James LaPlant, Michael Baun, Mandi Bates Bailey, Napolean Bamfo, and Marc Pufong. For me, one of the most important presentations of this research was at my job talk at VSU, which turned into a free-flowing debate in which colleagues enquired about virtually every major theory on American third parties. The questions they posed to me became central questions I repeatedly asked myself as I worked through the research behind the book. I would also like to thank VSU for consistently providing funding towards completing this project through a First Year Faculty Grant, Faculty Research Seed Grant, several Faculty Scholarships, and additional funds from the office of Connie Richards, VSU's Dean of Arts and Sciences.

I am very appreciative of the professional and supportive guidance I received from the editors and reviewers at Routledge, who have consistently allowed me the freedom to maintain my vision for this book. In particular, I wish to thank Jennifer Knerr, Ze'ev Sudry, and Natalja Mortensen.

I reserve special thanks for my father-in-law, Debabrata Chakraborti, who not only helped me better understand the intricacies of Indian electoral politics but through our discussions also led me to fundamentally change my perspective on Duverger's Law.

Finally, I wish to thank my wife and partner, Rie Debabrata Tamas, for the physical and emotional support she provided me as I conducted this research, along with the intellectual contributions she made through every stage of the book. Having earned her PhD in Sociology at UK's Essex University, Rie chose not to pursue an academic career and instead joined the United Nations Development Programme, in order to work at the grassroots towards improving the lives of those most vulnerable. This also drives her engagement with

STOP, an anti-trafficking movement in India founded by her mother, Roma Debabrata. Watching Rie's inexhaustible commitment to others, whether it be the well-being of her family, including our daughter, Kaashvi, or her work with trafficked survivors, I am continually reminded that the research questions I ask need to focus on issues that affect people's lives and futures. For these and many other reasons, and with the greatest depth of love, I dedicate this book to Rie, my comrade-in-arms.

Bernard Tamas

INTRODUCTION

A Third-Party Revival?

It has become almost a truism in American political science that third parties in the United States have largely vanished and are unlikely to ever again play anything beyond the most marginal role. Indeed, while third parties repeatedly disrupted American elections a century ago, currently they barely have any electoral impact. In elections to the House of Representatives from 1870 to 1940, third parties received over 10% of the vote four times: in 1878 (15%), 1894 (11%), 1912 (21%), and 1914 (13%). Since 1940, however, third-party House candidates received over 3% of the vote only twice: in 2000 (3.33%) and 2006 (3.01%).[1] The data seemingly gives strong reason to believe that American third parties have become obsolete organizations with little chance of having any future impact on US politics.

Political scientists have explained this apparent disappearance of American third parties with a large array of reasons: that the American winner-take-all elections as well as the Electoral College undermine small parties (Rosenstone, Behr and Lazarus 1984), that state election laws are designed to hinder all third-party efforts (Winger 1997), that Americans have a cultural predisposition to support only two political groups and are therefore weary of third parties (Romance 1998), and that whenever third parties become too strong, the major parties simply co-opt their rhetoric and issues (Gillespie 2012). Indeed, there is a long list of explanations that scholars who study third parties (who I will refer to simply as "third-party scholars") provide as to why these parties virtually disappeared by the middle of the twentieth century. These explanations consistently point to a permanent end to American third parties.

I find that there are two critical problems with these arguments. The first is that they are mostly based on little statistical research. These explanations can often be traced to the 1940s or 1950s, and yet political scientists have only begun testing them statistically in the last decade or so. As I will demonstrate in

2 Introduction

this book, the evidence for these commonly held explanations are often weak at best and non-existent at worst. The second problem is that the consensus image of third parties is outdated by half a century. While third parties did indeed become largely inactive outside of New York State by 1950, they have since begun a revival that has gone largely undetected by third-party scholars.[2] Starting during the contentious 1968 election, third parties began gradually running more and more candidates for elected office. By the 2000 election, third parties ran candidates in 71% of races to the House of Representatives, a level that had not been reached since 1916. Over the same period, when given a third-party option, voters are selecting third-party candidates at significantly higher rates than half a century ago. The median vote for third-party House candidates when there is at least one on the general election ballot, for example, spiked in 2016. Indeed, the median vote for third-party candidates when at least one is on the ballot is now at the highest level since the 1910s.

In other words, unnoticed by most political scientists, third parties have entered a new period. While in the late nineteenth and early twentieth century they staged waves of disruptive electoral attacks against the major parties, and while in the mid-twentieth century they were largely dormant outside of New York State, the beginning of the twenty-first century sees them becoming active again but not as of yet producing the waves of voter support that characterized American electoral politics a century ago. Still depending on arguments formulated over half a century ago, third-party scholars now face a new set of questions and conundrums, including why American third parties are reviving, and why these revived movements do not receive the level of voter support that they used to? The answers to these questions, I conclude, lead directly to the prediction that third parties will likely once again play the type of disruptive electoral role that they did a century ago.

In this book, I explain why third parties declined by the middle of the twentieth century, why they are in the midst of a significant rebound, what barriers they still face in attracting voters, and why evidence, including from the 2016 presidential election, suggests that they will likely once again play a significant role in American politics.

While third-party scholars have provided a slew of explanations as to why third parties are weaker today than a century ago, I argue, to the contrary, that there are two critical factors that affect the strength of third parties: polarization and resources. The level of third-party activity, including running candidates for office, is mostly a consequence of the level of political polarization in the United States, and as American politics has gotten more polarized over the past few decades, third parties have gotten more active. The critical problem facing third parties today is that they are unable to mobilize the resources needed to compete in election campaigns waged over expensive, modern mass media. However, continued political polarization combined with changes in ways that campaigns both raise money and advertise themselves (which were highlighted in the 2016 nomination campaigns of Bernie Sanders and Donald Trump) suggest that third parties may be at the cusp of again playing a significant role in American politics.

Indeed, the first Trump presidential term is a moment of considerable uncertainty in American politics. It is not clear, for example, whether the Republican Party can remain intact, or whether it will split between its populist and traditional conservative wings. A party split fueled by internal wars over severe policy divisions and by Trump's brash leadership style could easily echo the divide that led Roosevelt's Progressives to leave the Republican Party in 1912. Even without a split, the intensity of these divisions may produce an opening for the Libertarians or another third party on the right to gain the support of disenchanted Republican voters. That possibility is increased further by high levels of partisan polarization, since Republicans unhappy with their own party will be less likely to consider Democratic candidates a viable alternative than they would have been a few decades ago. On the Democratic Party side, the high percent of young voters open to Sanders's social democratic message may suggest a developing crisis for that party as well. Indeed, at a time when democracies across the globe are seeing major parties being challenged by new and extreme parties, including with a third party (Emmanuel Macron's En Marche!) winning control over the French government in 2017, it is no longer possible to assume that the Republicans and Democrats will retain the electoral domination that they have held since the 1950s. Instead, the evidence I will present in the following suggests an increased probability of the American party system entering a new era in which third parties again play a significant, disruptive role.

Third-Party Revival

The decline of third parties is one of the most fundamental changes in American politics during the twentieth century. Traditionally, third parties had played a disruptive role through repeated waves of voter support that threatened the political careers and legislative majorities of both the Democratic and Republican parties. In the early 1890s, for example, the challenge by the Populists, often running under the label of the People's Party, helped push the Democrats towards more progressive stances by the 1896 election. Similarly, in 1912, the Progressive Party further damaged the Republican Party, which had lost control of Congress in 1910 presumably because of the reactionary policies of President Taft, and may have helped pressure the government towards more progressive reforms. Since then, however, a handful of high profile third-party and independent candidates aside, no third-party movement has had this type of effect nationally.

4 Introduction

This change is demonstrated graphically in Figure I.1. It shows the percent vote for third-party[3] and independent House candidates since 1870. While independent candidates have consistently had little impact on congressional elections,[4] third parties have gone from playing a significant role to effectively none at all. In the first half of this period, from 1870 to 1940, the average percent vote for third-party House candidates was around 5%. In the second half, from 1942 to 2012, that figure was a mere 1%. The more significant difference is the variation in the vote. In House elections before 1940, the votes for third parties were more like a wave. While it could sink to as low as 1%, in elections such as those in 1878 and 1912, third parties could receive as much as 21% of the vote. After 1940, however, the vote for third-party candidates in congressional elections was largely flat and virtually always under 3%.

But there is a caveat to this observation. Third parties are in the midst of a revival. This revival is demonstrated visually in Figure I.2, which shows the average percent of House races with third-party candidates by decade from 1870 to 2016. As the graph shows, third-party candidates regularly ran in 70% or more of the House races in the period from 1880 to 1918. In 1892 and 1894, at the height

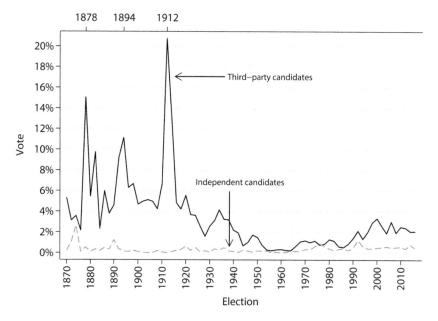

FIGURE I.1 Percent vote for third-party and independent House candidates, 1870–2016. The graph shows the total percent vote of all third-party and independent candidates in races to the House of Representatives from 1870 to 2016. It demonstrates that the percent vote for third-party candidates was much higher in the period before 1920 and that this third-party vote often came in waves. The graph also demonstrates that the percent vote for independent candidates has been consistently low throughout this 146 year period.

of the Populist movement, there were third-party candidates in nine out of every ten House races. But after 1916, that campaign activity dropped steadily. By the 1950s, on average fewer than 20% of House districts had at least one third-party candidate. As Figure I.2 also shows by separating between districts in New York State and the rest of the country, during the 1960s one-third of House districts with third-party candidates were in New York. A low point was reached in 1962, when there were third-party candidates in only thirty-three House races, or 8%. Fourteen of these districts, or 42%, were in New York State.

In 1968, during one of the most contentious years in American history, the percent of House districts with third-party candidates began rising. Initially jumping from 13% to 30% of districts from 1966 to 1968, the activity of third parties gradually rose in the decades that followed. During the 2000 election, there were third-party candidates in over 70% of the districts, a level that had not been reached since 1916. Since then, on average, third-party candidates have been running in half of House districts each two years.[5]

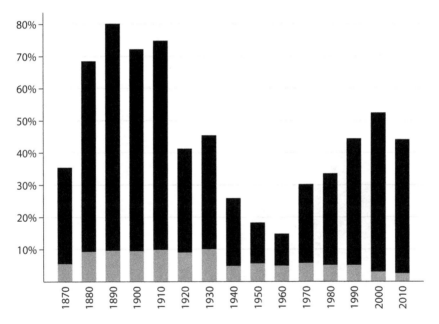

FIGURE I.2 Percent of House districts with third-party candidates by decade, 1870–2016. The graph shows the average percent of House districts with at least one third-party candidate from 1870 to 2008. The gray section shows when the district is in New York State while the black section is when that district is from any other state. The graph demonstrates that after the 1910s, third-party activity gradually declined and reached a low of 15% of House districts in the 1960s; one-third of these House districts were in New York State. The graph also shows that in the 1970s, the percent of districts with third-party candidates began to climb. In the 2000s, on average 53% of House districts had at least one third-party candidate.

6 Introduction

This revival is also occurring in the vote for third-party House candidates, when voters have the option of voting for a third-party candidate. Indeed, to some degree Figure I.1 hides this change in the third-party vote because it shows the percent vote overall for third-party House candidates, including when there is no third-party candidate running in a district. Figure I.3 focuses on districts with third-party candidates. It shows the median total percent vote for third-party candidates by district in House elections when there was at least one third-party candidate on the ballot. This graph shows that the median vote for third-party candidates was high in the last decades of the nineteenth century and early decades of the twentieth century, especially the 1910s. In the 1920s, this figure began to drop, reaching a low point in the 1950s at around half a percent (0.6%). Starting in the 1970s, the median vote for third-party candidates began rising again. In the 2010s (the House elections from 2010 to 2016), that figure reached 3.6%, or the highest point since the 1910s. Indeed, this measure of the third-party House vote is higher in the 2010s than every other decade since the 1880s except two: 1890s (4.1%) and 1910s (6.7%).

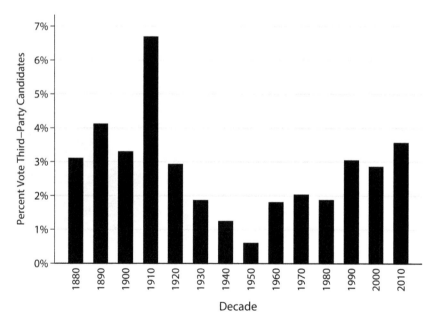

FIGURE I.3 Median percent vote for third-party House candidates by decade, 1870–2016. The graph shows the median total percent vote for third-party candidates in each House district by decade *if there was at least one third-party candidate on the ballot*. The graph demonstrates that the vote for third-party candidates had been high in the late nineteenth and early twentieth century, declined dramatically by the 1950s, and then slowly rose again over the next half century. As the graph shows, this measure of third-party vote is currently higher than during all other decades since the 1880s except the 1890s and 1910s.

In other words, the critical difference in third-party support between today and a century ago is the lack of waves. In the period from 1870 to 1918, a dramatic jump in voter support for third-party candidates happened once every decade or two, but the last such wave ended in 1914, just over a century ago. Beyond that, the amount of third-party activity and voter support today looks more like that of the 1880s than the 1950s.

The Third-Party Conundrum

This evidence of a decline and then revival of third parties over the past century produces a new set of questions for third-party scholars. Instead of simply disappearing by the middle of the twentieth century, third parties have instead demonstrated a significant decline by the mid-1940s, only to be followed by a gradual rebirth that began in the late 1960s. But, as of yet, that rebirth has not translated into the type of large waves of voter support that regularly occurred a century ago.

This book attempts to solve these interrelated conundrums: why are third parties so much weaker in the United States than in other countries with similar electoral systems? Why did third parties nearly disappear by the middle of the twentieth century? What is driving the revival of these parties at present? And why has that revival not translated into more votes for third-party candidates?

My answers to these questions challenge much of what has been written by political scientists about third parties over the past half century. I argue and present evidence that the demise and rebirth of American third parties was driven not by oft-touted factors like ballot access laws[6] or primary elections,[7] but by a decline and reemergence of partisan polarization in the United States over the same period. I also find that third parties have not as yet been able to capitalize on their newfound activity and presence because electoral campaigning has changed fundamentally in the last century. While political parties a century ago could run campaigns like social movements, fueled primarily through passionate commitment and dedicated workers (Klinghard 2010), today they are run largely by professional consultants that rely heavily on cutting edge, modern communications technology. This requires raising a significant amount of money, a prerequisite that is much more difficult for today's third parties to reach.

There is also an underlying reason why third parties in America have so few resources vis-à-vis the major parties. I argue that having elections in single-member districts leads to critical resources gravitating to the two largest parties, which in turn helps those two parties win more elections. I argue that this explanation adds to the widely cited theory often referred to as Duverger's Law (Duverger 1954, 216–28).

Duverger argued that the single-member plurality system (SMP), like in the United States, favors the two-party system for three reasons. (1) The simple mechanics of SMP reduces the vote for smaller parties. While a party that receives

8 Introduction

10% of the vote in a proportional representation (PR) system will likely receive something more than 10% of the seats in the parliament or congress, in an SMP system that party will likely receive no seats at all unless that vote is geographically concentrated. (2) Voters want to avoid wasting their vote and therefore gravitate to one of the top two candidates. (3) Parties also want to avoid dividing the vote between multiple parties in a disadvantageous way. Therefore, when there are more than two parties, smaller parties tend to fuse with a larger party in order to avoid handing the election to the least liked major party.

Duverger's Law is an important theory that provides a clear, simple explanation for why there tends to be fewer parties in countries with SMP instead of PR systems. Nonetheless, the theory has its limitation. It cannot explain, for example, why the vote for third-party candidates in the United States is so much lower than in other SMP countries such as the UK, Canada, and India; why in these other SMP countries voters often "waste" their vote in exactly the manner that Duverger argued that they would not; why small parties regularly do not join larger parties in most SMP systems, as he had predicted; and why the vote for third-party candidates in Australia is no higher than in most major SMP countries, even though Australia's preferential voting electoral system eliminates all rational concerns about vote wasting.

I argue that SMP does reduce the vote for third parties, but that Duverger underestimated the number of ways that electoral systems affect the competition among political parties. Specifically, I argue that electoral systems also impact the distribution of resources across parties. As Duverger argued in his mechanical explanation, smaller parties are generally allocated fewer seats in SMP than PR systems even when they receive the same percent of the vote. Party resources, I argue, then gravitate towards those parties that have won seats, including any money automatically given to winning parties by the government, public exposure gained by having representatives in the congress or parliament, and funding by interest groups hoping to influence policy. The more elected positions the party wins, generally speaking, the more resources it is likely to acquire. This produces a self-reinforcing process: parties that win seats tend to gain more resources, and those resources then help those parties to continue winning seats.

Thus, while the mechanics of SMP as well as the strategic behavior of both voters and parties in SMP systems can weaken smaller parties, as Duverger argued, the method for allocating elected positions in SMP (and other single-member district systems) also tends to reward the largest parties with greater political resources. This distribution of resources away from third parties, I argue in Chapter 8, is especially pronounced in the United States. Unlike third parties in other SMP systems, American third parties are competing in a campaign environment that requires significant financial resources at the same time that there is neither public financing of campaigns nor caps on campaign spending.

Introduction **9**

Despite facing these resource challenges, I contend in my concluding chapter that third parties are now in a position to again begin making significant inroads into American electoral politics. This is because, one, the political polarization that fuels these parties and their agendas is clearly continuing, and all current indicators, including widespread support for candidates like Bernie Sanders and Donald Trump during the 2016 nomination campaign as well as the Trump victory, suggest that it is only intensifying. Two, while one can expect the Democratic and Republican parties to retain significant resource advantages over third parties, new doors for gaining critical resources and challenging the major parties are opening. As the past few presidential nomination campaigns have demonstrated, especially the 2016 Sanders nomination campaign, candidates with an anti-establishment appeal can raise significant funding over the internet as well as use social media as a much less expensive approach for advertisement and outreach. To date, however, third parties have not capitalized on these changes. The critical question therefore becomes whether third parties can also learn to effectively apply these approaches. While one can expect that the major parties will always have a significant funding and advertisement advantage, I predict that third parties can realistically make enough inroads to return to their previous disruptive role.

Chapters Outline

The remainder of this book is presented in eight chapters and a conclusion. My detailed argument is presented in Chapter 1, which commences with an overview of the many theories put forward to explain why American third parties are so weak. The chapter then explains why some of these popular explanations can be rejected and put to the side. For example, some scholars have argued that the Electoral College is a primary reason that third parties are so weak. I argue and present evidence that the Electoral College cannot explain the weakness and especially the decline of American third parties. This chapter similarly demonstrates how "American political culture," which some scholars believe is intrinsically opposed to third parties, cannot explain why third-party support was once high and then declined. In this way, the chapter whittles the discussion down to a handful of much stronger arguments.

Chapters 2–8 examine other third-party theories in more detail. Chapter 2 explores Duverger's Law, or the argument that SMP electoral systems favor the two-party system. The chapter outlines the strengths of Duverger's Law as well as some of its key weaknesses, including that the theory as it currently stands cannot explain why third parties are weaker in the United States than in other SMP countries.

Chapter 3 explores the theory that ballot access laws undermine third parties. Many third-party scholars have argued that since the 1890s, when states began instituting the Australian ballot, states have been making ballot access

10 Introduction

laws steadily harder to the point that it is nearly impossible for third parties to get their candidates onto the ballot. In this chapter, I show that while these laws have indeed gotten more arduous over the twentieth century, they have had little impact on the ability of third parties to either get their candidates onto the ballot or to win votes. Moreover, I demonstrate that the ballot access law explanation is clearly wrong, since over the past few decades steadily more third-party candidates have been getting onto the ballot across the country despite these requirements remaining high.

Chapter 4 investigates the argument that the prohibition of fusion undermined third parties. Fusion is a campaign strategy in which a single candidate is co-nominated by multiple parties, often the Democrats or Republicans and one or more third party. A number of third-party scholars have argued that fusion was widely used in the late-nineteenth century and that this was a primary reason why third parties were effective then. As the argument continues, state legislatures across the country, especially those dominated by Republicans, overwhelmingly prohibited fusion, which undermined third parties. This chapter demonstrates that a decline in the use of fusion cannot explain the decline in third-party support, since fusion was in fact not widely used in the last decades of the nineteenth century, except in two elections: 1872 and 1896. The evidence I present also suggests that third-party success most likely leads to fusion candidacies, and not the other way around: fusion is mostly a co-optation strategy employed by the major parties when third parties are already strong.

Chapter 5 delves into the primaries, or when major parties began nominating candidates through public votes instead of party caucuses. Following an argument often attributed to V.O. Key (1956), third-party scholars often make the argument that primaries led to third parties being undermined. Since opposition groups can challenge the establishment within the nomination process itself, there is no incentive to run third-party candidacies. While this argument is consistent with candidate behavior in presidential primaries, including both Bernie Sanders and Donald Trump's nomination bids in 2016, at the state level there is no statistical relationship between when primary laws were enacted and when third parties declined. For example, Minnesota and Wisconsin were among the first northern states to require major party nominations for House elections (1901 and 1903, respectively), but they also had among the most vibrant third-party movements, which in both cases lasted into the 1940s.

Chapter 6 explores co-optation, or the argument that whenever third parties become a threat to a major party, that major party undermines the third party's agenda by adopting its issues and rhetoric and sometimes by joining forces with it, such as by running fusion candidacies with it. Proponents of this argument often point to the 1896 election, when William Jennings Bryan ran as a Democrat and Populist fusion candidate while adopting many of the Populists' stances. But, a key piece of evidence touted in support of the argument that co-optation led to the decline of third parties is FDR and the New Deal, which some believe undermined third parties on the left by expanding the social safety net and by allowing the Democratic Party to adopt the rhetoric of labor and socialist parties. As this chapter shows, there are a number of problems with using co-optation as an explanation for the decline of third-party vote, including that third-party support was already on the decline by the time FDR took office and that this co-optation in the 1930s cannot explain why eighty years later third parties had still not recovered.

Chapter 7 explores the polarization explanation for the decline and reemergence of third parties. The chapter shows that third-party activity and partisan polarization, as measured by DW-NOMINATE scores for members of the House of Representatives, are closely related. They both follow the same long-term pattern. Both polarization and third-party activity were very high in the late nineteenth and early twentieth century, both declined dramatically by the middle of the twentieth century, and both began rising again around the 1970s and 1980s. Moreover, as I will demonstrate in this chapter, these polarization levels are also closely related to third-party activity (and before the 1950s, the third-party vote) at the district level. Indeed, a highly polarized political environment can increase public support for third parties in a number of ways, including because the increased intensity of conflict among politicians can decrease public trust in the political system and because polarization might be closely related to other forms of political discontent, such as rising income inequality.

Chapter 8 explores the resources argument. The chapter shows how the rise of candidate-centered campaigning in the United States produced a political environment in which it became nearly impossible for third-party candidates to compete against their major party rivals. It also shows how the consolidation of the news media over the twentieth century helped lead to third parties having virtually no avenues open for advertising themselves to the mass public. The chapter also demonstrates how the mechanics of SMP reduces resources third parties acquire and why this adds to a strategic advantage of the two largest parties. Finally, the chapter shows how the rise of the internet and social media is creating a political environment that no longer produces an overwhelming resource advantage for the two largest parties.

The concluding chapter focuses on how both the rising polarization of American politics and the changes in communication technologies, especially the rise of the internet and social media, suggest that third parties are likely on the cusp of playing a significant, disruptive role in American politics again. On the resource side, the key is that the Democratic and Republican establishments are losing their gatekeeping ability. Bernie Sanders demonstrated in 2016 that opposition candidates can raise large sums of money over the internet from small donors. Additionally, with the proliferation of the news media and especially the rise of social media, the political elite can no longer control the information that is reaching the public, especially among the current generation of

12 Introduction

young voters, who receive most of their news through social media platforms. I conclude my findings and analyses by looking ahead and outlining the barriers that third parties still face and why these will likely be overcome in the near future, paving the way for a significant rebirth of third parties in the United States.

Notes

1 This data was gathered from Dubin (1998) as well as the Federal Election Commission's website at www.fec.gov. The data for the 2016 election was gathered from www.thegreenpapers.com.
2 A notable exception is Collet and Wattenberg (1999), who found that the percent of House districts with third-party candidates increased from 1968 to 1986. Even Collet and Wattenberg, however, did not realize that in 1968 that percent was already an increase from the low in 1962 or that this percent would continue rising.
3 For all elections since the late 1960s, third-party vote is calculated as 100 times the total vote for all House candidates nominated by a political party other than the Democratic and Republican parties divided by the total vote for all House candidates. However, this simple approach biases the results towards certain states before 1967, when Congress passed the Single-Member District Mandate. Before this point, states often had a combination of regular districts and at-large districts, and sometimes these at-large districts elected multiple House seats. In 1912, for example, Pennsylvania had thirty-six House seats, with four of those seats selected through at-large elections. This effectively meant that Pennsylvania voters voted five times for House races, and since Pennsylvania was a state with active third parties, this repeated voting would effectively inflate the third-party vote. For this reason, in each state, the third-party vote and the total vote were divided by the number of seats the constituents were electing before the final calculation was made.
4 The consistently low percent of districts with independent candidates over the last century and a half (as compared to candidates nominated by a third party) is important because it helps us define what "third party" means. Many third-party scholars, including Rosenstone, Behr, and Lazarus (1984), define a third-party candidate as any candidate who is not nominated by the Democratic or Republican party, even if that candidate is independent of any party label. I argue, to the contrary and following the general norm in the party politics literature (Downs 1957; Epstein 1967; Pomper 1992), that political parties are organizations that run candidates for elected office under a single label. If candidates are not running under a party name—indeed, the term "independent" quite literally means not affiliated with a political party—then they by definition are not third-party candidates. To further this point, Figure I.1 demonstrates empirically that third-party and independent candidates are in different categories: In House races since 1870, even as the impact of third parties have changed dramatically, independent candidates have consistently received a very small fraction of the vote.
5 Since the 2000 election, much of this revival has been driven primarily by two third parties: The Libertarians and the Greens. In the 2016 elections, for example, just over 52% of third-party House candidates were Libertarians, and another 23% were Greens. This domination by one or two third parties has been common since the Civil War, including during the moments of significant third-party activity. For example, in 1878 and 1880, the Greenbacks ran 62% and 70% of the House third-party candidates. During the 1894 election, the Populists/People's Party and

the Prohibitionists together ran 89% of the House third-party candidates. Similarly, in 1914, the Progressives and Socialists together ran over two-thirds of the House third-party candidates, and they also together received over 80% of the third-party vote. Indeed, since 1870, one party ran over half of the third-party House candidates in just under one-third of the elections.

6 Ballot access laws are state requirements that a political party must meet in order to place candidates' names on the ballot. These laws vary widely by state and generally include requirements like submitting a petition signed by a certain number of registered voters. Third-party scholars often argue that these laws have gotten much more difficult over the twentieth century and have made it nearly impossible for most third parties to get onto the ballot (Winger 1997).

7 Some political scientists argue that once major parties began selecting nominees through primary elections instead of closed party caucuses, opposition movements stopped running third-party candidates since they could simply run their candidates for major party nominations (Herrnson 1997).

1

UNRAVELING THE CONUNDRUM OF THIRD-PARTY DECLINE

A century ago, third parties played a critical role in American politics. Today, their impact is largely inconsequential. In this book, I ask why. And I refute the traditional explanations that have been provided to date for the decline of third parties.

For many third-party scholars, the near disappearance of third parties is no mystery. Anyone who has read or even skimmed through much of the American third-party literature, or for that matter even taken any undergraduate courses in American politics, may assume that this is an easy question with a well-established set of answers. Doesn't the American electoral system lead inevitably to a two-party system? Aren't ballot access laws so difficult that third-party candidates can rarely get on the ballot? Hasn't fusion been banned by most state legislatures, and hasn't this undermined these parties? Doesn't the Electoral College discourage voters from supporting third parties? Isn't the two-party system simply a consequence of American political culture?

These arguments and the others cited as follows are all well-entrenched in the current third-party literature. Political scientists have provided a dizzying number of explanations for why third parties are weaker today than a century ago, often in long chapters that seem to outline every reasonable argument the authors know without an attempt to determine which of these explanations might be more consistent with empirical evidence. Over the past decade or so, some political scientists have begun testing these explanations statistically, like Hirano and Snyder (2007), for example, and their results have called into question some of the arguments put forward by third-party scholars. I demonstrate, however, that the problems with this literature go beyond the details of which rules set by state legislatures do greater damage to third parties. Instead, I contend that third-party scholars have fundamentally misunderstood why third parties largely stopped running candidates and winning waves of voter support in the mid-twentieth century.

My conclusions are based on statistical analyses of an extensive amount of data related to third-party activity in races to the House of Representatives. Election results for all House races from 1870 to 2016 (78,000 candidates in 30,000 district-level elections) were collected using Dubin (1998) as well as data provided by the Federal Election Commission at www.fec.gov. Unofficial results from the 2016 House elections were downloaded from www. thegreenpapers.com.[1] The data also includes ballot access laws for each state from 1890 until the present, most of which was gathered by tracing through the session laws of each state stored on microfiche at the University of Illinois Law School library. This book also tests the veracity of Duverger's Law, which I present along with a comparative analysis of electoral systems similar to those of the United States. Consequently, I have gathered district-level election data for parliamentary elections in Australia (2013), Canada (2011), India (2009), and the UK (2010).

I chose to analyze elections to the House of Representatives instead of presidential or senatorial elections because the focus of this book is on third-party movements, not individual candidates. At both the presidential and senatorial levels, data on third parties can be heavily influenced by a small number of exciting candidacies, both because there are so few cases and because the higher profile offices can attract more individuals with their own political or financial resources. The success of an individual third-party candidate does not necessarily reflect or translate into success for a third-party movement. For example, in 1992 and 1996, Ross Perot ran one of the most successful independent and then third-party bids for the White House in American history. Yet, despite having Perot heading the ticket, the Reform Party ran candidates for only a small percent of other offices. At its height, in 2000, the Reform Party had candidates in 8% of House elections, compared to the Libertarian Party, which fielded candidates in 55% of districts. The Reform Party effectively collapsed during that election, while the Libertarians continue to run a large number of candidates. Thus, while Perot's bid for the White House was important—it certainly provided strong evidence against the argument that Americans are predisposed to always vote against third-party candidates—the more important evidence on the electoral fortunes of third-party movements comes from lower offices in which many candidates are running for many seats.

Senatorial races produce even more problems. There are only 100 US senators, and only around thirty-three run during each two-year election cycle. Unlike House elections, the number of senatorial races in each cycle are very low, and the locations of these races change every two years. Senate election results have another problem for a study on third parties. The 17th Amendment to the Constitution, which requires that senators be elected by the people instead of appointed by state legislatures, was ratified in 1913, after the last great

16 Chapter One

third-party wave. In other words, there were no senatorial elections before third parties largely disappeared from American politics, and therefore, there is no way to use this data to determine why the vote for third parties declined starting around 1920. For these combined reasons, my analysis focuses on the House of Representatives, or the lowest legislative races for which there is adequate and consistent data since the Civil War.

This analysis has led me to conclude that the standard narrative on American third parties is mostly wrong and falls significantly short of explaining the full potential that third parties present. I establish instead that the decline of third parties was a temporary phenomenon and predict, based on the evidence I gathered, that third parties are very likely to commence playing a significant role in American politics. The current turmoil driven by Donald Trump's unexpected victory simply adds fuel to a process that has been already developing over decades.

The first step in analyzing long-term changes in third-party behavior and the electoral impact of these movements requires working through the many arguments that have previously been proposed by political scientists and sorting out the most robust from among them. In this chapter, I commence that analysis.

Current Theories on Third-Party Decline

Explanations for third-party decline fall into roughly five categories. The first are structural explanations. Proponents argue that the underlying structure in how the United States runs elections undermines all but the top two parties. These structural reasons are usually blamed on the American founders, who inadvertently created these while writing the US Constitution. The second are state election laws. According to these arguments, states changed their election laws over the twentieth century in ways that undermined third parties, sometimes on purpose, sometimes as an unexpected consequence. The third is the notion of major parties taking strategic steps that undermine third parties, including delegitimizing these parties at the same time that they co-opt their issues. The fourth category is cultural; it is the argument that Americans have a cultural predisposition to favor two major parties. The final, fifth category are political resources, such as money, media attention, and the ability to attract competent politicians.

My focus is on arguments published by political scientists on the weakness of American third parties. I am addressing only theories about the decline of third parties presented by multiple scholars in academic books and peer reviewed articles. Similarly, I am not addressing larger philosophical debates within political science as a field. For example, in rejecting the political culture argument for the decline of American third parties, I am not making a general statement about the influence of political culture on the workings of democratic political systems, nor am I arguing for or against the existence of American political culture. I am instead addressing specific arguments within the third-party literature that claim that these parties are weak because Americans have a cultural predisposition to vote for only two parties, an argument that I believe has no empirical foundation. Indeed, as I will discuss in the following, I am critical of much of what has become the established literature over the past half century on American third parties.

Structural Explanations

There are two main structural explanations for weak third parties. The first is the electoral system, or the underlying rules that govern how American elections are run, or what might be called the full process of translating votes into seats (Farrell 2011, 4). Globally, there are a wide variety of electoral systems, with most countries employing some form of PR. The United States follows the British model of SMP, often called "first-past-the-post." In this system, for any legislature, the region or country is divided into districts that elect a single politician to represent them; whichever candidate receives the most votes, even if it is not a majority, wins the seat. According to Duverger's Law (Duverger 1954, 216–28), this electoral system is supposed to favor two major political parties except in cases when the support for a smaller party is concentrated in one region.

Most books on third parties begin their analysis with Duverger's Law, and even publications that do not explicitly discuss the theory implicitly treat it as a starting point. Under the heading "Constitutional Biases," Rosenstone and his coauthors summarize the argument as follows:

> The only way for a party [in a single-member plurality electoral system] to receive any immediate rewards (other than psychic ones) is for it to gain a plurality of votes. Unlike a proportional representations system where 20 percent of the votes usually yields some seats in the legislature, in a single-member-district plurality system a party can receive 20 percent of the votes in every state and yet not win a single seat. Because citizens know third parties have very little chance of winning, they prefer not to waste their votes on them. Small parties become discouraged and either drop out or join with another party.
>
> *(Rosenstone, Behr and Lazarus 1984, 16)*

It is important to note that, contrary to Rosenstone and his colleagues' implication, the single-member plurality electoral system was never specified in the US Constitution. Indeed, until 1842, one out of every four congressional seats was elected in multimember districts (Tamas 2006). Nonetheless, electoral systems are extremely difficult to reform (Katz 2005), both because they tend to

18 Chapter One

have a high level of legitimacy—few Americans, I would argue, are even aware of the various ways legislatures are elected around the globe—and because those who are winning seats generally do not have an interest in reforming a system that benefits them. In this way, the single-member plurality electoral system in national and most state and local elections is very much a structural part of American politics in a way that, for example, specific ballot access laws (which states regularly revise) are not.

The second structural explanation is the Electoral College, which many third-party scholars argue also harms the prospects of third parties (Rosenstone, Behr and Lazarus 1984, 17; Herrnson 1997, 24; Bibby and Maisel 2003, 62; Gillespie 2012, 23–25). In the most common version of this argument, the most important election for third parties is for the presidency, which helps determine how successful these parties will be for lower offices. However, the Electoral College makes it nearly impossible for third-party and independent presidential candidates to gain success. Since all electoral votes in most states are allocated to the candidate that won the most votes in that state, all candidates except the top two are likely to receive absolutely no electoral votes, unless support for that candidate is highly concentrated in one region. This complete failure at the presidential level translates into little momentum at all in the other levels of party building, making it yet harder for that party to sustain itself and win elections at any level. Gillespie provides one version of the Electoral College argument:

> The winner-takes-all principle [by state for presidential electors] still is firmly entrenched in forty-eight states and the District of Columbia; and because under it no party receives electoral votes without coming in first in some jurisdiction with electoral votes to cast, this means that even those third parties with substantial popular backing are unlikely to receive any share of electoral votes. In 1992 Perot received not even 1 of the 538 electoral votes, despite having taken nearly one in every five popular votes cast...Winner takes all underlies the recurrent charge in mainstream media that popular votes for third-party presidential campaign are likely to accomplish nothing more than to spoil the election for one major-party candidate by tipping to the other major nominee the electoral votes of one or more crucial state.
>
> *(Gillespie 2012, 24)*

State Election Law Explanations

The next set of explanations for third-party weakness are *state election laws*. Generally, these explanations are related to reforms made by state legislatures in the late nineteenth and early twentieth century that had both accidental and intentional consequences on minor parties. Ballot access laws are probably the most widely argued example of state laws that undermine third parties (Rosenstone, Behr and Lazarus 1984, 19–21; Herrnson 1997, 24–25; Winger 1997, 164; Bibby and Maisel 2003, 70; Gillespie 2012, 25–28). Before the Australian ballot, or secret ballot, was instituted in most states between 1890 and 1900, political parties printed their own ballots and handed them out as voters entered the polling places. This approach made various forms of corruption, especially voter fraud and voter intimidation, extremely easy, which led to the introduction of the secret ballot in most states in the 1890s. However, the Australian ballot required states to write their own ballot, which also required states to set rules to decide which candidates and parties would be listed on the ballot. As the argument goes, once state legislatures had established these basic rules, it became very easy for them to make the requirements so hard that it was almost impossible for third parties and independent candidates to get onto the ballot. With such stringent rules, it is argued that it became virtually impossible for third parties to get onto the ballot, effectively eliminating their ability to challenge the major parties.

Some third-party scholars further argue that the outlawing of *fusion* by many states has also undermined third parties. Fusion is a strategy in which a single candidate is co-nominated by multiple parties, often the Democratic or Republican party and at least one third party. It is common in New York State, for example, where both Republicans and Democrats are usually listed by several party names on the ballot. For third parties, fusion produces a way to gain exposure and legitimacy; by nominating major party candidates in some races, they help boost the prospects of their own candidates in other races. However, according to this argument, fusion was abolished by Republican-controlled legislatures in the late nineteenth century, taking this key strategy away from third parties (Argersinger 1980). This decline in fusion, they argue, also helped lead to the decline in third-party strength.[2] This is the primary argument of Lisa Disch in *Tyranny of the Two-Party System* (2002), and it is an argument that has gained wide circulation among third-party scholars (Scarrow 1986; Winger 1997, 164; Gillespie 2012, 28–30).

A third state election law explanation, often attributed to V.O. Key, is the introduction of *primaries* (Epstein 1986, 129–32; Herrnson 1997, 25; Bibby and Maisel 2003, 62–63). Before states began requiring the Democratic and Republican parties to hold primaries to select their nominees, those candidates were generally selected through a caucus system often controlled by the state or local party leadership. Opposition candidates were effectively excluded. Once states began requiring major parties to select their candidates via primaries in the early decades of the twentieth century, the argument goes, opposition became internalized into the two major parties. Instead of having to form a third party and challenge major party candidates in a general election, interest groups could instead promote candidates to run for major party nominations, which both increased the chances of their candidates getting into office and created

20 Chapter One

pressure on major parties to submit to their demands. In this way, primaries became a major reason for the decline of third parties.

A final state law explanation is what are commonly referred to as *sore loser laws*, which disallow candidates who have lost a major party primary to run as an independent candidate. As Bibby and Maisel explain this argument:

> "Sore loser" laws also work to protect the two major parties in many states. Such laws are designed to keep those who lose primary elections from turning around and running in the general election as independents. If candidates were allowed to follow such a strategy, those without firm ties to political parties would have two chances at victory, whereas party loyalists would have only one. Sore loser laws have been upheld by the courts on the grounds that they protect the integrity of the electoral process. There is no question that these laws protect the major parties from fringe candidates who might try to capture major party nominations knowing that they can always run as independents if they lose the first time around.
>
> *(Bibby and Maisel 2003, 71)*

The Co-optation Explanation

The third type of explanation for third-party decline is *co-optation*, an argument made by a wide group of third-party scholars (Rosenstone, Behr and Lazarus 1984, 43–44; Herrnson 1997, 30; Hirano and Snyder 2007; Gillespie 2012, 18). According to this explanation, whenever third parties become a serious threat to one or both of the major parties, those parties respond by stealing the issues or rhetoric that fuel third-party support, thereby winning back supporters who had abandoned them for third-party candidates. This argument hinges mainly on two historical examples: 1896 and 1932. As the 1896 election approached, populist parties were making significant electoral inroads and becoming a significant challenge to the Democratic Party. It was at this point that the Democrats nominated Williams Jennings Bryan, adopted much of the Populist rhetoric, and ran many Democrat-Populist fusion candidates. As an electoral movement, the Populists mostly disappeared after that election. Similarly, in 1932, one of the political advantages of the New Deal for the Democratic Party was that it helped co-opt many of the key demands of progressive and labor parties. Many, including Hirano and Snyder (2007), argue that the New Deal was a critical moment of co-optation that helped eliminate left-wing and pro-labor third parties by the post-World War II era.

A related explanation is *de legitimization* (Rosenstone, Behr and Lazarus 1984, 41–42; Gillespie 2012, 33–36). At the same time that the Democratic Party was adopting issues promoted by third parties, the major parties were also taking steps to undermine the credibility of minor parties. In some cases, like those highlighted by Rosenstone and his coauthors, major party candidates argued against third parties as being a waste of a vote or touted their powerlessness to produce any real policy changes. At the other extreme, third parties were treated as being anti-American or a threat to democracy. The best example of this was the Cold War period, when the conflict against the Soviet Union and anti-communist rhetoric was also used to subvert the standing of third parties, especially socialist, labor, and other workers' parties. Nonetheless, Gillespie shows, there was a long history of this type of attack on third parties that extends back to at least the first Red Scare during the First World War.

The Political Culture Explanation

Some third-party scholars argue that there are cultural reasons why third parties are so weak in the United States. Rosenstone and his colleagues summarize this argument as follows:

> A second prevalent belief is that the two-party system is a sacred arrangement—as American as an institution as the Congress, the Super Bowl, or M★A★S★H. Third party candidates are seen as disrupters of the American two-party system. Thus minor parties do not start out on an equal footing with the Democrats and Republicans; they must first establish their legitimacy—something the voters do not demand of the major parties. This two-party sentiment, of course, reinforces itself: minor parties do poorly because they lack legitimacy, their poor showing further legitimates the two-party norm, causing third parties to do poorly, and so on.
> *(Rosenstone, Behr and Lazarus 1984, 40)*

Others place the argument more within a historical context (Herrnson 1997, 22–23; Romance 1998; Bibby and Maisel 2003, 58–60). The most common argument in this case is that the United States has always divided itself into two ideological camps, and for that reason two large political parties emerged. Some, like Romance, argue that this division dates back to the Foundation, first with the division between the Federalists and Anti-Federalists, then with the division between mercantile interests behind Alexander Hamilton and agriculture interests behind Thomas Jefferson.

Gillespie (2012, 19) presents the culture argument from a different angle. He argues that the reason for this dualism in American politics was the lack of a strong labor movement. While in most Western European countries the labor movement led to the development of socialist and social democratic parties, the much weaker American labor movement had little choice but to be co-opted into the Democratic Party. The labor movement in Great Britain built the Labour Party, which eventually became more dominant than the Liberal Party as well as becoming the key opponent of the Conservative Party. The once

22 Chapter One

dominant Liberals, now the Liberal Democratic Party, remains active in British politics, however, and even won enough seats in Parliament in 2010 to form a coalition government with the Conservatives. Since the labor movement in the United States was never that strong, owing to a lack of class consciousness, Gillespie argues, socialist and labor parties in the United States were never supported enough to effectively challenge the major parties, or survive, much less win enough seats to form coalition governments.

The Political Resources Explanation

The final category of explanations is the disparity of *political resources* between the major and minor political parties (Rosenstone, Behr and Lazarus 1984, 27–39; Herrnson 1997, 25–28). The primary issue here is money. While major party candidates are capable of raising large sums of campaign funding from various sources, third-party candidates are generally unable to garner support from these sources for two main reasons. Most major donors to campaigns see donations as an investment with a hope to influence politicians once they enter office. Since third-party candidates are seen as unlikely to win, they are viewed as a bad investment. Moreover, corporations and other big donors see third parties, especially those politically on the left, as bad investments because they are less likely to promote the interest of these potential sources of money. Third parties are therefore far more dependent on raising money from small donors, although even in this way they are clearly far less capable than major party candidates at gathering significant funding.

Similarly, third parties have tremendous difficulty attracting political professionals and consultants (Rosenstone, Behr and Lazarus 1984, 33–37). Rare, high-profile exceptions like Angus King aside, ambitious politicians are unlikely to run as third-party candidates because running under a third-party label against two major party candidates generally reduces their chances of victory. Similarly, professional consultants are unlikely to work for a third party, since running a failing campaign does not help build one's professional reputation, and, moreover, it can make it impossible for these consultants to build relationships within the two major parties. Third parties are often therefore relegated to attracting activists and idealists who are ill-prepared for intensive political battle against the political professionals in the Democratic and Republican parties.

A third resource issue is media coverage (Rosenstone, Behr and Lazarus 1984, 33–37; Bibby and Maisel 2003, 69–70). With their inability to get public exposure through paid media like television and radio commercials due to lack of funds, third parties become especially dependent on the news media for getting their campaign message to the public. However, third parties and their candidates rarely get much attention from the prominent news outlets. As Rosenstone and his coauthors argue, this lack of media coverage is closely related to a general perception, and the perception of newspaper editors, that third parties are unlikely to win anyway. Since they are unlikely to win, they are also generally considered an uninteresting news story, particularly since news organizations often focus heavily on the "horse race" among competitive candidates.

Finally, third-party scholars sometimes also argue that the rules governing presidential debates also harm third parties (Bibby and Maisel 2003, 67–69; Gillespie 2012, 30–32). Specifically, the televised debates during general election campaigns virtually always include only the Democratic and Republican party nominees. Only Ross Perot in 1992 was able to debate against both major party candidates, while in 1980 John Anderson debated Ronald Reagan in a debate that President Jimmy Carter chose not to attend. The inability of third-party presidential candidates to debate on the same stage as the major party candidates significantly reduces the public exposure those parties receive.

Within the political resources category, while Rosenstone and his colleagues provide a long list of explanations for third-party weakness in Chapter 2, they give their most interesting contribution to the question of third-party decline in Chapter 4:

> Although the third parties of the 1800s closely resembled the major parties, the same cannot be said for those of the twentieth century. The most prominent movements of the 1900s... are all more accurately labeled independent campaigns than political parties... These changes had their parallels within the major parties, which also became more candidate-centered. Both the major and minor parties responded to an evolving environment: technology replaced organization as the crucial ingredient, with less reliance on formal party apparatus.
>
> *(Rosenstone, Behr and Lazarus 1984, 81)*

One could read this analysis to mean that the resources that were deemed important had changed over time. In the period before the rise of modern communication technology, including television, radio, and direct mail, the party organization itself, including the number of active rank-and-file members, was probably the most important party resource. Parties and their campaigns could run more like social movements, and they could piggyback on other movements, such as the labor unions. Today, in contrast, the key resource is probably money. While third parties have always had difficulty raising funds, that problem has become much more serious now that campaigns are often run by consultants over the airwaves.

Shortcomings of these Arguments

I argue that, overall, the current third-party literature has two main problems. The first is lack of parsimony. Instead of whittling theories down to a few

24 Chapter One

key factors, third-party scholars have tended to go in the opposite direction and instead follow more of a "kitchen sink" approach to theorizing. This approach, it seems, fits into a general narrative that third parties are overwhelmed by so many biases in the American political system that there is virtually no chance that they could again have an impact on American politics. Second, the widespread support for these arguments seems to be based not on clear and demonstrable evidence, as one might assume, but instead on little substantiation. Many explanations for third-party decline have been proposed over the past half century, but since evidence for testing these explanations has been so limited, it has been difficult to rule any out.

Why has there been so little statistical testing of key arguments on the weakness of American third parties? One reason might be that reliable data on third parties is difficult to find. For example, much of the research on American voting behavior is based on an ongoing series of detailed, extensive surveys called the *American National Election Study* (ANES). Housed at the University of Michigan's Inter-university Consortium for Political and Social Research (ICPSR), a giant library of social science data, political scientists at most universities and colleges can simply download the ANES and begin conducting analyses, provided that questions related to their research were asked. The ANES, however, rarely includes questions about third parties; there is no way to use this data to track changes in views about, for example, the Greens or the Libertarians in ways that one can track movement in feelings towards or identification with the Democratic and Republican parties.

Another example is the *United States Historical Election Returns, 1824–1968*, which provides district-level returns for elections to the House of Representatives and other offices. In an obvious show of priorities, this study excludes data on all candidates (nearly one out of every four[3]) who did not receive at least 5% of the vote, effectively rendering that data useless for third-party research. Third-party scholars face similar hurdles in other research areas, for example, in gathering information on the history of state election laws that may affect minor parties.

There is likely a historical reason for this paucity of data on and statistical research about American third parties. While the study of politics has a very long history, most scientific research on politics and especially the use of statistical methods began only after the Second World War. This shift in approach to what we now call political science, often called the "Behavioral Revolution," was spearheaded by Charles Merriam and his students at the University of Chicago in the 1940s and then driven further by researchers at the University of Michigan in the 1950s and 1960s (Ricci 1984). Many of the key theories about government and politics that political scientists use today originated during this period.

The problem was that American third parties had already largely disappeared by the time that the Behavior Revolution had been launched. They were already a historical relic and therefore required very little research focus. Political scientists therefore seemed content with presenting explanations that assumed that third parties had permanently disappeared from American politics. For example, E.E. Schattschneider (1942) presented an argument very similar to Duverger's Law, stating that the way the United States runs elections undermines third parties. Similarly, the argument that ballot access laws undermined third parties can also be traced back to the 1940s ("Legal Obstacles to Minority Party Success" 1948). With third parties having largely disappeared by the time political scientists began large-scale data collection, and with prominent political scientists already arguing that their weakness was structural and therefore effectively permanent, there may have been little incentive to commit resources towards further measuring the demise of these organizations.

This historical incongruence may be one reason why other political changes have gained so much more attention by political scientists than the decline of third parties. As a comparison, one might consider research on the incumbency effect, or the tendency of politicians holding certain elected positions, especially as members of the House of Representatives, to win reelection. For members of the House, the incumbent reelection rate began rising rapidly around the 1950s or 1960s. Today, reelection rates to the House of Representatives are almost 100%. When political scientists discovered this development in the 1970s (Mayhew 1974), that topic became a significant research focus. The declining competition for elected positions was clearly seen as a threat to the workings of American democracy, and political scientists began significant research over the possible causes of this phenomenon. In response, in 1978, the ANES revised its procedures to improve the study of congressional elections. Congressional districts became the primary sampling unit, and it significantly expanded the number of survey questions on congressional elections, including candidate thermometers and incumbent job ratings (Hinckley 1980; Mann and Wolfinger 1980).

The great irony here is that the rise of incumbency and decline of third parties in legislative elections are in many ways very similar phenomena. Both are cases of reduced electoral competition, and both pose the same threat to the workings of American democracy. Representative democracy functions best when politicians in office face constant electoral challenge. Without that challenge, and without rotation of who is in power, those in office become more capable of ignoring the needs of the public in favor of the interests of elite groups and the dynamics of intra-party politics. Moreover, a lack of third-party challenge is one factor that helps maintain electoral security and especially safe districts. If third parties today were able to muster the public support that they had gained in 1914—for example, if the Libertarians and Greens gained a much higher percent of the vote—then these challenges would most likely be strongest in exactly the districts that are currently safest for the Republican and Democratic parties.

Of late, there has been an increase in the amount of empirical research, mostly published in peer review journals, exploring third-party weakness or

26 Chapter One

decline statistically. While these studies have increased our understanding of third-party decline, the number of these studies remains comparatively low. A notable example is ballot access laws, one of the cornerstones of third-party theory. Third-party scholars and activists have long argued that state governments have made ballot access laws extremely difficult for third parties, making it almost impossible for these parties to even run in general elections. While Dowling and Lem (2009) found that signature requirements reduced the number of minor party candidates in gubernatorial elections from 1980 to 2005, most other studies (Collet and Wattenberg 1999; Strattman 2005; Burden 2007; Schraufnagel and Milita 2010; Tamas and Hindman 2014) have found little relationship between ballot access laws and either the number of third-party candidates running or the votes that third-party candidates received. Hirano and Snyder (2007) similarly found no evidence that electoral reforms such as the Australian ballot or primary elections helped cause the decline of third parties. More than anything, this new literature raises the question of whether we should continue to accept this long-held consensus on why third parties became so weak in the United States.

My rejection of this consensus is the main driving force behind this book. I begin by treating the demise of third parties as not an easily explained phenomenon but rather as a conundrum that needs investigating and unraveling. My method is scientific and statistical: I pose possible explanations for this phenomenon—and consider possible explanations already posed by others—and then test them, one by one.

While I use multivariate statistics to run these tests, I also include straightforward and easily understood approaches to test each theory. I take this approach because while I believe that multivariate statistical testing is critical for judging the merit of an empirical theory, I also believe that an empirical theory should lead to simple predictions that can also be tested. For example, if difficult ballot access laws are making it much harder for third parties to run candidates and attract voters, then this should be reflected in election results: as the laws have gotten harder, the number of third-party candidates running should have declined. Moreover, third parties should be less active in states with the most difficult ballot access laws. My investigation however finds that this is not the case. In the end, I reject many of the arguments made by third-party scholars over the past half century, and this culminates in me presenting an alternate set of explanations for this phenomenon.

Alternative Explanations

As discussed before, there are a wide range of explanations as to why third parties have become so weak in the United States. These arguments are not only widely cited within the political science literature and in undergraduate texts on American politics, but are also regularly presented in the popular press. My research, however, demonstrates that these popular and prevalent explanations are mostly wrong or insufficient.

Electoral System

There is a great deal of evidence, presented elsewhere (Taagepera and Shugart 1989, 142–55; Lijphart and Aitkin 1994, 95–117) as well as in the next chapter, that third parties do indeed receive fewer votes and win fewer seats in countries with SMP electoral systems as compared to those with PR systems. If the United States were to somehow switch to some form of proportional representation, there is a very good chance that third parties would become more successful. The more interesting question is why third parties are so much weaker in the United States than in other countries that also use SMP. As I will demonstrate in the following, the difference becomes especially clear when one compares election results at the district level. In the United States, only 2% of the vote in House elections is cast for candidates other than the top two in each district. In Canada, India, and the UK, at the district level, approximately 20% of the vote is cast for candidates other than the top two.

There are also limitations to Duverger's explanation as to why SMP systems favor the two-party system. Duverger argued that voters in SMP systems gravitate towards the top two parties because they want to avoid wasting their votes. This would mean that if voters could select third-party candidates without the danger of wasting their vote, they would vote for these parties in much higher numbers. Australia provides an ideal comparison. It is a single-member district system, but instead of plurality voting, it uses a ranking system that eliminates any negative impact of selecting a minor party first. As I will show in the following, contrary to this aspect of Duverger's argument, voters in Australia are no more likely to vote for third parties than in Canada, India, and the UK, even though the latter have SMP systems. Indeed, in Canada, India, and the UK there is clearly a great deal of voting for candidates other than the top two that could disrupt elections in exactly the way that Duverger argues voters are trying to avoid.

Duverger's Law as it currently stands also cannot be used to explain the decline of third parties over the twentieth century, since the American electoral system has remained largely unchanged during this period. The mechanics of translating votes into seats are the same today as they were a century ago, and one can assume that both voters and political parties were just as strategic in the late nineteenth century as in the early twenty-first century. In this way, while Duverger's Law can explain why the United States has fewer parties than countries that use PR, it cannot explain why third parties in America are so weak even in comparison to other SMP countries, nor can it explain why they are so much weaker today than a century ago.

28 Chapter One

Other Explanations

As I demonstrate in later chapters, other major explanations have even more serious shortcomings. While ballot access laws have gotten more difficult over the twentieth century, as Winger (2000) argues, I have found that they have had little impact on third parties in House races. The reduction in fusion candidacies (or candidates nominated by more than one party) was also not a significant cause of third-party decline. Contrary to the theses of Disch (2002) and Scarrow (1986), fusion was never widely used in American elections, with the exceptions of the 1872 election, 1896 election, and, to a lesser extent, the 1916 elections. Therefore, the prohibition of fusion could not have caused the decline of third parties. My evidence further suggests that the introduction of primary elections in the early decades of the twentieth century did not hurt third parties. And while Rapoport and Stone (2008) are likely correct that major parties often co-opt the rhetoric and policy stands of more successful third parties, this argument cannot explain why third parties stopped challenging major parties at all by the middle of the twentieth century. Moreover, if co-optation is such an effective strategy for undermining the strongest third parties, why don't the two major parties in other countries with SMP electoral systems co-opt all the other minor political parties? Why, for example, has Labour not co-opted the Liberal Democrats in the UK?

Furthermore, some explanations for third-party decline, I find, are presented so poorly that they cannot be studied in-depth. These include the following:

American Political Culture Argument

As discussed before, some third-party scholars have argued that American political culture predisposes voters in the United States to support only two political parties. The key to this argument, as it is often presented in the third-party literature, is dualism. American political culture always divides itself into two large factions, which can be traced back to the struggles between Hamilton and Jefferson, and these divisions are represented by the two major parties. For this reason, Americans are unlikely to ever support candidates except for those nominated by one of the two major parties (Romance 1998).

The evidence for this very specific interpretation of American political culture, or the argument that United States citizens divide themselves into two instead of many political groups, is anecdotal and selective, and one can easily find historical examples that contradict it. For example, in the 1992 presidential election, third-party candidate Ross Perot received nearly 20% of the vote, and right before the Democratic convention, he led both Clinton and Bush with nearly 40% voter support. In the late nineteenth and early twentieth century, as I demonstrated in the introductory chapter, a significant portion of Americans were voting for third parties like the Greenbacks, Populists, and Progressives as

Unraveling the Conundrum of Third-Party Decline **29**

well as parties like the Socialists and Prohibitionists. Third parties have at times even become dominant within particular states, such as Farmer-Labor in Minnesota in the 1930s and 1940s. In sum, the culture argument for third-party weakness, at best, requires a broad stroke that ignores a great deal of specific evidence.

Moreover, the American political culture theory for third-party weakness, as it is usually specified within this literature, cannot be tested. Scientific research requires variation. For example, if a scholar was to argue, as Robert Putnam (1993) has, that the amount of civic engagement that citizens are involved in affects how well representative democracy works, then one can measure the amount of civic engagement and the effectiveness of democracy across regions or countries to see if there is a relationship. In sharp contrast, the "American political culture" argument about third parties is a narrative that describes the entire United States since its inception. There is no underlying factor theorized that is driving this American political culture, and so there is no way to measure variation across groups within or regions of the United States, nor is there a way to measure change over time. This sweeping narrative of American political culture also makes comparative analysis across countries impossible. Instead of measuring some cultural characteristic that the United States and some other countries have and then determining if countries with this characteristic tend to have only two major parties, this theory leads to a variable with two values: the United States and all other countries, since only the United States has "American political culture." In this situation, one could attribute any difference between the United States and other countries to American political culture.

Yet another problem with the American political culture theory, as it is usually presented in the third-party literature, is that "American political culture" is treated as a constant, such as a characteristic that dates back to the Foundation. A constant cannot explain a change, and for this reason this theory cannot explain the dramatic decline in third-party support during the twentieth century. Instead, most versions of the American political culture explanation seem to paint third parties over United States history with a very broad brush, ignoring significant changes that occurred at various moments.

For these reasons, Gillespie's argument (2012) about social class and the labor movement is likely stronger than the other versions of the political culture argument presented by third-party scholars. In Western Europe, one can see clear links between the socialist parties of the late nineteenth century and the rise of multiparty politics. One can even see how the co-optation of third parties in the New Deal era was related to the co-optation of the labor movement into the Democratic Party. However, the three major third-party movements after the Civil War—the Greenbacks, the Populists, and the Progressives—were not, strictly speaking, labor parties. Their disappearance was clearly not caused by the decline of the American labor movement. Similarly, this argument does not

30 Chapter One

explain why other third parties, such as those focusing on conservative social values, have also not been stronger.

Electoral College Argument

The *Electoral College* argument for third-party weakness is another theory that is poorly specified. This theory can be summarized as follows. (1) In a presidential system, a minor party needs to gain success in presidential elections in order to be successful in lower-level elections. (2) In the Electoral College system, success is defined as winning electoral votes. (3) Since electoral votes are much more difficult to gain then simply a percent of the vote, third parties are unable to gain the electoral votes needed to build or sustain national organizations.

This argument hinges on the assumption that electoral votes are in some way a key resource for political parties. But proponents of this theory never specify why votes in the Electoral College are so much more important than, for example, actual votes or even victories in lower offices. Gaining a certain number of electoral votes, like winning a certain percent of actual votes, is a form of symbolic capital. Unlike, for example, actually winning elected positions, political parties gain no concrete resources from winning either electoral votes or actual votes. But proponents of this theory present no evidence that demonstrates that the symbolism of winning electoral votes is so central to third-party success. Why, for example, is it a failure for a third-party presidential candidate to win 20% of the vote but no electoral votes but a victory for another third-party presidential candidate to win 5% of the vote as well as the electoral votes from one state?

Beyond this, the Electoral College explanation has exactly the same problems as the American culture argument. Like American political culture (as it is defined by some third-party scholars), the Electoral College is a constant. The Electoral College system, as it is currently used, dates back to the Jacksonian era. Since it has not changed, it cannot explain a decline in the vote for third parties during the twentieth century. Also, like the American political culture argument, since it does not vary across regions within the United States or across time, there is no statistical way to determine if it is related to levels of support of third parties. In order to compare it across countries, there would need to be more than one nation that has the same Electoral College system. Otherwise, there is no way to tell if fewer votes for third parties was influenced by the Electoral College or some other unique characteristics of the United States.

Presidential Debate Argument

The Presidential Debate argument can be easily ruled out as a possible explanation for third-party decline. While keeping a third-party presidential candidate out of presidential debates surely hurts the chances of that candidate and even eliminates a useful source of free advertisement for the party of that candidate, it is hard to see how this can explain the large-scale changes in third-party fortunes over the last century. In particular, one must consider that presidential debates became common during the 1976 election and then were effectively institutionalized in the 1984 election, when Ronald Reagan debated Walter Mondale even though Reagan had little to gain. The decline of third parties began around 1920, and they had almost completely disappeared by 1950. Televised presidential debates were certainly not a factor in that decline.

Polarization and Party Resources: A New Perspective

Current evidence, I demonstrate, does not support most of what third-party scholars have theorized about third parties. The evidence instead points us in two other directions.

The first is that third-party candidacies did not simply disappear in the mid-twentieth century, as most of the third-party literature implies and as one would have expected from several of the prevalent explanations. Instead, the percent of House districts with third-party candidates follows more of a "U" shape since 1900: high at the beginning of the century, dropping low by the middle of the century, and then climbing back upwards during the last few decades of that century. That curve matches closely to the change in congressional polarization shown in Poole and Rosenthal's DW-NOMINATE scores, and it is also consistent with the decline and reemergence of inequality in America (McCarty, Poole and Rosenthal 2016). Changes in partisan polarization, not changes in state election laws, seem to be the main driver in how many third-party candidates are on the ballot. However, this change in polarization cannot explain why third parties still receive such a small percent of the vote, despite more third-party candidates getting onto the ballot.

Second, this increased third-party activity has not translated into significant increases in voter support for third-party candidates because these parties have not been able to muster critical party resources, including campaign finances. This resources explanation does not exist in a vacuum. Instead, it is related to the electoral system. Duverger argues that in SMP systems, voters want to avoid wasting their votes and therefore vote for only the top two parties. He argues further that political parties also want to avoid splitting the vote in a disadvantageous way, and for that reason smaller parties will generally fuse with larger parties that hold similar ideological positions. In addition to this, I argue that SMP systems shift political resources, especially money, to a few large parties. It is a self-reinforcing process. The mechanics of electoral systems affect how many seats each party wins; 10% of the vote for a party will translate into seats in most PR systems, for example, but often no seats when there are single-member districts. The more seats a party wins, the more resources it is capable of acquiring, which it can then use to win further seats. In other words,

32 Chapter One

since single-member district systems tend to allocate seats to fewer parties, they effectively distribute political resources in a way that makes it easier for fewer parties to remain in a dominant electoral position.

This addition to Duverger's Law not only explains why there tends to be fewer successful parties in SMP than PR systems; it also helps explain why the vote for American third parties declined over the twentieth century. While the key resource for parties in the late nineteenth century was people/activists, making them more akin to social movements, by the late twentieth century the primary resources have become money, professional consultants, and access to the mass media, all of which are more difficult for third parties to acquire. This thesis is similarly consistent with the finding that the most successful third-party candidates in the late twentieth century have entered their campaigns with significant financial resources that most third parties cannot muster.

Finally, this addition to Duverger's Law can also explain why third parties are weaker in the United States than in countries with similar electoral systems such as Canada, the UK, and India. A critical secondary factor linked to the electoral system is campaign finance laws. These other countries have some combination of public funding for campaigns, tighter campaign contribution restrictions, and campaign spending caps, all of which effectively make the distribution of party resources less unbalanced. In sharp contrast, however, private funding of campaigns in the United States makes parties and candidates more dependent on donors who have a vested interest in giving all their money to likely winners. This addition can also explain why third parties in Australia are just as weak as in other single-member district systems like Canada and the UK, even though its preferential voting system eliminates any need for strategic voting. Effectively, having single-member districts will drive down the vote for third parties, regardless of whether or not that vote creates a spoiler effect, because it impacts the distribution of resources. Indeed, this theory predicts that electoral reforms based on the Australian system such as rank choice voting, which Maine adopted by referendum during the 2016 election,[4] are likely to have limited impact because they do not address a fundamental reason why the Democratic and Republican parties are so dominant.

Notes

1 Results from elections to the US House of Representatives were used instead of similar data for presidential or senatorial elections because the latter would have been significantly influenced by the popularity of a small number of high profile third-party candidates, whereas my focus here is on third parties as party organizations. Election results to state legislatures were not used because gathering this data since 1870 would have produced potentially insurmountable data collection issues without providing any clear leverage improvement over House data. State legislative elections would have also produced analysis issues due to the need to combine election results from fifty states with varying election laws (e.g., Illinois's use of cumulative voting until 1980 and New Jersey's policy of state legislative election in odd-numbered years).

2 To be clear, I am using the term "third-party strength" here simply as a shorthand that combines both the vote for third parties and their capacity to run candidates in the general election. I am in no way addressing arguments related to party organizational strength presented by Aldrich (1995) and others.

3 Of the 67,079 House candidates from 1870 to 1988, 15,126 (or 23%) received less than 5% of the vote and were therefore excluded from the ICPSR study. This conclusion is based on more extensive data gathered from Dubin (1998) and House election results reported by the Federal Election Commission at www.fec.gov.

4 Katharine Q. Seelye, "Maine Adopts Ranked-Choice Voting. What Is It, and How Will It Work?", *New York Times*, December 3, 2016.

2

DUVERGER'S LAW AND THE AMERICAN ELECTORAL SYSTEM

The 2000 presidential election came down to whether George W. Bush or Al Gore had received more votes in Florida. A range of issues were raised about the Florida election that year. Arguably the most famous was the "butterfly ballot." The butterfly ballot was the ballot in Palm Beach County, Florida during the 2000 election, which was structured in a way that many voters found confusing. That confusion led thousands of them to accidentally vote for Pat Buchanan instead of Al Gore or to vote for two presidential candidates, which made their votes invalid. A number of political scientists have argued that this ballot structure led directly to Bush winning the presidential election that year (Wand et al. 2001). Bush also gained an advantage through Florida's infamous felon lists. Before the 2000 election, Florida collected names of all people who had been convicted of felonies in Florida or Texas and then made anyone who had a name similar to one of those felons ineligible to vote. The process disenfranchised a disproportionately high number of African-American voters, which also significantly deflated the vote for Al Gore (Stuart 2004).

For our purposes, the most important factor was the Green Party candidacy of Ralph Nader. Nader ran to the ideological left of Al Gore, and most political analysts assume that the vast majority of his supporters would have voted for Gore had there been no Green Party candidate. In Florida, Bush beat Gore by 0.01% of the vote; Nader received 1.67%. The Nader vote therefore most likely reduced the Florida vote for Gore enough to help produce a Bush victory. Four years later, the focus of many Democrats as well as outside organizations like MoveOn.org was to put an end to the Bush presidency. Support for the Green Party collapsed. In 2000, Nader received 2.7% of the vote nationally. In 2004, running as an independent, Nader received less than half a percent of the vote (0.4%) while Green Party presidential candidate David Cobb received a tenth of a percent of the vote.

Duverger's Law and the American Electoral System **35**

The Ralph Nader explanation for the 2000 victory of George W. Bush, as well as the subsequent decline of Green Party voter support, is consistent with Duverger's Law (Duverger 1954). This theory, in brief, argues that the overarching rules that govern elections, or the "electoral system," largely determine how many parties that country will have in government. The primary comparison is between SMP and PR systems. SMP, used by the United States, the UK, and a number of other countries, is a winner-take-all system. For the national parliament or congress, an SMP country is divided into single-member districts. The candidate who gets the most votes wins the seat, even if it is not a majority of votes. PR systems have multimember districts; each district sends multiple candidates to the national legislature. In each district, the party is awarded a number of seats in the legislature based on the proportion of votes it receives. Some PR systems, like in elections to the Swedish Riksdag, include compensatory seats, which are meant to offset imbalances across districts so that, in the end, the percent of seats each party receives in the national legislature is roughly proportional to the votes it had gotten.

Duverger argued that SMP favors the two-party system. He gave three reasons. The most famous and possibly most important reason is that voters want to avoid wasting their votes. In other words, if a voter has a choice between a much liked third-party candidate with little chance of winning and a less liked but still acceptable major party candidate, he or she will tend to vote for the major party candidate. The reason is that voting for the weak third-party candidate effectively reduces the chances that the acceptable major party candidate will win. Thus, a vote for Nader instead of Gore was equivalent to helping George W. Bush win.

Following this logic, many political scientists, maybe especially those with a comparative politics background, argue that the American electoral system is the primary reason why the Democrats and Republicans are so dominant. Many third-party scholars begin their analysis by citing Duverger's Law (Rosenstone, Behr and Lazarus 1984, 16; Bibby and Maisel 2003, 60–61; Gillespie 2012, 21–23).

Does Duverger's Law solve our puzzle and explain the decline of third parties over the past century? The short answer is that it cannot, not in its current format. The American electoral system is almost definitely a factor in the weakness of American third parties; if somehow the system was suddenly changed to a PR system like the ones in countries like Austria or Norway, the number of parties in Congress would likely rise dramatically. But, Duverger's Law has two significant limitations in its ability to explain the problems facing American third parties. First, since the American electoral system remained virtually unchanged during the twentieth century, it cannot explain why support for third parties rapidly declined in the middle of that century. Second, while it can explain why third parties are much weaker in the United States than in most PR systems, the theory cannot explain why American third parties are also so much weaker than in other SMP systems like the UK, Canada, and India.

36 Chapter Two

Duverger's Law—A Synopsis

An electoral system is a set of overarching rules that a country uses to govern its election. Sometimes, it is defined as the full process a country uses to translate votes into seats (Farrell, 2011, 4). Electoral systems have fascinated political scientists for many decades and political thinkers for at least a century and a half, and it has evolved into a rather large field of research with its own section within the American Political Science Association and a range of journals that regularly publish its findings (including *Electoral Studies*, *Representation*, and *Party Politics*). The two most important findings of this area are that the type of electoral system can affect the number of parties that enter government and that some electoral systems can significantly inflate or deflate the percent of seats a party gets in government related to the percent of votes it receives (Gallagher, 2005).

The starting point of this field is generally considered the classic by Maurice Duverger (1954), *Political Parties: Their Organization and Activity in the Modern State*, first published in French in 1951. In it, Duverger famously argues that the electoral system largely determines how many parties that political system will have in government. He also made three predictions. The first is that SMP favors the two-party system; this, he said, is close to a sociological law, which is how it got the name "Duverger's Law" (Duverger 1954, 217). The second is that PR tends to lead to multiparty systems, with these parties largely independent of each other (Duverger 1954, 245–55). The third is that a two-ballot majority system, like the one used by France, will tend to lead to a multiparty system in which parties produce electoral alliances (Duverger 1954, 239–45).

Duverger's Law has had a dramatic impact on political scientists. Expanding on Duverger's framework, electoral studies scholars generally analyze these systems using three categories. First, they look at district magnitude, or how many positions are elected in each district. In the US House of Representatives, the district magnitude is one, since only one politician is elected per district. At the other extreme, in Israeli elections to its parliament, the Knesset, the entire country is treated as a single district; since the Knesset has 120 members, the district magnitude is 120. Second, these scholars examine the ballot structure, or how each voter actually votes. In the United States, the ballot has a list of candidates and their respective parties, and each voter selects a single candidate for each office. In closed-list proportional representation systems, the voter will usually see only a list of parties and be able to choose one. Third, electoral system scholars examine how these votes are translated into seats. In SMP systems, like the United States, whichever candidate gets the most votes in each district wins, regardless of whether he or she received a majority. In proportional representative systems, the percent of seats that a party is allocated in a legislative body is supposed to be roughly proportional to the percent of votes that party received, although the exact method of calculating the number of seats vary (Rae 1967).[1]

Duverger's Law and the American Electoral System **37**

PR is the electoral system used by the largest number of representative democracies, and because it is employed by a small number of very large countries, SMP is the system used by the most people globally. There are, however, a wide variety of electoral systems beyond SMP and PR. The lower house of Parliament in Australia, for example, uses preferential voting, or a system with single-member districts in which voters rank candidates instead of simply selecting one. The upper house in Australia uses single-transferable vote, as does Ireland, in which voters rank candidates but the districts are multimember, which produces results more like proportional representation. France uses a two-stage system in which there are single-member districts and citizens can vote in two rounds. Whenever a candidate does not receive a majority of the vote in the first round, every candidate with at least 12.5% of the vote gets to run again in a second round, and then whoever wins the most votes in the constituency wins. There are also a range of mixed electoral systems. For example, in Japan, 300 seats in Parliament are elected through PR, while 180 are through SMP. Germany does the same for the Bundestag, its lower house of Parliament, except that seats are calculated in such a way that they become roughly proportional to the overall votes each party received. Thus, there are vast differences in the way that democracies govern their elections, with the United States and a small number of countries, often former colonies of the UK, using SMP. By most accounts, SMP systems have fewer parties in government than other types of electoral systems.

Duverger gives three reasons why SMP favors the two-party system. The first is mechanical: The very structure of SMP (that is, of having a country divided into single-member districts in which the candidate receiving the most vote in each district wins) translates into fewer parties winning seats, provided that levels of party support do not vary greatly across regions. To give a simple example, let us say that there is a party that receives 15% of the national vote in a parliamentary election. If elections to that parliament are run through a PR system, chances are that the party will receive something more than 15% of the seats, provided that the minimum vote threshold is less than 15%.[2] If those elections are run through SMP, and therefore the country is divided into districts with only the top candidate receiving a seat, that party would likely receive no seats if its support is equally distributed across the country. The only way that the party can win any seats in an SMP system is if that support is highly concentrated in smaller geographic areas (Duverger 1954, 224–26).

Duverger calls the second reason "psychological," although current political scientists would probably refer to it as strategic. A significant problem with SMP is that it often forces voters into making a strategic decision. To extend the above example, if there are three candidates running in a district, two representing parties on the ideological left who respectively receive 15% and 40% of the vote, and one representing a party on the right who receives 45% of the vote, the candidate on the right wins the seat even though voters in this

38 Chapter Two

district are presumably more ideologically to the left. This puts the supporters of smaller parties into a strategic bind. They can either vote for the party that they most prefer but then, in terms of influencing the outcome, effectively waste their votes, or they can choose between the two candidates who have a chance of winning the election. Duverger and proponents of this framework argue that most voters do the latter: they shift their support to the top two parties, which drives the country towards a two-party system. As Duverger put it:

> In cases where there are three parties operating under the [SMP] system the electors soon realize that their votes are wasted if they continue to give them to the third party: whence their natural tendency to transfer their vote to the less evil of its two adversaries in order to prevent the success of the greater evil. This "polarization" effect works to the detriment of a new party so long as it is the weakest party but is turned against the less favoured of its older rivals as soon as the new party outstrips it.
>
> *(Duverger 1954, 226)*

The third reason has to do with the reaction of political parties to this pressure. The problem for third parties is that by running candidates they often accomplish little more than undermining the electoral prospects of a larger party with a similar ideology. So, there is an inherent advantage for both of these parties to reach an agreement in which they run together or the candidate for the smaller party steps aside. As Duverger puts it:

> Take for example a British constituency in which the Conservatives have 35,000 votes, Labour 40,000, and Liberal 15,000: it is obvious that the success of Labour is entirely dependent on the presence of the Liberal party; if the Liberal party should withdraw its candidate it can be assumed that a majority of voters supporting him will transfer to the Conservative, the minority being divided between Labour and abstention. Two alternatives are therefore possible: either the Liberal party may reach agreement with the Conservatives to withdraw its candidate (in exchange for some form of compensation in other constituencies), in which case the two-party system is restored as a result of fusion or of an alliance very like fusion; or else the Liberal party may persist in its independent line, the electors will gradually desert it, and the two-party system will be restored by elimination.
>
> *(Duverger 1954, 223–24)*[3]

To be clear, Duverger does not argue that SMP always leads to two parties in government. Instead, he argues that there is significant pressure at the district level in SMP systems towards two dominant parties. Thus, the rise of the Scottish National Party in Great Britain or the Bloc Québécois in Canada does not necessarily contradict Duverger's Law.

It is also worth pointing out that while Duverger gets most of the credit for this theory, it has actually existed long before he presented it in *Party Politics*. William Riker (1982) argues that the first known argument for the law was by Henry Droop, inventor of the Droop quota, in 1869, nearly a century before Duverger published the argument. More recently, E.E. Schattschneider (1942) made roughly the same argument in two chapters of *Party Government*. Riker (1982, 754) claims that it

> is customary to call the law by Duverger's name, not because he had much to do with developing it but rather because he was the first to dare to claim it was a law. The memorial honors, therefore, a trait of character as much as a scientific breakthrough.

My own guess is that Duverger, like Schattschneider a decade before, presented the theory without citation because it was already widely known at the time. It is a compact, clear theory that has significantly influenced how political scientists understand elections globally as well as explain why the Democrats and Republicans are so dominant in the United States.

Analyzing Duverger's Law

But, this does not mean that Duverger's Law is universally accepted by political scientists or even specialists in electoral systems. Early criticism came from Grumm (1958), who argued that the causal arrow should be reversed: political culture influences how many parties will exist in a country, and the country will then pick an electoral system that fits that culture. Rae (1967) similarly pointed out that Duverger's Law is a poor predictor of Canadian elections, with third parties often receiving around 10% of the vote. Most electoral studies scholars, though, would likely argue that the electoral system is not determinant: while there is a tendency for SMP systems to produce fewer parties in government, other factors also influence the number of parties. Benoit (2006) argues further that Duverger himself felt that the "law" had been accidentally overstated, that he had never intended it to seem deterministic.

Indeed, one of the key questions is whether the evidence of Duverger's Law is strong enough to justify the framework. It clearly does not work perfectly, certainly not at the level of being a "sociological law." But does it work well enough to help us understand the weakness of third parties in the United States?

Analyzing this question, however, cannot be adequately conducted using the main data for this book, which focuses on elections to the House of Representatives since 1870. There are two problems. The first is that SMP is used throughout the United States for all House races. There is no variation across districts and therefore no way to see if third parties do better in a different type

40 Chapter Two

of election. Two, there is also no variation across time. SMP has been in place since the 1840s, once the Apportionment Act of 1842 outlawed multimember House districts. It is true that before this point, around one in five districts were multimember. Elections were conducted in what at the time was called "general elections" but today would be called block voting: citizens could vote for as many candidates as there were seats, and then whichever candidates got the most votes got those seats. This generally led to a single party winning all the seats (Tamas 2006). In other words, even though a high percentage of House seats were elected through multimember districts, the elections were still majoritarian and therefore more like elections in SMP than PR systems. Moreover, these changes happened long before the decline of third parties. By the late nineteenth century, the vast majority of representatives were elected in single-member districts. There is no way to test whether the American electoral system may have affected third parties over time since there was no significant change in that electoral system during the period that third parties declined.

Since there was effectively no variation in the American electoral system during the period of third-party decline, this part of the analysis will employ a more comparative approach. To do this, I will first compare elections in countries with SMP and PR systems, and then I will compare American elections against those in other SMP countries as well as a nation with a similar system, Australia. The primary question will be whether and to what degree Duverger's Law can solve our puzzle about the decline of American third parties.

Single-Member Plurality versus Proportional Representation

One of the most basic predictions of Duverger's Law is that the top two parties will win a higher percentage of seats in SMP than PR systems. Indeed, as the left side of Figure 2.1 shows, this is the case. In SMP systems, the top two parties hold an average of 87.4% of the seats. The confidence interval is from 76.3% to 96%. In PR systems, the top two parties hold an average of 65.6% of seats with a confidence interval of 59.7% to 71.6%. As Duverger has predicted, the top two parties gain more votes in SMP than PR systems.

These results are consistent with the general findings on the differences between SMP and PR systems (Taagepera and Shugart 1989, 142–55; Lijphart and Aitkin 1994, 95–117). Nonetheless, the results shown in Figure 2.1 are based on an analysis that was conducted using a different approach than in much of the electoral systems literature. This was done in order to solve two problems. One, since my focus is on the domination of the top two parties, I used a different measure than most studies of Duverger's Law. Two, because there are a small number of countries that employ SMP, I employed a bootstrapping technique to determine whether the top two parties are significantly stronger in SMP than PR systems.

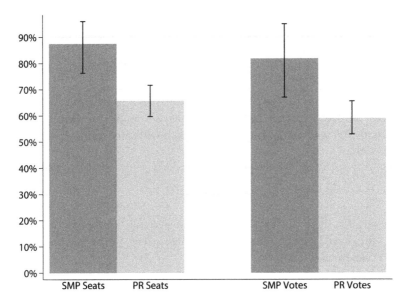

FIGURE 2.1 Average percent seats won and votes received for two strongest parties in SMP and PR systems. This graph shows the average percent seats won and the average votes received in elections to the national congress or parliament by the two largest parties in countries with SMP and PR electoral systems. It demonstrates that the two largest parties generally win significantly more seats and votes in SMP than PR systems. On average, in SMP systems, the two largest parties won 87% of seats as compared to 66% of seats in PR systems. Similarly, in SMP systems, the two largest parties received a combined mean vote of 82% as compared to 59% in PR systems. This analysis was based on four independent bootstraps of one million runs each on the electoral results of eight SMP and forty-two list-PR systems.

Measurement

For this analysis, I measured the electoral and legislative strength of the two largest parties in each country by focusing on the combined percent of votes the top two parties gained and the combined percent of seats the top two parties won. In the United States, where currently no third-party or independent candidates hold any seats in the House of Representatives, the combined percent of seats won by the top two parties is 100%. Similarly, after the 2014 election in India, when the top two parties won 51.9% and 8.1% of the seats, this figure was 60%. If SMP systems have the impact that Duverger predicted, then one would expect this figure to be significantly higher for SMP than PR systems.

Most electoral systems scholars define the question in a slightly different manner, focusing on the number of political parties, or more specifically, the number of "effective" parties, or the number of parties that can actually impact

42 Chapter Two

policy outcomes. The most widely used measure of the number of effective parties was developed by Laakso and Taagepera (1979), who use the equation:

$$N = \frac{1}{\sum s^2}$$

In this equation, s is the proportion of seats that each party holds and N is the effective number of parties. To give two related examples, if there is a parliament with 100 seats and only two parties, each with fifty seats, N would equal two because

$$N = \frac{1}{\left(0.50^2 + 0.50^2\right)} = 2$$

However, if in the next election, one of these parties lost a single seat to a third party, this would not be calculated as a three-party system but, instead, just over a two-party system:

$$N = \frac{1}{\left(0.50^2 + 0.49^2 + 0.01^2\right)} = 2.04$$

As the percent of seats held by the third party increases, so does N. So, if in the following election, the third party won 3% of the seats, all of it taken from the second party, N would now equal 2.11:

$$N = \frac{1}{\left(0.50^2 + 0.47^2 + 0.03^2\right)} = 2.11$$

In this way, Laakso and Taagepera have provided a method for counting the number of parties without having the numbers wildly inflated by the introduction of a new party with a few seats.

But for a study on third parties, or an analysis of Duverger's Law, this measure has an important limitation. For third parties, we are concerned only with the parties after the first two; yet, Laakso and Taagepera's measure is sensitive to the movement of all the parties, including the top two. Similarly, Duverger's Law leads to the conclusion that the top two parties would gain most of the votes as well as win most of the seats. It says nothing about the relative strength of the two largest parties. Yet, if during the following election, the first party has much higher voter support vis-à-vis the second party but the third party's level of support is unchanged, the measure nonetheless shifts:

$$N = \frac{1}{\left(0.65^2 + 0.32^2 + 0.03^2\right)} = 1.90$$

In other words, even though the third party is equally strong in this scenario and the previous, this measure provides a lower score than any of the previous

Duverger's Law and the American Electoral System **43**

examples, including when the top two parties held every single seat. In this way, while Laakso and Taagepera's measure is a significant improvement over counting the number of parties, it has an important limitation when testing whether SMP increases the power of the two strongest parties.

The combined percent of seats won by the two largest parties, which I employ, is a much simpler measure that can be easily interpreted. It also measures much more clearly the combined strength of the top two parties in a political system. Both Lapaakso and Taagepera's measure and this measure can also be easily applied to how an electorate voted, but again the latter is more appropriate for a study on third parties. To say, for example, that third parties received 3% of the vote one election and then 15% of the vote the next says something about the vote beyond support for the top two parties. To say that the measure shifted from 1.90 to 2.46 does not. Finally, this simple measure of third-party strength can be easily applied to other aspects of this study, including comparing the vote across countries at the district level. While Duverger's Law implies that a country using SMP would be dominated by two large parties, it more specifically predicts that the vote would gravitate to the top two candidates in each district.

Analysis

The second problem with comparing the impact of SMP and PR systems on two party strength is that there are only a small number of countries that use SMP. That problem becomes even more serious if one takes two other factors into consideration. The first is that authoritarian regimes, especially what are now referred to as "competitive authoritarianism" (Levitsky and Way 2010), also hold elections and therefore employ electoral systems. The impact of those electoral systems on election results, however, are most likely overwhelmed by other factors, including opposition leaders being intimidated or not being able to present their positions and candidates through the mass media. A second concern is with the size of the legislative body. If a national legislature has only twenty seats, for example, then it becomes much more likely for a single party to gain a large majority of seats, since there might be less variation across districts in a way that would diminish the chance of second and third parties to gain significant electoral support.

Because there are so few cases, I decided to conduct a simple comparison of SMP and PR systems without examining the various other types of electoral systems. I also limited the data to systems that were defined as "free" by Freedom House (2014) and have at least forty seats in the lower house of the national legislature. For SMP systems, this produced only eight cases[4] while for PR it produced forty-two.[5]

However, there is another problem with these eight cases that make conventional statistics, like a T-Test, inappropriate. The distribution of seats across

44 Chapter Two

SMP countries clearly does not look like a normal curve: there is an upper limit for countries like the United States and Jamaica, where the top two parties hold 100% of the seats, and more importantly the percent of seats held by the two strongest parties is much lower in India than other SMP countries.

In order to circumvent these problems, I used a bootstrapping technique. I repeatedly, randomly selected eight data points from the SMP countries and calculated their mean. After repeating this a million times, I calculated the mean of these means, or 87.4%. In other words, on average the top two parties in SMP systems will hold 87.4% of the seats. I then determined the range of the middle 95% of these million means, which leads to a confidence interval of 76.3% to 96.0%. I performed the same approach for the PR countries, which led to a mean of 65.6% with a confidence interval of 58.7% to 71.6%. Since the lowest point on the SMP confidence interval, 76.3%, is higher than the highest point on the PR confidence interval, 71.6%, I can be 95% sure that overall the top two parties hold significantly more seats in SMP than PR systems.

Ultimately, the analysis presented in Figure 2.1 adds more evidence to the argument widely made by electoral studies scholars. Even when taking India into consideration, the evidence strongly suggests that the two largest parties tend to be more dominant in SMP than PR systems. The question we are left with is why there is this difference, and whether that explanation helps us understand why third parties are so weak in the United States.

Mechanical Explanation

One possibility is that Duverger's first proposition alone explains most of the weakness of third parties in SMP systems. In other words, while some voters are gravitating to one of the top two parties in order to avoid wasting their votes and some political parties are making strategic decisions in order to avoid vote splitting, it is possible that this has only a small impact on election outcomes. Instead, it is possible that most of the difference between SMP and PR shown in Figure 2.1 is caused by the mechanics of how votes are translated into seats.

From a strictly logical perspective, Duverger's first explanation is very hard to argue against. In many ways, the mechanical explanation is really nothing more than basic math. Specifically, the very structure of dividing a country into single-member districts produces a potential bias in the system. If, for example, there were two parties running in an election, and one receives 55% of the vote while the other received 45%, but that vote was absolutely consistent across all districts (that is, in every district, the first party received 55% while the second receive 45%), the first would win all the seats. The only way that the number of seats could be proportional to the percent of votes is if that party support varies across the country in a way that, almost by accident, more voters support the first party than then second party in exactly 55% of the districts.

That problem becomes even more serious for smaller parties. Let's say that this system has three parties, and the third party is supported by 10% of voters. In an SMP system, that party will likely win zero seats, unless its support is highly concentrated within a particular region. The simple mechanics, in other words, work very much against smaller parties and very much in favor of the larger parties.

Indeed, this form of disproportionality is one of the critical characteristics of SMP systems. Gallagher and Mitchell (2005, 12) have referred to this as "one of the most robust findings in electoral systems research, namely that the smaller the average district magnitude, the greater the disproportionality." SMP systems tend to increase the percent of seats some parties receive, often giving winning parties much larger victories than the votes that they had received and warping the relationship between votes and seats in various other ways. In the 2014 Indian elections to the Lok Sabha, for example, the Bharatiya Janata Party (BJP) received less than a third of the vote (31%) but a majority (51%) of the seats. Similarly, in the 2015 parliamentary elections in the UK, the Conservatives received 37% of the vote and a majority 51% of the seats.

This has also become a larger issue in the United States over the past few elections. At this point, the electoral system within the House of Representatives has a clear Republican bias, making it much easier for them to win majorities and producing a harder road for the Democratic Party. In the 2012 elections to the House of Representatives, for example, the Democrats received 48.8% and Republicans received 47.9% of the votes. But, the American electoral system translated this into a thirty-one seat Republican majority. This biased translation of votes to seats became the foremost reason that Obama was not able to push much of his agenda forward during the beginning of his second term. The 2016 election also inflated the number of Republican seats in the House vis-à-vis the percent of votes its candidates received—the Republicans received 49% of the vote and 55% of the seats—although in this case the party had actually won more votes than the Democrats and would have gained control even without the bias.

The more general trend across SMP systems is that this system inflates the number of seats for the two strongest parties within a region while deflating the number of seats that smaller parties win. In the 2015 parliamentary elections in the UK, the two largest parties, the Conservatives and Labour, both won a higher percentage of seats than the percent of votes they received. Combined, they received 67% of the vote, which this SMP system translated into 86% of the seats. Similarly, the Scottish National Party, which runs candidates exclusively in Scotland, received 4.7% of the vote and 8.6% of the seats. On the other hand, the UK Independence Party, which came in third place with 13% of the vote, won a single seat in the 650-seat parliament, or one-seventh of one percent. Similarly, the Liberal

46 Chapter Two

Democrats received 8% of the vote but only eight seats, or just over 1% of the 650 seats in Parliament.

The question is whether the mechanics of how votes are translated into seats in SMP systems explains most of the reason why third parties are so much weaker in these countries than in countries with PR. The answer is that it cannot. If the difference between SMP and PR systems was simply an issue of the allocation of seats from votes, then there would be no significant difference in the voting pattern between SMP and PR systems. As the right side of Figure 2.1 demonstrates, voters in SMP systems cast a significantly higher percent of votes to the top two parties than voters in PR systems. As the graph shows, in SMP systems the top two parties receive an average of 81.8% of the vote with a confidence interval of 67% to 95%. For PR systems, the mean vote for the top two parties is 58.9% with a confidence interval of 52.9% to 65.5%. Clearly, other factors are also reducing the votes received and seats won by third parties in SMP systems.

Comparing SMP Systems

For Duverger, those other factors are the strategic behavior of both voters and political parties. As outlined before, Duverger argued that voters in SMP systems want to avoid wasting their votes and therefore gravitate towards whichever of the top two candidates they consider less offensive. Similarly, political parties recognized that there is a strategic disadvantage of multiple parties with similar ideologies running against each other in SMP systems. Therefore, Duverger argues, smaller parties tend to reach electoral agreements with larger parties in order to avoid dividing the vote in ways that lead to both of their candidates losing.

While the idea that voters are strategic and want to avoid wasting their votes makes a compelling argument, how much evidence actually exists that voters make these types of strategic decisions? More exactly, do *enough* voters take this type of strategic step to drive political systems towards two parties? Certainly, one can find historical examples of third parties joining forces with a larger party instead of dividing votes with them. In the 1940s, for example, Minnesota's Farmer-Labor Party joined the Democratic Party to become the Democratic-Farmer-Labor-Party, or DFL. But is this strategic behavior a driving force in SMP systems?

Figure 2.2 compares the percent vote received by the two strongest parties to elections to the lower house of the congress or parliament for the four major SMP systems (Canada, India, the UK, and the United States) from 1945 to 2015. The graph, in many ways, shows two different periods after the end of World War II. In the first period, from 1945 until the early 1970s, there was a clear pattern: the two strongest parties were dominant in the United States and the UK, weaker in Canada, and weakest in India. In

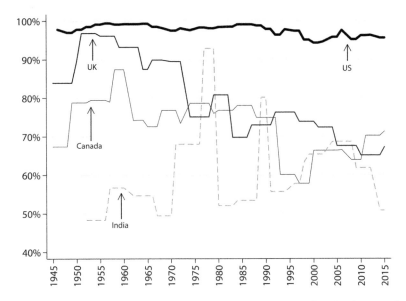

FIGURE 2.2 Average percent votes for two strongest parties in four SMP countries, 1945–2015. This graph shows the combined percent vote for the two parties that received the most votes to the lower house of Congress or Parliament in elections from 1945 to 2015 in four SMP countries: Canada, India, the UK, and the United States. The graph demonstrates that from the 1950s until the 1970s, the United States and the UK were each dominated by two major parties, while the top two parties received a lower combined share of the vote in Canada and especially India. Since then, the electoral dominance of the Conservatives and Labour in the UK has declined to the point that it is no longer distinct from Canada and India. The graph suggests that consistent two-party electoral dominance, as measured by the percent of the vote received, over the past half century is a US phenomenon.

the Indian case, this was because the Indian National Congress (INC) was an extremely dominant first party; the second party consistently received a fraction of the votes that went to the INC. But, starting in the 1970s, the distinction among the Westminster systems largely disappeared. On the one hand, in the UK, the domination of the Conservatives and Labour began to wane, partially because the Liberal Party (now the Liberal Democratic Party) gradually gained public support, and partially because of the rise of regional parties, like the Scottish National Party. In the Indian case, the one-party domination of the INC gradually disappeared. Today, the two largest parties are the INC and the BJP. In the 2014 election, for example, the BJP won a plurality of votes and a majority of seats in the Lok Sabha, the lower house of the Indian parliament.

48 Chapter Two

It is easy to see, considering this history, why political scientists writing in the 1970s and 1980s would consider the United States and the UK clear cases of Duverger's Law working and Canada and India requiring explanation. The problem is that the UK results were period specific. While Labour and the Conservatives were together gaining 90% or more of the vote in parliamentary elections, that combined electoral strength turned out to be temporary. The same was true in terms of seats in Parliament. In the two elections after the defeat of Germany in World War II, the Conservatives and Labour won around a combined 90% of the seats. By 1955, and until 1974, they won 98% to 99% of the seats. But in 1974, these numbers started to drop, and by the 2005 election, third parties and independents had won nearly 15% of the seats. For this reason, one cannot treat the United States and the UK as evidence for Duverger's Law and then treat Canada and India as exceptions. It is quite the opposite: Canada, India, and the UK appear to be the norm and the United States might be the exception.

An obvious example of how the party system in the UK differs from that of the United States is the Liberal Democratic Party. This party, then called the Liberal Party, was a prime example Duverger used to illustrate his argument about the strategic behavior of voters and parties. As I had quoted before:

> Take for example a British constituency in which the Conservatives have 35,000 votes, Labour 40,000, and Liberal 15,000: it is obvious that the success of Labour is entirely dependent on the presence of the Liberal party; if the Liberal party should withdraw its candidate it can be assumed that a majority of voters supporting him will transfer to the Conservative, the minority being divided between Labour and abstention. Two alternatives are therefore possible: either the Liberal party may reach agreement with the Conservatives to withdraw its candidate (in exchange for some form of compensation in other constituencies), in which case the two-party system is restored as a result of fusion or of an alliance very like fusion; or else the Liberal party may persist in its independent line, the electors will gradually desert it, and the two-party system will be restored by elimination.
>
> *(Duverger 1954, 223–4)*

The electors, however, did not desert the Liberal Party. Quite the opposite, the Liberals gradually climbed into being a formidable third strongest party in the UK. While the party received 9% of the vote in the 1945 and 1950 elections, that public support collapsed to under 3% in the election of 1951, the year Duverger's *Party Politics* was first published. From there, public support for the Liberal Party climbed. In the February 1974 election, it received 19% of the vote. In 1983, when it ran as an alliance with the Social Democratic Party, it received over 25% of the vote. That support dropped into the mid-teens in the

Duverger's Law and the American Electoral System **49**

1990s, but in the 2005 and 2010 general elections, the party, now calling themselves the Liberal Democrats, received 22% and 23% of the vote and became a coalition partner with the Conservatives in 2010. In 2015, that public support dropped back down to 8%, although this appears to have much more to do with anger over joining that coalition government than with voters wanting to avoid wasting their votes.

While election results in the UK and Canada seem to have produced problems for Duverger's Law, the most serious counterevidence may have come from India. While Canada and Great Britain can be safely defined as "two-and-a-half" party systems, India is very clearly a multiparty system. The Indian parliament, or Lok Sabha, currently has thirty-six parties. The top two parties, the BJP and the INC, hold only around 60% of the seats combined.

Some proponents of Duverger's Law have taken theoretical steps to try to explain why all SMP systems do not simply lead to two very strong parties. Following an argument made by Anthony Downs (1957), William Riker (1976) tried to explain the difference between the US and Canada by dividing voters into three categories. The first is the "naïve" or "sincere" voter, who always votes for the party that they prefer the most. The second is the "sophisticated" voter,

> by which is meant that the voter takes account of anticipated votes by others and then votes so as to bring about the best realizable outcome for himself, regardless of whether or not his vote is sincere, i.e., for his preferred alternative.

In other words, they will vote for the candidate that they most support among those with an actual chance of winning. The third is the "disillusioned" voter, who normally supports a major party, but since that party has so many constituents to satisfy, will sometimes be disappointed by the major party and then shift his or her support to a smaller party. The second two produce the drive behind Duverger's Law: some voters become disillusioned by the major party, driving them towards a third party, but then they return to the major party within an election or two either because that party is their first preference or because they are "sophisticated" enough to recognize that voting for a small party in an SMP system is a losing proposition.

To explain the India results away, Riker takes another tactic, which was also later employed by Nikolenyi (2010). Riker argues that Duverger's Law does not hold if the country is dominated by a single, widely supported party. At the time, the INC was by far the most dominant party. Since it held the ideological central position, Riker argued, voters on its left and right had no reason to be concerned about wasting their votes, since the INC would win regardless. Therefore, they voted in much the same way as "naïve" voters in systems like Canada and the United States.

50 Chapter Two

Riker's argument is problematic on multiple grounds. In the Indian case, it simply does not hold up to historical change. In the period from 1952, India's first free election, until 1971, the INC did dominate the country's electoral politics, repeatedly receiving between 40% and 50% of the vote while the next strongest party received less than 10% of the vote. In 1977, the election after Prime Minister Indira Gandhi lifted the state of emergency and reinstituted representative democracy, the INC was soundly defeated by the Janata alliance of parties. In the early 1980s, the INC return to their electoral dominance, again winning between 40% and 50% of the vote in 1980 and 1984 with the next strongest party receiving less than 10% of the vote. But then, this one-party domination ended. Since 1991, the INC and BJP became the two strongest parties, and while the INC had won more votes (but not always the most seats) in most of these elections, the vote difference between the INC and BJP was usually less than 10%. Finally, in 2014, the BJP soundly defeated the INC, winning both a plurality of the votes and a majority of the seats.

Despite the rise of the BJP and India no longer being a country dominated by a single political party, there has been little evidence of Indian voters gravitating towards the top two parties in order to avoid wasting their votes. Instead, around 50% or more of Indian voters consistently select a party other than the INC or BJP.

This leads to the question: why is there this variation across SMP systems? Riker chose to use the unfortunate term "naïve" for those voters not following the predictions of Duverger's Law, but he never gave an explanation as to why Canadian, British, and Indian voters are more naïve than American voters.

Another approach is to simply dismiss these variations across SMP systems as random fluctuations. As Benoit (2006) argued, Duverger's Law is not deterministic, and so one should expect variation across SMP systems. On its face, this is understandable; social science research has a muddiness to it, and so scholars tend to focus on patterns with the understanding that there will also be many, many factors that cannot be accounted for in a theory. But if this is the case, then we can already see the limitation of Duverger's Law for explaining the problems of American third parties. The more that the theory is not deterministic, the more that factors other than the electoral system are driving the disappearance of these parties.

Strategic Behavior and the Two-Party System

But there is a critical limitation in the analysis thus far as well as any research on this topic that studies elections in a country as a whole. Duverger's Law does not lead to the conclusion that two parties will dominate in the national legislature or win most of the votes in a country; it leads to the conclusion that two parties *will dominate within each region of a country*. In other words, the theory predicts that a strategic voter will choose one of the two candidates who are most likely to win the election; it does not predict that across every district in the country those candidates will come from the same two parties (Gallagher, Conclusion 2005, 547). In this way, the difference across SMP countries could be regional. The critical difference between the United States and the UK, for example, could be that the latter includes Scotland, Northern Ireland, and Wales. Similarly, Canada includes Quebec, and India is an extremely diverse country with different parties being supported in different regions.

To take this to its logical extreme, a way to test Duverger's Law across SMP systems is to measure vote differences not across the entire country but across individual districts. In other words, one can treat the third-party vote as the percent vote for all candidates who (a) were nominated by a political party and (b) did not receive the most or second most votes in the district. In this way, the top two parties can vary significantly across districts. For example, in a district near London, the third-party vote might be the vote for all candidates nominated by a party other than Labour or the Conservatives, but in a Scottish district the third-party vote might be all the votes for candidates nominated by parties other than Labour or the Scottish National Party. If the fear of wasting votes is driving the weakness of third parties in the United States, then the third-party vote measured this way should be roughly the same across all four major SMP countries.

This logic can be taken one step further. How does one know that the differences in voting behavior across different electoral systems are actually being caused by strategic voting? To put this another way, Duverger's second argument is that in SMP systems, voters have to consider not only which candidates they most prefer but also what the consequences are if they choose a candidate who is unlikely to win. But, what if voters were not forced into this type of choice? For example, an electoral system could be designed in which there are single-member districts, but instead of selecting a single candidate, the voter ranks them. If a majority of voters have the same most preferred candidate, then that candidate would win. If not, the system would go through automatic runoffs. In each runoff, the votes for the candidate with the fewest highest rankings would then be redistributed to each voter's second highest rankings. If no candidate has a majority of highest rankings, then this process keeps repeating itself until one candidate has a majority.

This electoral system, often called "preferential voting" or "alternative voting," is used in elections to the lower house of the Australian parliament (Farrell and McAllister 2006). Proponents of electoral reform in the United States often argue for a slightly modified version of this system called instant runoff[6] or ranked-choice voting, as had been approved by voters in Maine during the 2016 election.[7] The great advantage of this system, proponents argue, is that voters do not have to vote strategically. Florida voters in 2000 could have selected Nader first, for example, and when no candidate got a majority of the vote, then those ballots could be redistributed to their next highest selection, presumably Al Gore.

The strategic voter aspect of Duverger's Law can therefore be tested rather easily. If voters are not forced to avoid wasting their votes, like in Australia, they should be selecting a significantly higher percent of third-party candidates as their first choice than voters in SMP systems. In other words, by treating Australians' most preferred candidate as their "vote," it can be easily integrated into the district-level test presented before and used as a method for testing the strategic voter aspect of Duverger's Law. If Duverger was right, then votes at the district level for third parties should be consistently low in Canada, India, the UK, and the United States but much higher in Australia.

As Figure 2.3 clearly shows, this is not the case. Third parties receive a mean of 20.3% of the vote in Australian parliamentary districts. This figure is

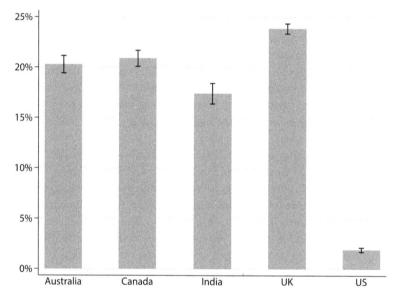

FIGURE 2.3 Mean percent vote for third parties at district level. This graph shows the average district-level vote for third-party candidates in four SMP system elections (Canada in 2011, India in 2009, the UK in 2010, and the United States in 2010) as well as the 2013 elections in Australia, which uses preferential voting for its lower house of Parliament. Duverger's second proposition leads to the prediction that voters in Australia would be more likely to vote for third-party candidates because preferential voting eliminates the concern about splitting the vote. Instead, Australians vote for third-party candidates at generally the same rate as voters in Canada, India, and the UK. In sharp contrast, far fewer votes are cast for third-party candidates in the United States. For the purposes of this comparative analysis, third-party candidate is defined as any candidate who was nominated by a political party and did not receive the most or second most votes in a district. For Australia, a "vote" means their first preference.

Duverger's Law and the American Electoral System **53**

statistically equal to districts in Canada, where third-party candidates receive an average of 20.9% of the vote. It is also less than in the UK, where third-party candidates receive an average of 23.8% of the vote. The only Westminster system in which voters select third parties less often then Australians is, ironically, India. Despite Indian voters repeatedly electing a large number of parties to the Lok Sabha, at the district level, an average of 17.4% of the vote went to third-party candidates.[8]

It is worth pointing out that the difference between India and these other three systems has more to do with voting for independent candidates and less to do with voting for the top two candidates. In Australia, Canada, and India, the mean combined district-level vote for the top two candidates are, respectively, 78.9%, 79.0%, and 78.3%. This mean combined vote for the top two candidates is slightly lower in the UK: 75.7%. In other words, once one removes the impact of regional variation, the vote for third parties is roughly equal across these four countries, despite Australia using preferential voting.

Figure 2.3 also shows that the exception is not Australia but the United States. Measuring the third-party vote this way (the total percent vote for all candidates in a district who were nominated by a party but did not receive the most or second most votes), the mean third-party vote is 1.9% with a confidence interval of 1.7% to 2.1%. Similarly, the mean combined vote for the top two candidates in each House district is 97.7%, far higher than these other single-member district systems. Compared to other major single-member district systems, the vote for third-party candidates in the United States is extremely low. In the average district in the United States, third parties receive one-tenth of the vote that third-party candidates receive in the average district in Australia, Canada, India, and the UK.

Figure 2.4 makes this point another way. Duverger's primary argument is that voters want to avoid dividing the vote between two parties with similar ideologies and therefore gravitate to the top two candidates. Figure 2.4 shows the percent of districts in which the vote had been potentially split, which in this case is measured as percent of districts in which the vote for the second and third candidate combined was greater than the vote for the winning candidate. In other words, had all the votes for the third strongest candidate been cast for the second strongest candidate, including if the third candidate had dropped out of the race, would the second candidate have won the election?

This measure, to be sure, likely includes a significant percent of Type 1 errors, or false positives. It is quite possible that supporters of the third strongest candidate would be more inclined to support the strongest instead of the second strongest candidate, or that vote could be split evenly between the two largest parties. This measure also does not take into consideration any other candidates running in that district. While all the supporters of the third strongest candidate might support the second strongest candidate over the winner, for example, supporters of the fourth strongest candidate might have supported the

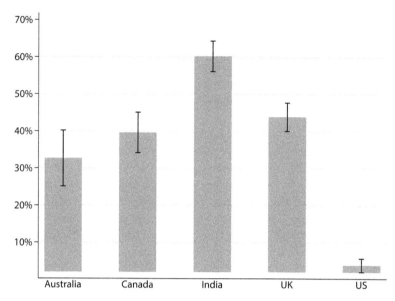

FIGURE 2.4 Percent of district-level elections that third-party candidate could have spoiled. This graph shows the percent of districts in which the combined vote for the second and third most supported candidates exceeds the vote for the winning candidate. For Australian elections, a vote is defined as the voter's first preference. The graph demonstrates that, despite having a preferential voting electoral systems, Australian voters are not more likely to "split" their votes than voters in Canada, India, and the UK. However, vote splitting is much less common in the United States than in these other countries. This graph is based on election results for the lower house of Congress or Parliament in Australia (2013), Canada (2009), India (2011), the UK (2010), and the United States (2010).

winner over the second strongest candidate. However, that bias in the measure is consistent across the countries; therefore, it still provides a useful way to compare these systems.

The graph shows two results consistent with the findings in Figure 2.3. First, the graph suggests that voters in Canada, India, and the UK are not avoiding dividing their votes because it is a SMP system. To the contrary, they are potentially more likely to be dividing their votes than in Australia, despite the latter having a preferential voting system. If one treats a first preference as if it were a vote in a SMP system, then 32.7% of Australian districts had potentially spoiled elections. In Canada, India, and the UK, those figure are respectively 39.6%, 60.2%, and 43.8%. Second, a much smaller percentage of elections to the House of Representatives in the United States are spoiled by third-party candidates. In the 2010 election, 3.9% of district-level elections were potentially spoiled by the third candidate. Based on this evidence, there is little reason to believe that SMP systems favor two dominant parties because voters are avoiding wasting the vote.

Conclusion

The evidence presented in this chapter leads to the conclusion that the American electoral system does deflate the vote for third parties, but that this factor certainly does not explain why the vote for third parties in the United States is so much lower than in other SMP systems. There is no evidence to the contention that third parties cannot succeed in the United States because voters will always gravitate towards the top two parties in order to avoid wasting their votes. Instead, some other factors are deflating the vote for American third parties.

This evidence, I would argue, is consistent with Duverger's prediction that SMP electoral systems increase the strength of the two largest parties. However, this evidence also suggests that Duverger's Law is incomplete. On the one hand, this phenomenon cannot be explained as simply a function of how seats are allocated, since the two largest parties also receive more votes in SMP than PR systems. On the other hand, the strategic behavior of voters and parties is not enough to explain this phenomenon. In most SMP countries, a significant percent of voters is voting for third parties and potentially wasting the vote in exactly the manner that Duverger argued that they would not. Thus, the evidence leaves an unanswered question: how does SMP deflate the vote for third parties if not through the strategic behavior of voters and parties?

It also does little to solve the puzzle of why third parties are so much weaker in the United States than other SMP systems, or why third-party support declined in the United States over the twentieth century. The outlier among the SMP systems is not India. While India is a vibrant multiparty political system, at the district level the voting looks relatively similar to that of Canada and the UK. The outlier is instead the United States. While roughly 20% of the vote at the district level are going to third parties in these other SMP systems, only around 2% of the vote in House elections goes to third parties. (If we measure it more generously as the total percent of the House vote for candidates nominated by a party other than the Democrats or the Republicans, that figure is closer to 3%.) In order to solve this puzzle, one needs to look at other factors that might be affecting third parties.

Notes

1 To be clear, in this analysis I am speaking strictly about list-PR and not making a distinction between open and closed lists. (It gets the name list-PR because parties running in this system publish a list of candidates, get allocated a number of seats based on the election results, and then allocate the specific seats based on the order

56 Chapter Two

of that candidate list.) I am also not speaking about single transferable vote, which is another type of proportional representation system.

2 All list-PR systems have a minimum vote threshold that parties need to win any seats. In Germany, that minimum is 5%, for example, while it is 2% for the Danish Folketing. This minimum is designed to reduce the number of parties in parliament as well as keep fringe parties from winning seats. Since there are virtually always parties that run candidates but get fewer votes than the threshold requirement, successful parties will generally receive a higher percentage of seats than votes.

3 It is worth pointing out that by "fusion," Duverger means that the two parties join together and form one political party (Duverger 1954, 344–5). In American politics, and in most of this book, "fusion" is when a single candidate is co-nominated by multiple parties; the term in no way implies that these party organizations join together.

4 Botswana, Canada, Ghana, India, Jamaica, Trinidad and Tobago, the UK, and the United States.

5 Argentina, Austria, Belgium, Benin, Brazil, Bulgaria, Cape Verde, Chile, Costa Rica, Croatia, Cyprus, Czech Republic, Denmark, Dominican Republic, El Salvador, Estonia, Finland, Greece, Guyana, Iceland, Israel, Italy, Latvia, Luxembourg, Montenegro, Namibia, Netherlands, Norway, Panama, Peru, Poland, Portugal, San Marino, Serbia, Slovakia, Slovenia, South Africa, Spain, Suriname, Sweden, Switzerland, and Uruguay.

6 Australia requires voters to fill out the entire ballot, that is, rank every single candidate for each office. If a voter does not rank a particular candidate, the vote for that office is thrown out. The key difference in instant runoff is that this requirement is removed.

7 Henry Grabar, "Maine Just Voted for a Better Way to Vote", Slate, November 9, 2016.

8 The election results for each district in each country were gathered from the following sources: for Canada, Parliament of Canada, "History of Federal Ridings Since 1867", www.lop.parl.gc.ca/About/Parliament/FederalRidingsHistory/hfer. asp?Language=E&Search=Gres&genElection=41&ridProvince=0&submit1=Search; for India, Election Commission of India, "Election Commission of India, General Elections, 2009 (15th Lok Sabha), 25-Constituency Wise Detailed Result", http:// eci.nic.in/eci_main/archiveofge2009/Stats/VOLI/25_ConstituencyWiseDetailed Result.pdf; for the UK, file "Results(XLS)" for UK Parliament general election on 6 May 2010 at The Electoral Commission, "Election data", www.electoral-commission.org.uk/our-work/our-research/electoral-data; for Australia, file "First Preferences by Candidate by Voting Type" at Australian Electoral Commission, "House of Representatives Downloads", http://results.aec.gov.au/17496/Website/ HouseDownloadsMenu-17496-csv.htm. All data retrieved April 20, 2015.

3

THE IMPACT OF BALLOT ACCESS LAWS

One of the most widely supported explanations for the decline of American third parties is the difficulty of ballot access laws. These state laws determine which candidates and parties will be on the ballot each election and which will be excluded. Generally speaking, in order to get onto the ballot, a candidate or party needs to gather a specific number of signatures from registered voters. If a party already on the ballot receives a minimum percent vote set by some states, then its candidates will be automatically put onto the ballot during the next election. Otherwise, that party will have to once again gather the requisite signatures in order to run a candidate in the general election. The difficulty of these laws varies widely by state, and overall, these requirements are higher today than they were a century ago.

Many third-party scholars argue vigorously that as these laws got more difficult, third parties have been almost completely shut out of the political system. Indeed, there has been a wide range of scholarship arguing that ballot access laws undermine third parties, including by political scientists (Rosenstone, Behr and Lazarus 1984, 19–21; Herrnson, 1997, 24–25; Bibby and Maisel 2003, 70; Gillespie 2012, 25–28) and legal scholars (Daybell 2000; Cofsky 1996; Smith 1999; Evseev 2005; Hall 2005–2006). Indeed, much of the writing on ballot access laws has been in law journals, in which the authors generally begin by assuming that ballot access laws have been unnecessarily harsh and a hindrance to third parties and democracy in general, and then proceeding to elaborate on legal issues related to these laws.

A good example comes from Oliver Hall in an article titled "Death by a Thousand Signatures." Hall argues that ballot access laws create a conflict of interest for the major parties. Because these parties receive significant voter support each election, they do not need to collect signatures to get their candidates onto the ballot. The Republicans and Democrats therefore have every

58 Chapter Three

incentive to make ballot access laws very difficult for third parties, that is, their competitors. Hall concludes that, indeed, "as ballot access laws have become more restrictive, the formerly 'permanent minor parties' in the United States have appeared on fewer and fewer state ballots" (Hall 2005–2006, 415–16).

The most widely cited researcher on ballot access laws is probably Richard Winger, an activist associated with the Libertarian Party who is also the editor of *Ballot Access News*, an online source on the most updated issues on ballot access laws. Winger writes extensively on these state laws (Winger 1997; Winger 2000; Winger 2004) and has consistently argued that excessively difficult ballot requirements have significantly hurt the ability of third parties to get onto the ballot and win votes. Winger claims, for example, that third parties are "much more likely to win elections when such laws are lenient" and, moreover, that in some states "a minor party may need to spend several hundred thousand dollars just to get on the ballot" (Winger 1997, 165).

But there is a problem with this argument. Most statistical research by political scientists on ballot access laws shows that they have little if any impact on third-party success. While Dowling and Lem (2009) found that from 1980 to 2005 signature requirements reduced the number of third-party candidates in gubernatorial elections, the majority of empirical studies have demonstrated that ballot access laws have had little impact on third parties. Stratmann (2005) found no evidence that signature requirements reduced the number of third-party candidates in state legislative elections. Examining the effect of ballot access restrictions on third-party and independent candidacies in the 2006 senatorial and gubernatorial elections, Burden (2007) found that signature requirements reduced the number of candidates on the ballot but had no impact on the votes these candidates received. Collet and Wattenberg (1999) found that in the 1996 presidential election ballot access laws explained little of the variance in the number of third-party candidates on the ballot or the vote for them. Schraufnagel and Milita (2010) similarly found that Florida's Revision 11, which dramatically improved ballot access requirements for third parties in that state, produced only a small increase in the number of third-party candidates and the percent vote received by these candidates. Tamas and Hindman (2014) also found little evidence that ballot access laws have had much of an impact on the strength of third parties. The general findings of those who conduct statistical tests on the relationship between ballot access laws and third-party success have probably been summarized best by Collet and Wattenberg (1999, 230), who express surprise for finding "that ballot access laws explain very little of the variance in either the number of minor party candidacies or the vote for them," and suggesting that both activists and scholars are "overstating the importance of ballot access as the key to minor party and independent candidate success."

In this chapter, I take the next step in attempting to determine why third parties became so much weaker over the twentieth century. I will show that while ballot access laws have indeed gotten much more difficult since 1900, there is little evidence that their level of difficulty significantly reduces the number of third-party candidates on the ballot or had much to do with the decline of third parties over the past century. The claim that these laws make it almost impossible for third parties to get onto the ballot is clearly untenable. Third-party candidates are getting on the ballot across the country, and over the past few decades the number of third-party candidates getting onto the ballot has steadily risen even though ballot access laws have not gotten significantly easier. Maybe most damaging to the theory, the evidence even suggests that forcing third parties to gather signatures *might actually increase their vote share*, though marginally. Ballot access laws, I argue, do not help us explain why third parties are much weaker today than a century ago.

This analysis is based primarily on ballot access laws for each state from 1888, when Massachusetts was the first state to enact the Australian ballot, until today. I focus on two key aspects of those laws: the number of signatures a party needs to get its candidate onto the House ballot and the percent of the vote that a party needs to remain on the ballot without having to repeat the process of acquiring signatures. I refer to the former as signature or petition requirements and the latter as previous vote requirements, since it is the vote during the previous election that determines whether a party will be automatically put onto the ballot. This data was gathered by tracing the changes in ballot access laws in the session laws of all fifty states since the 1890s, or more specifically, from when the Australian ballot was enacted (or when the state joined the union) until today.

What are Ballot Access Laws?

Ballot access laws are state laws that determine what candidates are listed on the ballot during a general election. They are a necessary consequence of the Australian ballot, which states began using in the 1890s. Before the Australian ballot, or the secret ballot used in the United States and much of the world, American elections were famous for significant corruption by the major political parties. One factor was the lack of voter registration, which made it very easy for a single voter to reenter the voting area multiple times, repeatedly voting for the same candidates. Another factor was that each political party printed its own ballot and handed it out at polling places. So, whenever a citizen wanted to vote, he had to go to one of the party representatives, ask for a ballot, and then throw that ballot into the ballot box in full view of everyone in the room. This system made voter intimidation easy. One purpose of the secret ballot, of course, was to eliminate this opportunity for voter coercion (Evans 1917, 1–16).

The requirement for voting in secret meant that each state would have to print its own ballot. Requiring the voter to request a ballot from a party

60 Chapter Three

representative would still be a public act and effectively undermine any advantage gained by casting that ballot in a secret location. However, this also meant that the government would have to play a gatekeeping role. It could not simply place any name on the ballot, since the list would become far too long and make voting extremely complicated for most people.

Indeed, the need for requirements that limited the number of candidates on the ballot was made especially clear during the recall election in California in 2003. While the recall itself required a significant number of signatures, getting onto the ballot as a gubernatorial candidate required only sixty-five. The number of people registering to be gubernatorial candidates ballooned to nearly 200, with 135 finally being put onto the ballot, including forty-nine Democratic and forty-one Republican candidates. These candidates included movie star and former weight lifter Arnold Schwarzenegger, political commentator Ariana Huffington, former child actor Gary Coleman, pornographer Larry Flynt, and pornographic film actress Mary Carey. The size of the ballot was, to say the least, confusing, which may have contributed to Schwarzenegger's victory (Gerston and Christensen 2015).

Since the 1890s, as the states were gradually writing laws to run elections using the Australian ballot, they were also writing laws to determine which candidates would be allowed on the ballot. While these laws vary widely by states, they generally have four types of requirements. The first is signature requirements, sometimes also called petition requirements, which often falls under two headings within the law: "Definition of political party" or signature requirements for individual candidates. Idaho provides a standard example of a signature requirement for third parties:

> A "political party" within the meaning of this act, is an organization of electors under a given name. A political party shall be deemed created and qualified to participate in elections in any of the following three (3) ways... (c) By an affiliation of electors who shall have signed a petition which shall... have attached thereto a sheet or sheets containing the signatures of at least a number of qualified electors equal to two per cent (2%) of the aggregate vote cast for presidential electors in the state at the previous general election at which presidential electors were chosen.[1]

These laws also add a group of specifications that political parties must meet for submitting these petitions, including a due date. In the Idaho case, for example, the petition must "be filed with the secretary of state on or before August 30 of even numbered years."[2]

The second type is a previous vote requirement. Specifically, if the candidates of a political party gain a certain number or percent of the vote during an election, that party will automatically be put onto the ballot the next election. One advantage of this requirement is that it excuses the Democratic and

Republican parties in most states from having to collect signatures and apply again for party status; their candidates are automatically put onto the ballot. It also means that more successful third parties can also automatically place their candidates on the ballot. At the same time, this requirement limits the number of parties that are on the ballot by making the hurdle more difficult for the smallest parties. Illinois, for example, set its previous vote requirement of 5% in 1931 and has maintained that level ever since. The wording within the Illinois state code is common for previous vote requirements:

> A political party, which at the general election for State and county officers then next preceding a primary, cast more than 5 per cent of the entire vote cast within any congressional district, is hereby declared to be a political party within the meaning of this Article, within such congressional district, and shall nominate its candidate for Representative in Congress, under the provisions hereof.[3]

The third type of requirement, used by some states, is party membership. Delaware, for example, requires that a political party gain membership by 0.1% of the state population before it can place candidates on the general election ballot.[4] It is the only state in which membership provides the only method for parties to run general election candidates.

Finally, some states require that a political party demonstrate that it is "organized." One example of this approach is South Carolina. In 1950, South Carolina became the last of the forty-eight continental states to implement the Australian ballot. In its original law, it mandated that new parties must gather 10,000 signatures statewide in order to be certified as a political party; this requirement did not apply to any party that had candidates on the ballot in 1948, that is, the Democratic or Republican parties. In 1977, the state modified the law to include "organizational tasks" that the party must perform to retain certification and therefore run candidates. These tasks include that new parties must organize at the precinct level by holding county conventions before March 31 of each general election year, that these parties must hold a state convention before May 15 each election year, and that they certify their candidates in at least one of two consecutive general elections each even-numbered year.[5]

Ballot access laws not only vary widely in terms of these types of specific issues. They also vary widely in terms of their difficulty. At the easy end are states like Hawaii, which requires a petition containing a number of signatures equaling 0.1% of the number of voters registered at the last election.[6] While many states require parties to produce a certain percent of signatures, others require a specific number. A number require 1,000 signatures or fewer for a party to be recognized or get its initial candidates on the House ballot: Louisiana (1,000), New Jersey (200), Nevada (100), Rhode Island (500), Vermont (500), and Washington (1,000).[7]

62 Chapter Three

On the opposite end are states that have a very high signature requirement for an organization to be recognized as a political party and run candidates for office. Maine requires third parties to gain signatures equaling or greater than 5% of the total number of votes cast for governor in the last gubernatorial election.[8] In New York, for a new party to put a candidate onto the ballot for the House of Representatives, it must produce either 3,500 signatures or signatures amounting to 5% of the vote in the last congressional election.[9] For California, which has an open primary, that figure is 10% of the last gubernatorial vote. To make matters even more difficult for third parties in California, that high number of signatures gets the candidate onto the ballot for the open primary, not the general election. Only the primary candidates who received the most or second most votes, regardless of party or even if they come from the same party, can run in the general election.

This variation is also true for previous vote requirements, although the number of votes needed to remain on the ballot are generally higher than the number of signatures to first get onto the ballot. Two states, South Carolina and Vermont, effectively have no previous vote requirements; in both cases, for parties to remain on the ballot, they must be "organized" in a manner specified by the law. The next lowest is New Mexico. In this state, to remain a qualified political party, at least one of its candidates for president or governor over the previous two elections must have received at least half a percent of the vote. Seven other states allow a party to stay on the ballot if in a previous statewide race, usually for governor or president but sometimes for secretary of state, it had received at least 1% of the vote. On the other extreme include Hawaii and Virginia, which require 10% of the vote statewide, as well as Alabama and Georgia, which require 20% of the vote statewide.[10]

In other words, ballot access laws vary significantly across states. While there are states with extremely difficult ballot access requirements, there are other states with requirements that are far less harsh. If difficult ballot access laws have undermined third parties, then one would expect third parties to have been weakened or completely disappeared where ballot access laws are very difficult but remaining vibrant where those laws remain easy.

How Have Ballot Access Laws Changed?

Figure 3.1 shows the evolution of ballot access requirements since 1886. Specifically, it shows the mean signature and previous vote requirements for a party to run candidates in races for the House of Representatives. (While in most states the law is consistent regardless of what office is being sought, some change the requirement by the level of the office, especially when that requirement is a raw number instead of a percent.) These means are calculated by district instead of state, so a change in populous states like California or Texas will have a much greater impact than a change in, for example, Montana or North Dakota.

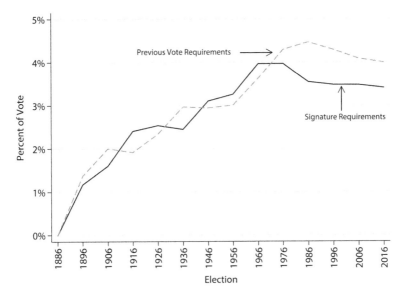

FIGURE 3.1 Difficulty of ballot access laws, 1886–2016. This graph shows the difficult of ballot access laws from 1886, just before states began instituting the Australian ballot, to 2016. Specifically, for each election year ending with the digit "6," it shows (1) the mean signature requirements third-party candidates needed to get onto the House ballot and (2) the mean vote third parties needed to have their candidates automatically placed on the ballot during the next election. (When a state defined a requirement as a raw number, it was translated into a percent of the vote.) These figures are shown by House district, not state; for this reason, ballot access laws in larger states like New York would have a greater impact on these figures than in smaller states like Vermont. The graph shows that overall ballot access laws became more difficult until around 1976. Since then, on average, previous vote requirements have gotten more difficult, while signature requirements have gotten less challenging.

As this graph clearly indicates, ballot access laws have become more difficult over the past century. The mean signature requirement for getting a House candidate on the ballot in 1900 was 1.4%, and the mean previous vote requirement to stay on the ballot was 1.6%. By the 1950 election, when third parties had largely disappeared from American politics outside of New York State, the mean signature and previous vote requirements had doubled to 3.3% and 3.1%, respectively. In 1972, the mean signature requirement for House districts peaked at 4% and then began declining again. Since the 2000 election, the mean signature requirements have been approximately 3.4%. Similarly, the mean previous vote requirement for House elections peaked in 1986 at 4.5% and have since declined to around 4%.

64 Chapter Three

These changes in ballot access laws came gradually, as Figure 3.1 suggests. When the states began instituting the Australian ballot, the number of signatures required to initially get onto the ballot was generally low. Of the thirty-nine states that had enacted the Australian ballot before 1900, four initially had no petition requirements (Connecticut, Florida, Michigan, and Virginia) and twenty-two had petition requirements that were raw numbers by district (Tennessee with 15; Delaware, Iowa, and Kansas with 25; Arkansas, Mississippi, Nebraska, Oregon, and Washington with 50; Colorado, Louisiana, Montana, North Dakota, Utah, and Wyoming with 100; Indiana and Maryland with 200; New Hampshire, New York, and Rhode Island with 250; Kentucky with 400; and Alabama with 500). In the rest of the states, third parties were required to gather signatures from 1% (Maine, Massachusetts, Minnesota, Missouri, Ohio, Vermont, West Virginia, and Wisconsin), 2% (Illinois), 3% (California, Nevada, and Pennsylvania), or 5% (New Jersey) of the voters. In other words, only New Jersey initially had a very high petition requirement, and even it soon reduced that petition requirement to 1%.

From this point onward, states varied a great deal in terms of how often they changed these laws. On the low end, Kentucky instituted the Australian ballot in 1891 with a signature requirement for House candidates of 400 and previous vote requirement of 2% statewide. The only significant change in this law since its enactment has been to specify that the previous vote requirement is based on turnout in the last presidential election.[11] At the other extreme, New York changed its ballot access laws repeatedly until the mid-1970s. It instituted the Australian ballot in 1890; for the House of Representatives, the petition requirement to get onto the ballot was 250 signatures. In 1891, that figure doubled to 500. In 1896, that figure was doubled again to 1,000, which was increased again in 1911 to 1,500. In 1918, it was doubled yet again to 3,000. (Technically, at this point the requirement was 5% of the total number of votes cast in the district, but in reality the 3,000 figure was the key.) That signature requirement remained stable for congressional candidates in New York until it was increased to 3,500 in 1971, which is the current requirement for independent candidates to get onto the ballot.[12]

After this initial set of ballot access laws, the requirements became more difficult in most states. Like New York, some states increased those requirements quickly around 1900. For example, Kansas initially required parties to provide twenty-five signatures in order to place its candidate on the ballot for the House of Representatives. Four years later, third parties had to provide signatures of 5% of qualified voters from that House district. When Minnesota enacted the Australian ballot in 1893, parties could place candidates on the House ballot if they acquired signatures equaling 1% of the total vote in the district during the previous election. In 1899, that requirement was increased to 10%. Nevada, North Dakota, Oregon, and West Virginia also dramatically increased their petition requirements during this period.

However, these extreme examples are not representative of the over-all change in ballot access laws. The widely held image of state legislatures across the United States creating insurmountable ballot access restrictions is a significant overstatement. For much of the country, ballot access requirements rose slowly. Of the forty-five states that gained statehood before 1900, twenty-eight, or around 62%, did not increase their previous vote requirements from 1900 to 1940, or during the period that third parties almost completely disappeared from House elections. Five even reduced their previous vote requirements. Similarly, just over half of the states either kept their signature requirements the same or reduced them during this period. Among states in the South, where third parties almost completely disappeared around 1900, only four had significant ballot access restrictions before 1940: Florida, Louisiana, North Carolina, and Texas. The other six (Alabama, Arkansas, Georgia, Mississippi, South Carolina, and Virginia) had absolutely no previous vote requirement and did not require more than a few hundred signatures. Instead, third parties often had to hold conventions or demonstrate that they were organized as a party.

Indeed, the results in Figure 3.1 are skewed by a small number of states with extremely high ballot access requirements. During every election since 1900, the mean signature and previous vote requirements were respectively higher than the median signature and previous vote requirements. Indeed, these means were often twice as large as the medians, suggesting that a few cases were pulling the results upward. Similarly, while the mean signature and previous vote requirements rose rapidly, the median for both rose much slower and remained much lower. In 1892, as states were beginning to enact ballot access laws, the median signature and previous vote requirements for House districts was 1%. The median previous vote requirement did not reach 2% until 1934 and then 3% in 1986, where it remains today. Similarly, the median signature requirement to get onto the House ballot rose to 2% in 1938 and then dropped to 1.5% in 2008, where it is today.

Figure 3.2 demonstrates this in a different way. It shows the percent of House districts with easier ballot access laws by decade from 1900 to 2016, with "easier" defined as signature requirements or previous vote requirements of 1% or less. The graph demonstrates that while there was a decline in the percent of districts with easier ballot access laws, that decline was gradual and did not sweep the entire United States. In the 1910s, during the last great third-party wave, 52% of House districts were in states with easier signature requirements. In the 1950s, when third parties had largely disappeared from American politics, 41% of districts had easier signature requirements. Reaching a low in the 1970s and 1980s, some state governments have since been reducing the difficulty of signature requirements. By the 2010s, the percent of House districts with easier signature requirements rose back to 47%, almost as high as in the 1910s.

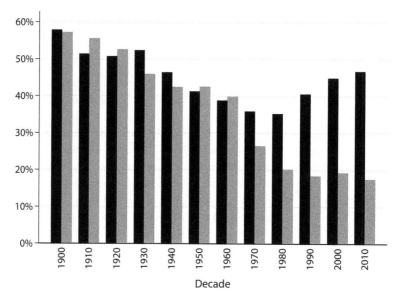

FIGURE 3.2 Average percent of districts that have easier ballot access requirements. This graph shows the percent of districts each decade with easier ballot access requirements, defined as signature or previous vote requirements of 1% or less. (The black bars are signature requirements while the gray bars are previous vote requirements.) The graph shows that while the percent of districts with easy ballot access laws declined by the middle of the twentieth century, that decline was not as dramatic as it is often portrayed in the third-party literature. Moreover, while previous vote requirements continued to get more difficult, the percent of districts with easier signature requirements has increased since the 1980s.

The change in previous vote requirements since 1900 was more severe, but much of that changed happened after third parties had already largely disappeared. In the 1910s, third parties would have been placed back on the ballot after receiving 1% of the vote in 56% of House districts. In the 1950s, that figure dropped to 43%. After the 1950s, the percent of districts with easier previous vote requirements continued to drop. Today, a third party can secure a spot on the ballot with 1% of the vote in only 18% of House districts.

In other words, for most House districts, there was not a dramatic decline in easier ballot access laws during the period that third parties disappeared. Instead, the decline was gradual. In the case of signature requirements, in the 1990s that decline reversed itself.

The first problem with the ballot access law argument, then, is that it is based on a faulty narrative. While these laws have indeed gotten more difficult over the twentieth century, dramatic increases in requirements are isolated to a small number of states. For a majority of House districts since 1900, the signature and previous vote requirements have increased from 1% to 2% of the vote. Like the decades from 1890 to 1918, when third parties were thriving, these parties can still get candidates onto the ballot in a significant percent of congressional districts with signatures from 1% or less of the voting population.

Ballot Access Laws and the Change in Third-Party Candidacies

The second problem with the ballot access law argument is that it is not consistent with the long-term changes in how many third-party candidates got onto the ballot.

Figure 3.3 shows the evolution in the mean percent of signatures needed to get onto the House ballot and the percent of House districts with third-party candidates in the general election since 1900. On average, signature requirements became significantly more difficult from 1910 to 1914 and then

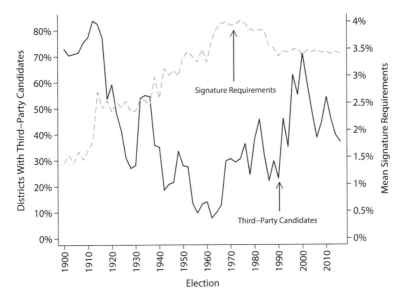

FIGURE 3.3 Percent third-party candidates on House ballot compared to signature requirements. This graph compares the percent of House districts with at least one third-party candidate with the difficulty of signature requirements since 1900. As the graph suggests, there is very little historical relationship between these ballot access requirements and the likelihood that third parties would get their candidates on the House ballot. While ballot access laws got steadily more difficult from 1900 to around 1970, the percent of districts with third-party candidates followed a different pattern. There were many third-party candidates in the beginning of the century; the percent of districts with candidates steadily dropped after the 1916 election, reaching a low in the 1950s and 1960s, and then began rising again in the late 1960s. During the 2000 election, there were third-party candidates in more House districts than during any election from 1918 to 1998, despite only a small drop in the mean signature requirements since the 1970s.

68 Chapter Three

gradually climbed in difficulty until around 1970. After 1990, those regulations became slightly easier, on average, but nonetheless remain very high by historical standards.

The percent of districts with third-party candidates, however, follows a different pattern. During the first two decades of the twentieth century, between 70% and 80% of House districts had third-party candidates each election. Then, beginning in 1918, the percent of districts with third-party candidates began dropping rapidly and continued to decline until it reached its low point in the 1950s and 1960s. However, starting in 1968, the number of third-party candidates began to rise again. While in the 1960s there were on average third-party candidates in 17% of the districts, there were third-party candidates in 31% of the districts in the 1970s and 35% of the districts in the 1980s. In the 2000 election, despite no significant change in ballot access laws, third parties ran candidates in over 70% of House districts.

In other words, even a cursory examination of the data suggests that signature requirements for getting onto the ballot and the actual percent of districts with third-party candidates on the ballot are not related to each other. If ballot access laws were causing third-party candidacies to disappear, one would expect that they would have declined as these laws got more difficult and then remained absent from American politics. Instead, third-party candidacies rapidly declined after 1918 and then began rebounding after the 1960s, despite ballot access laws remaining consistently very high.

This point can be illustrated another way. In the period from the 1930s to the early 1950s, when third parties were already very weak through most of the country, five states played a disproportionately large role in third-party activity: California, Minnesota, New York, Pennsylvania, and Wisconsin. In 1940, for example, 76% of House districts in these five states had third-party candidates, but only 20% of the House districts in the rest of the country had third-party candidates. However, none of these states had easy ballot access requirements in 1940. In Minnesota, for example, the signatures required to get onto the ballot had to be "equal to at least (5) percentum of the total number of votes cast at the preceding general election in the county where the application is made." In California, the signature requirement was "at least ten per cent of the entire vote of the State at the last preceding November election at which a Governor was elected." In New York, the signature requirement was "five per centum of the total number of votes cast, excepting that not more than three thousand electors shall be required to make an independent nomination in any political subdivision." The signature requirements were "at least two per centum of the largest entire vote for any officer elected at the last preceding general election" in Pennsylvania. In Wisconsin, the signature requirements were 17%, or "not less than one-sixth of the electors within any senatorial, assembly or congressional district." If the introduction of unreasonably high ballot access

The Impact of Ballot Access Laws **69**

laws had caused the disappearance of third parties, one would not expect third-party candidacies to be concentrated in a handful of states with often very difficult ballot access requirements.[13]

Impact of Ballot Access Laws at the District Level

The third problem with the ballot access law argument is that there is not a strong relationship between the difficulty of these laws and how well third parties perform at the House district level. While there is a statistically significant relationship between ballot access laws and whether third-party candidates get onto the House ballot, ballot access laws had only a small impact on how often third-party candidates were running for House seats. Similarly, while there is a relationship between the difficulty of ballot access laws and the percent of votes third-party candidates received, the impact of these laws on the vote outcome was also very small. For these reasons, ballot access laws could not have been a primary reason for the demise of third parties over the twentieth century.

Table 3.1 presents the result of random effects logistic and linear regressions with district-level election results from 1890 to 2016 organized as time-series cross-sectional data. It shows the relationship between the difficulty of ballot access laws and the success of third-party candidates in House elections. The analysis is based on district-level House election data from 1890, when ballot access laws were first enacted by the states, to 2016. The dependent variable for the logistic regression, in the left column, is whether the district had at least one third-party candidate. The dependent variable for the linear regression, on the right, is the total percent vote received by third-party candidates in each district. Both equations include five sets of independent variables. The first set, the focus of this chapter, includes variables for signature and previous vote requirements. The second, fusion, will be discussed in the next chapter. The third set, which includes four measures of DW-NOMINATE scores, will be discussed in Chapter 7, which explores the relationship between political polarization and third-party activity. The fourth, two-party margin, is simply the percent difference in the vote between the candidates who received the most and second most votes. Thus, if a Republican candidate won the seat with 52% of the vote and the Democratic candidate receive 47% of the vote, then the two party margin would be 5. The purpose of this variable is mostly to see if voters are less likely to vote for third-party candidates when there is a competitive race between the top two candidates, and therefore there is a greater chance of spoiling the election. The final variable, for the regression equation only, indicates whether there was at least one third-party candidate running in that district. This variable is meant to offset any impact of the third-party vote increasing for no other reason than that there is a third-party candidate on the ballot.

70 Chapter Three

TABLE 3.1 Impact of ballot access laws on third-party success in House elections, 1890–2014

	Districts with a Third-Party Candidate	Percent Votes Received by Third-Party Candidates
Signature requirements	−0.06★★★	0.09★★★
(Percent of vote needed)	(0.006)	(0.015)
Previous vote	−0.08★★★	−0.16★★★
requirements	(0.006)	(0.016)
(Percent of vote needed)		
Fusion	0.65★★★	2.33★★★
(1 = Fusion candidates in	(0.045)	(0.147)
state)		
(0 = No fusion candidates)		
DW-NOMINATE,	1.97★★★	4.75★★★
dimension 1	(0.121)	(0.386)
(Mean of state		
representatives)		
DW-NOMINATE,	−1.70★★★	−2.20★★★
dimension 1	(0.096)	(0.317)
(Representative)		
DW-NOMINATE,	0.80★★★	2.10★★★
dimension 2	(0.097)	(0.305)
(Mean of state		
representatives)		
DW-NOMINATE,	−0.31★★★	0.28
dimension 2	(0.063)	(0.208)
(Representative)		
Two-party margin	−0.008★★★	0.01★★★
	(0.001)	(0.002)
Minor party candidates		7.08★★★
		(0.101)
Constant	−0.95★★★	−1.30★★★
	(0.068)	(0.197)
Wald chi-square	2,233★★★	6,728★★★
Number of cases	28,669	28,669
Number of groups	570	570
Overall R^2		0.18

★$p \leq 0.05$; ★★$p \leq 0.01$; ★★★$p \leq 0.001$.

Both the logit and regression equations show statistically significant relationships between ballot access laws and third-party success. Specifically, the logit model demonstrates that as signature requirements and previous vote requirements got more difficult in the state that a House district was in, the likelihood of a third-party candidate running in that district declined. The relationship between ballot access laws and the percent vote for third-party candidates is not as direct. As the signature requirements got more difficult, the vote for third-party candidates increased, but as previous vote requirements got more difficult, the vote for third-party candidates declined.

However, the impact of these laws, while statistically significant, is very small. Indeed, these relationships are statistically significant in these equations partially because they are based on nearly 30,000 district-level elections, which dramatically reduces the size of confidence intervals as compared to an analysis of a single election, or 435 cases. While ballot access laws have had an impact on the success of third parties, that impact is far too small to explain why third parties had declined dramatically by the middle of the twentieth century.

The strength of the relationship between third-party candidacies and ballot access laws is shown graphically in Figure 3.3. Since the results of logistic regressions cannot be interpreted in the direct manner that one can analyze linear regressions, I ran a set of Monte Carlo simulations based on the results from the random effects logistic regression shown on Table 3.1 and presented those results in this graphic. In these simulations, all the independent variables except ballot access laws were held constant, the state the district was in is assumed to have had no fusion candidates, the top two candidates in the district received an equal number of votes, and all the DW-NOMINATE scores were held at their mean. In each run of 1,000 simulations, the signature requirements and previous vote requirements were assumed to be equal to each other, and the runs were performed with these requirements set from 0% to 20% of the vote. Effectively, each point with an error bar above and below it on this graph shows the predicted probability that there will be a third-party candidate on the ballot when both the signature and previous vote requirements are set at that percent; the error bar shows the confidence intervals for each of these predictions. These confidence intervals are very small because this logistic regression was run on nearly 30,000 district-level elections from 1890 to 2014.

As the graph shows, as ballot access laws got more difficult, the probability that a third-party candidate would be on the ballot declined. If there were no signature and previous vote requirements, there was a 0.59 probability (that is, a 59% chance) that the district would have at least one third-party candidate on the ballot. If both of these requirements were increased to 1%, that probability dropped to 0.55. At 2%, the probability dropped further to 0.52. If the signature and previous vote requirements were increased to 5%, then the chances of a third-party candidate running in that district reduced to 0.42. If those laws were increased to 10% of the vote, then the probability of a third-party candidate running reduced further to 0.26. At 20%, that probability reduced further to only 0.08. In other words, when there are no ballot access laws, there are likely to be third-party candidates in nearly 60% of the districts. When third parties have to gather signatures of 20% of the voting population or have had to receive 20% of the vote in the previous election, that likelihood drops to only 8%.

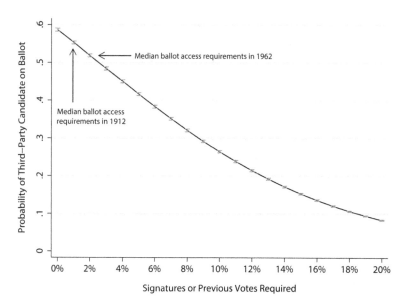

FIGURE 3.4 Impact of ballot access laws on probability a district will have a third-party candidate. This figure provides a graphical representation of the results from the random effects logistic regression shown in Table 3.1. The graph shows the results of a Monte Carlo simulation based on that logit model in which all the independent variables except ballot access laws were held constant. (The state was assumed to have no fusion candidates, the top two candidates in the district received an equal number of votes, and all the DW-NOMINATE scores were held at their mean.) In each run of 1,000 simulations, the signature requirements and previous vote requirements were assumed to be equal and an integer from 0% to 20%. The graph demonstrates that as ballot access laws get more difficult, the probability of a district having at least one third-party candidate declines. However, that decline has to be substantial before these requirements start significantly harming the prospects of third parties.

This comparison, however, hides the real story. In the history of ballot access laws in the United States, no state had both signature and previous vote requirements of 20%. The more appropriate comparison is between 1% and 2%. In 1912, during the last great wave of third-party activity, the median signature and previous vote requirements were 1% of voters. In the 1950s and 1960s, when third parties had virtually disappeared, the median of both of those requirements was 2% of voters. The model predicts that when both of these ballot access requirements are at 1%, the probability of third-party candidates getting on the ballot is 0.55. When those requirements are increased to 2%, the model predicts that the probability of third-party candidates getting on the ballot is 0.52. The difference between a 55% and 52% chance of getting onto the ballot

The same analysis can be made about the impact of ballot access laws on what percent of the vote third-party candidates received. Proponents of the ballot access law argument often claim that, besides keeping third-party candidates off the ballot, signature requirements also deflate the vote for these candidates if they get onto the ballot. As the argument is presented, third-party candidates have to put significant resources into collecting the signatures needed to get onto the ballot, which reduces their ability to actually compete in the general election campaign (Winger 1997). The linear regression equation, on the right column of Table 3.1, demonstrates that exactly the opposite is true. Signature requirements have a small, positive impact on the vote for third-party candidates. The more difficult the signature requirements, the more votes third-party candidates receive.

is very small, and it certainly cannot explain why in 1912 third parties were on the ballot in 77% of House districts, but fifty years later in 1962, they were on the ballot in only 8% of House districts.

There are a number of possible explanations for these seemingly self-contradictory results. The first is that the causal arrow may be reversed. In other words, it is possible that states make ballot access laws more difficult when third parties are more competitive. The strength of third parties therefore leads to higher ballot access laws, not the other way around. There is, however, a problem with this argument. If tougher ballot access laws are a reflection of stronger third parties in a state, one would expect those results to present themselves in all the relationships between ballot access measures and third-party success. Instead, the coefficients for both ballot access variables are negatively related to whether there are third-party candidates on the ballot, and the previous vote requirements are negatively related to the percent vote third parties receive each election.

A better explanation, I believe, is that gathering signatures effectively acts as a form of advertisement. When a third-party activist approaches a registered voter to request a signature, that voter has just been provided information about the party and possibly one or more of its candidates. In other words, while the signature requirements produce a hurdle that makes getting onto the ballot harder, it also creates a mechanism for promoting the party, even though this mechanism seems to produce only limited positive help.

More importantly, the linear regression strongly suggests that ballot access laws had very little impact on the vote. The dependent variable, percent vote for third-party candidates, is coded as 0 to 100. The coefficient for signature requirements is 0.09. This means that, on average and all else being equal, for every 1% increase in signature requirements, third-party candidates received a vote increase of 0.09%. This effectively means that even a 10% increase in signature requirements would not, on average, produce even a 1% increase in the vote towards third parties. Conversely, every 1% increase in previous vote requirements reduced the vote for third-party candidates on average by

74 Chapter Three

0.16%. If one performed an analysis, as I had before, with the assumption that signature and previous vote requirements were always equal, then each 1% increase of both signature and previous vote requirements would translate into an average drop in the vote for third parties by 0.05% of the vote—that is, by one-twentieth of a percent.

While these results are statistically significant, owing partially to the large number of cases being studied, they are clearly not politically significant. In the decade from 1900 to 1908, the average vote for third-party House candidates was 4.5%, and from 1910 to 1918 that average was 7.9%. In the decades from 1950 to 1958 and 1960 to 1968, those averages were 0.6% and 0.5%. The median of both ballot signature and previous vote requirements changed over that period from 1% to 2%, which would have produced a net loss in third-party votes of far less than 1%. Clearly, ballot access laws did not produce the decline in vote for third parties over this period.

Conclusion

The main finding of this chapter is that ballot access laws could not have been a major contributor to the decline of third parties by the middle of the twentieth century. While these laws got more difficult over the twentieth century, much of this change was driven by a minority of states producing extremely difficult restrictions. Moreover, the impact of these laws was small. They likely reduced the number of third-party candidates and percent vote that third-party candidates received, but not by much. Regardless of what the intent of state governments might have been, ballot access laws did not undermine third parties.

Beyond this, the evidence presented in this chapter conflicts with the narrative common throughout much of the third-party literature. A general view presented by some third-party scholars is that third parties were once vibrant and then were destroyed by mid-century by a range of factors, including ballot access laws. The greatest problem for the ballot access law argument is that it cannot explain why third-party candidacies began rising again in the 1970s. Even with some level of moderation in these laws over the past few decades, they remain much more difficult than they were in the first decades of the twentieth century. Ballot access laws do little to help solve the puzzle of why third parties nearly disappeared by the 1950s, and they certainly cannot explain why they began reviving over the past few decades.

Notes

1 Idaho Code Ann. §34–501 (1987).
2 Ibid.
3 10 Ill. Comp. Stat. 5/7–2 (1943).
4 Del. Code Ann. Tit. 15, §3001 (2010).
5 S.C. Code Ann. §7–9–10 (1984) to §7–9–100 (1989).

The Impact of Ballot Access Laws **75**

6 Haw. Rev. Stat. Ann. §11–62 (LexisNexis 2013).
7 La. Rev. Stat. Ann. §18–465 (2011); N.J. Stat. Ann. §19–23 (2013); Nev. Rev. Stat. §24–293.1715 (2016); R.I. Gen. Laws §17–1–2 (2013); Vt. Stat. Ann. tit. 17 §2402 (2016); Wash. Rev. Code §29A-20–141 (2016). For Nevada, the candidate can gain either one percent of the total votes cast at the last general election for the same office or 100 signatures.
8 Me. Rev. Stat. Ann. tit. 21–A, §303 (2016).
9 N.Y. Election Law §6–142 (Consol. 2016).
10 One could argue that Mississippi also has a 20% previous vote requirement, though Mississippi's law is more deceptive. Qualifying as a party is relatively easy in Mississippi. However, to place a candidate on the ballot, each party must nominate candidates through primary elections. But, the state will only pay for those primary elections if the party received 20% of the vote in the previous gubernatorial election or one of the two previous presidential elections. In other words, for all parties except the Democratic and Republican parties, the process of nominating candidates is extremely expensive. Miss. Code Ann. 25–15–301 (1986) and Miss. Code Ann. 23–15–291 (1986).
11 To be slightly more specific, Kentucky distinguishes between political party and political organization. A political party must receive at least 20% of the previous vote while a political organization must receive at least 2% of the vote. The only significant difference between a political party and political organization is that the former must nominate its candidates via primary whereas the latter can use a primary, caucus, or petition. Ky. Rev. Stat. Ann. §118.015 (LexisNexis 2015); Ky. Rev. Stat. Ann. §118.325 (LexisNexis 2015).
12 To be more specific, New York has no method for a party to form before it runs a candidate in the general election. Instead, a political organization must nominate a candidate for governor, and that candidate must receive at least 50,000 votes statewide to become recognized as a party. 1890 N.Y. Laws 482; 1891 N.Y. Laws 575; 1896 N.Y. Laws 929; 1911 N.Y. Laws 2717; 1918 N.Y. Laws 1040, 1058; 1971 N.Y. Laws 2706.
13 1915 Minn. Laws 224; 1937 Cal. Stat. 1220; 1918 N.Y. Laws 1058; 1893 Pa. Laws 419; 1913 Wis. Sess. 956.

4

THE PROHIBITION OF FUSION

The Working Families Party (WFP) is one of the newest third parties to have an impact on American politics. Founded in 1998 in New York by a coalition of community organizers, labor unions, public interest groups, and former members of the defunct New Party, the WFP has had rising success in New York and has begun spreading out to other states, including Connecticut, Oregon, South Carolina, Delaware, and Vermont. Its success appears to be tied to an electoral strategy based on fusion, or when a single candidate is nominated by multiple parties. The strategy, in brief, is to co-nominate some major party candidates in an effort to boost the prospects of those candidates as well as take some credit for their victories. The WFP then uses that help to lobby those major party candidates once they are in office. At the same time, co-nominating major party candidates is a way to gain free advertisement for the party that can be used to increase the support of non-fusion candidates run by the party. As Frances Moore Lappe wrote:

> The Working Families Party attributes its success to what is called its "secret weapon": fusion voting, which permits candidates to appear on more than one party's ballot line. Fusion—also known as cross-endorsement—was common in America until the end of the nineteenth century. It's now legal in seven states and up and running in New York and Connecticut. With effort, it could spread.
>
> "Fusion" means the Working Families Party can run its own candidate chosen by members to fight for their priorities or it can put another party's candidate on its ballot line. For the most part, the party has cross-endorsed Democrats, but occasionally it's backed a Republican. It has also run its own candidates when there seemed to be a fighting chance of victory.
>
> *(Lappe 2006, 54)*

Indeed, the WFP has clearly chosen states to organize in which this fusion strategy can be applied. New York is without question the main state in which fusion candidates run. Connecticut, Delaware, Oregon, South Carolina, and Vermont as also states where fusion is permitted.

Many third-party scholars argue that fusion is one method for third parties to gain success within the American political system. They argue further that the prohibition of fusion is a primary reason that third parties have nearly disappeared in American politics. In *Tyranny of the Two-Party System*, Lisa Disch explained the argument as follows:

> Also known as "cross-endorsement" or "multiple-party nomination", fusion is a nomination strategy third political parties commonly used in the nineteenth-century to sustain themselves within the winner-take-all system. In a fusion candidacy two or more parties combine forces to run a single candidate on multiple party lines in the general election. Fusion is not an endorsement. It is a multiple-party nomination in which typically a dominant-party candidate ran on the lines of an established party and a third party... All but lost to voters and parties today, the strategy was used throughout the nineteenth century, but most notoriously by the People's Party, to make organized opposition manifest at the polls.
>
> *(Disch 2002, 12)*

Did the widespread elimination of fusion as a strategy help cause the near disappearance of third parties by the middle of the twentieth century? My answer is that it did not. Third parties do run more candidates in House races in states where fusion candidacies are common, and third-party candidates do receive a higher percentage of the vote in those states. However, contrary to a widely argued claim in the third-party literature, fusion was not a widely used third-party strategy in the last three decades of the nineteenth century, except for two elections: 1872 and 1896. Since it was not a primary reason for third-party success in the decades from 1870 to 1918, its prohibition by state legislatures cannot explain the decline of third parties in the subsequent decades.

The Fusion Argument

In American politics, fusion is the co-nomination of a single candidate by multiple political parties. By any account, fusion plays a central role in New York politics today, far more than any other state in the union. Whenever a New York candidate is nominated by multiple parties, that candidate is listed separately on the ballot for each of these parties. For example, the winning candidate in the 2013 New York City mayoral race, Bill DeBlasio, was listed on two different lines, for the Democratic Party and the Working Families Party, and voters could choose him on either party line. Similarly, the Republican

78 Chapter Four

candidate, Joe Lhota, was also listed on the ballot for the Conservative Party. In Oregon and Vermont, however, the candidate's name as well as the name of all parties nominating that candidate appear on a single line on the ballot.

The argument, in sum, is that if most state legislatures permitted multiple parties to co-nominate the same candidates, like New York does, then third parties would be much more vibrant across the United States. This argument is based on what its proponents see as a significant change in American campaign politics. In the nineteenth century, according to this argument, co-nominations were extremely common. Because major party candidates were willing to allow their nominees to be co-nominated by third parties, these third parties gained public exposure and legitimacy that they would have otherwise not received. However, once state legislatures began instituting the Australian ballot, they also started prohibiting fusion. Specifically, since fusion was more of a Democratic then Republican strategy, the argument continues, it was Republican legislatures that generally outlawed it. The prohibition of fusion eliminated a critical third-party strategy, and this became a primary reason for the disappearance of these parties.

This line of reasoning has been made by a number of third-party scholars. Peter Argersinger, for example, made this argument in a detailed, historical analysis. After arguing vigorously that fusion had been a key component of nineteenth century American electoral politics, Argersinger then argued that Republican controlled state legislatures banned fusion, often in the process of instituting the Australian ballot. This, Argersinger claimed, led directly to the demise of third parties (Argersinger 1980, 303–4).

Howard Scarrow made a similar argument in an article often cited within the third-party literature. He too begins by arguing that in the nineteenth century "jointly sponsored candidacies were commonplace, with cooperation between a minor party and a major one being especially in evidence" (Scarrow 1986, 634). He then argued that the "institutional reforms enacted at the turn of the century had the effect of eliminating fusion candidacies, and with them the more complex party system they helped sustain" (Scarrow 1986, 634).

Thus, proponents of this argument make a consistent set of claims. Fusion was a widely used strategy in the nineteenth century, maybe especially during the Greenback Party era, or the late 1870s and the 1880s. This strategy, they argued, dramatically increased the vote for third-party candidates. However, because Democratic candidates were more likely to be co-nominated by third parties than Republican candidates, Republican-controlled state legislatures after 1896 used the new Australian ballot laws as an excuse to limit candidates to a single party nomination. With fusion having been banned through most of the country, they conclude, the vote for third parties rapidly declined around the time that the Australian ballot was being instituted.

In the process of making this argument, proponents of the fusion argument have effectively laid out a range of testable claims about the history of fusion and American third parties. (1) Many states banned fusion around 1900, putting an end to the practice through most of the country. (2) Fusion was a widely used strategy in the late nineteenth century, but it largely disappeared in the early twentieth century. (3) Fusion significantly increases the vote for third parties. The decline in its use is a major reason why the vote for third-party candidates declined over the twentieth century. As I will demonstrate in the following, none of these predictions are consistent with the evidence in House elections from 1870 to 2016.

Three Types of Fusion Candidates

While the third-party literature tends to treat fusion candidacies with a broad brush, focusing on candidates co-nominated by a single major party and at least one third party, I would argue that there are different types of fusion candidacies, and each type would have a different impact on third-party fortunes.

Figure 4.1 shows the percent of districts with three types of fusion candidates from 1870 to 2016. The first type could be called *third-party fusion candidates*, or when a candidate is nominated by two or more third parties but no major parties. Overall, from 1870 to 2016, there were 196 third-party fusion candidates, or 7% of all fusion candidates. As Figure 4.1 suggests, in most elections from the late 1870s until almost 1950 there were a handful of third-party fusion candidates, although rarely more than three or four across the country. The heyday for this strategy seemed to be in 1922, when twenty-seven House candidates (2.4%), or 39% of all fusion candidates, were nominated by more than one third party but not a major party. During this election, the Socialist and Farmer-Labor parties were co-nominating a significant number of candidates in New York and to a much lesser extent in Connecticut and Utah. Indeed, to the degree that this type of fusion had any impact, it was more important in the 1910s and 1920s than in the 1880s and 1890s—that is, after the Australian ballot was adopted in most states. In 2012, there were only two third-party fusion House candidates, and in 2014 there was one. All three ran in Oregon. In 2016, the single third-party fusion candidate ran in New York State.

The second type could be called a *major party fusion candidate*, or when a candidate was nominated by both the Republican and Democratic parties but not a third party.[1] Not only did this type of fusion not promote third parties; the fusion candidate running in this type of election was virtually guaranteed electoral victory by a very high percent of the vote. In the seventy-four elections examined in this study, major party fusion candidates won every single election. These types of candidates appeared most often in the 1940s and 1950s, and most commonly in California. Of the 178 major party fusion candidates from 1870 to 2012, 149 (or 84%) ran in California. The only other states to have had this type of candidate were Pennsylvania (fifteen times), New York (eight times), Vermont (thrice), Massachusetts (twice), and Georgia (once).[2] The most

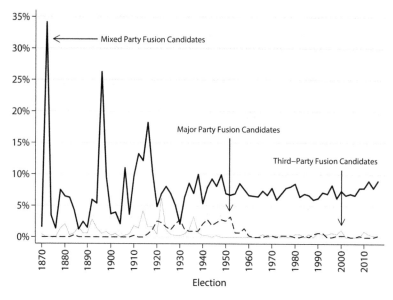

FIGURE 4.1 Percent of districts having different types of fusion candidacies, 1870–2016. This graph shows the percent of districts with at least one major party fusion candidate (when a candidate was co-nominated by the Democratic and Republican parties but no third party, shown as a thick, black line), third-party fusion candidate (when a candidate was co-nominated by two or more third parties but no major party, shown as a dashed line), or mixed party fusion candidate (when a candidate was co-nominated by at least one major party and at least one third party, shown as thin, gray line). The graph shows that mixed party fusion candidates were by far the most common type of fusion candidate, although major party fusion candidates also played an electoral role in the 1940s and 1950s.

famous of this type of candidate was Richard Nixon, who in 1948 ran for Congress with the nomination of both the Democrat and Republican parties, as did a large percent of the other major party candidates from California that year. The most recent House major party fusion candidate was Peter Welch in 2016, a progressive Democrat in Vermont who was also nominated by the Republican Party in that state.

As Figure 4.1 also shows, major party fusion candidacies played their greatest role in the middle of the twentieth century, at the time that third parties were already disappearing from American politics. From 1920 until 1952, one out of every five fusion candidates had been co-nominated by the Democratic and Republican parties. These major party fusion candidates were highly concentrated in California. In 1922, 1928, and 1930, over 70% of California House districts had a candidate running that was nominated by both the Democratic and Republican parties. Similarly, in the period from 1940 to 1952, from a third to just over half of districts had a major party fusion candidate. During this period, it was a central aspect of California electoral politics.

The third type is the *mixed party fusion candidate*, or when a candidate is co-nominated by at least one major party and at least one minor party. As Figure 4.1 shows, this type of fusion was the most commonly used in House races since the Civil War. From 1870 to 2016, 88% of all House fusion candidates were mixed party fusion candidates. In the first half of this period, there were three spikes in the percent of House candidates who were nominated by both a major party and at least one minor party. The first, and most prominent, was in 1872, when the Liberal Republicans became a splinter group that separated from the radical Republicans of Congress. 34% of all House districts had at least one mixed party fusion candidate. The second and best known spike was during the 1896 election, when Populist parties co-nominated the Democratic presidential candidate William Jennings Bryan as well as a large number of Democrats for lesser offices, including in the House of Representatives. Mixed party fusion candidates ran in 26% of House districts that year. The third spike was in 1916, when 18% of all House districts had at least one mixed party fusion candidate. By the second half of the twentieth century, the percent of candidates who were nominated by both a major party and at least one minor party stabilized, largely because this type of fusion became widely used in New York politics.

Each type of fusion candidacy should have a different impact on third parties. Third-party fusion candidacies, for example, are unlikely to increase the overall vote for third parties in a district. Instead, it most likely helps keep the vote from being divided between the two third parties that chose to nominate a single candidate. While this type of fusion might help an individual third-party candidate, this strategy does little to change the basic dynamics between major parties and third parties. Similarly, major party fusion candidacies would likely have no positive impact on third parties. If the two major party candidates run against each other and are likely to receive nearly the same number of votes, a third-party candidate has a greater chance of influencing the outcome and therefore having a disruptive effect. When there is only one major party candidate and this candidate is likely to receive approximately 90% of the vote, the impact of a third-party candidate is negligible at best.

Mixed party fusion, however, is a very different strategy. For major party candidates, it is a low cost way to increase voter support; if a candidate can gain a few extra votes by having another ballot line or having another party name placed after his or her name, those extra votes come without a single advertisement purchase or other cost. For third parties, it provides two possible advantages. The first is as a negotiating position with major party candidates. If a third party co-nominates a major party candidate, and that candidate wins the election, the third party can try to claim some part of the victory and use

82 Chapter Four

that interpretation to help lobby that officeholder. At the same time, there is an implicit threat within the strategy: the third party could co-nominate the major party candidate or it can run its own candidate in the next election, with the latter possibly reducing the vote for the major party enough to lead to a defeat by the other major party. In this way, the third party is acting something like a party and something like an interest group, more focused on influencing the policy outcomes than actually winning an election.

The second advantage is that co-nomination of major party candidates is a form of advertisement. The party gains a much easier way to get its name onto the ballot as well as into newspaper and other news outlets, and it is much more likely to be associated with electoral victory. One could argue, for example, that the primary reason the WFP has gained any recognition within New York State is that it has associated itself with major party candidates who have won significant elections, including both the governor of New York State and the mayor of New York City. That positive advertisement can then help boost other candidates from that party.

For our purposes here, the critical question relates to the second advantage of mixed party fusion candidacies. Does mixed party fusion have any impact on the percent of votes that third parties get, and is that impact enough to help explain why third parties have declined over the past century? For this reason, for the remainder of this chapter, when I speak of fusion candidates, I am specifically speaking about mixed party fusion candidates.

Did the States Ban Fusion?

The fusion argument for third-party decline, like the ballot access law argument, is mostly a legal explanation. The argument is that the prohibition of fusion in many states led to the decline of third parties. For this reason, one would expect that there should be a statistical relationship between whether states permit fusion and how strong third parties are in that state. However, this approach has a serious problem. There is, in fact, no relationship between whether a state supposedly banned fusion in the early decades of the twentieth century and whether parties actually stopped running fusion candidates.

Much of the research on these changes around 1900 are based on Arthur Crosby Ludington's *American Ballot Laws, 1888–1910* (1911), a monograph providing extensive information about the newly emerging ballot laws, including how they applied to fusion. Ludington's piece is similar to Charles Merriam's *Primary Elections* (1909): it is a book rich in specific details, including a history of ballot laws in each state until 1910 (Ludington 1911, 12–83) and a breakdown for each state of each legal ballot issue (Ludington 1911, 90–201). In these laws, as reported by Ludington, fusion was often banned by simply specifying that a candidate's name could be placed on the ballot only once or that there can be only one party placed next to a candidate name. Conversely, the law could

The Prohibition of Fusion **83**

specifically say that a candidate can have multiple party nominations or not mention the issue at all, which effectively permitted fusion.

A significant percent of the states that Ludington claimed had prohibited fusion had, in fact, not prohibited fusion. It is not clear whether Ludington had misinterpreted the laws, or subsequent political scientists had misinterpreted Ludington's analysis, or that the states had written these prohibitions but not enforced them. In any case, parties continued to co-nominate candidates during the period Ludington studied even in states that had presumably banned the practice. Scarrow recognized this problem in Michigan, for example. Stating that Michigan was one of the first states to require that candidate names appear only once on the party-column ballot, "that restriction did not prevent the Democrat and Populist parties in that state from presenting on the 1896 ballot a complete 'Democrat-People's' column of national, state, and local candidates" (Scarrow 1986, 634).

The problem extended far past Michigan. In the period Ludington studied, from 1890 to 1910, there were just over 4,000 district-level elections to the House of Representatives. During the elections in this period, 9% of districts in states that allowed fusion had fusion candidates, and 9% of the districts in states that prohibited fusion, according to Ludington, also had fusion candidates. In other words, during these crucial years for the fusion theory of third-party decline, the predictive value of whether there were fusion candidates based on whether fusion was allowed by law was zero.

While Argersinger used Ludington as one of his sources for determining when states banned fusion, he provided a different list of what states had banned fusion and when those prohibitions were put into law. He summarized the key period of change as follows:

> The lessons learned in, and the opportunity presented by, the sweeping 1896 Republican victory led Republican-dominated legislatures in many more states to enact antifusion laws quickly. Republican legislatures passed antifusion laws in 1897 in Illinois, Iowa, North Dakota, Pennsylvania, Wisconsin, and Wyoming as well as in Indiana. As Republicans gained sufficient legislative control elsewhere, the law spread still further: California and Nebraska in 1899; Kansas, Minnesota, and South Dakota in 1901; Idaho in 1903; and Montana in 1907.
>
> *(Argersinger 1980, 303)*

Argersinger stated that Kansas banned fusion in 1901; it had fusion House candidates in 1904. He claimed that Nebraska had also banned fusion in 1901. That state had fusion House candidates in every election from 1902 to 1916. Similarly, even though North Dakota presumably prohibited fusion in 1897, it had a House fusion candidate in 1898. Both Argersinger and Ludington stated that California had banned fusion in 1899, but Argersinger failed to state that

84 Chapter Four

California reversed this decision in 1902, despite providing other details about California ballot laws. From 1902 until the 1950s, California was one of the most important fusion states in the country.

Probably the biggest example of how this approach has failed is Pennsylvania. Both Argersinger and Ludington state that Pennsylvania banned fusion in 1897. Pennsylvania House races had fusion candidates during every election from 1898 until 1938. Often, 75% or more of the districts had at least one fusion candidate, and in 1912 over 90% of district-level races included at least one fusion candidate. Starting in 1940, the number of Pennsylvania House races with fusion candidates declined, but the state continued to have occasional fusion candidacies. The most recent Pennsylvania fusion House candidate ran in 2000, for example.

Because of this problem, one cannot realistically determine whether the prohibition of fusion undermined third parties by measuring the relationship between fusion laws and third-party success. There is a second problem as well. Unlike ballot access laws, which set requirements that third parties could attempt to meet on their own, fusion (or specifically, mixed party fusion) requires a major party to consent to allowing its candidates to be co-nominated by a third party. In other words, the law itself is not sufficient for third parties to apply this strategy. Instead, if candidates from both major parties simply refuse to be co-nominated, then it is irrelevant whether state election laws say that they are permitted to do so.

For this reason, I focus on the actual use of fusion as a strategy instead of whether a state permits co-nominations of candidates. I define a "fusion state" in the statistics that follow as a state that had at least one mixed party fusion House, senatorial, or gubernatorial candidate on the ballot during that election year. This definition ignores, for example, California elections during the middle of the twentieth century in which major party candidates were being co-nominated by the Democratic and Republican parties, and it ignores a state in which there is the occasional third-party fusion candidate but no candidate co-nominated by both a major party and a third party. In this way, this independent variable is a measure of the actual application of the fusion strategy as it is described in much of the third-party literature.

Has the Use of Fusion Declined?

A key prediction of the fusion argument for third-party decline is that its use decreased dramatically over the past century. Specifically, these scholars argue that fusion was a widely used strategy during the nineteenth century, but largely because of the enactment of Australian ballot laws that prohibited the practice, fusion quickly disappeared from American politics around 1900. As fusion disappeared as an option for third parties, these parties also quickly became irrelevant in American politics.

The evidence, however, presents a different story. Graph 4.1 shows that there were roughly two periods of mixed party fusion candidacies in post-Civil War United States. In the first period, from 1870 to around 1940, fusion candidacies came in spikes, much like the vote for third parties. The first spike was in 1872, when 34% of House districts had at least one fusion candidate. During this election, the Liberal Republicans became a splinter group that separated from the radical Republicans of Congress. While there were a handful of candidates nominated by only the Liberal Republican Party, this party mostly co-nominated Democratic candidates, including the Democratic presidential nominee, Horace Greeley.

The second and best known spike was during the 1896 election, when 26% of House districts had at least one fusion candidate. During this election, the Democrats nominated William Jennings Bryan as their presidential candidate and shifted ideologically towards the Populists. Bryan and a large number of Democrats running for other offices, including the House of Representatives, were co-nominated by a Populist party. Indeed, one out of every five Democratic candidates, or 22%, were also nominated by the Populist or the People's Party.

The third spike of fusion candidacies was in 1916, when 18% of House districts had candidates nominated by at least one major party and third party. These candidacies were heavily concentrated in New York, Pennsylvania, and Nebraska. Unlike the previous two spikes, both Republicans and Democrats had candidates being co-nominated by third parties, and there was a wide range of these third parties.

During this period from 1870 to 1940, except for these spike election years, fusion was generally used in only a small percent of House districts. Indeed, in the last three decades of the nineteenth century, there were fusion candidates in more than 10% of House districts only twice: 1872 and 1896. Often, fusion candidates ran in just over 1% of the districts. Contrary to the image often presented that the late nineteenth century was the heyday of fusion candidacies, they were more consistently active in the 1910s, despite the fact that the Australian ballot had already been instituted throughout most of the country. During the second period, starting around 1940, the percent of districts with fusion candidacies largely stabilized, primarily because fusion became a critical aspect of New York politics at the same time that it became less used in other states.

Figure 4.2 shows this another way. This graph shows the percent of districts with fusion candidates and third-party candidates by decade from 1870 to 2016. It demonstrates that fusion candidates ran in only a small percent of districts throughout this century and a half period. While third parties were regularly running non-fusion candidates in more than two-thirds of House districts in the late nineteenth and early twentieth century, 1910 through 1918 was the only decade in which fusion candidates ran in more than 10% of House districts. During that decade fusion candidates ran in 12% of districts while, in comparison, third-party candidates were running in 75%.

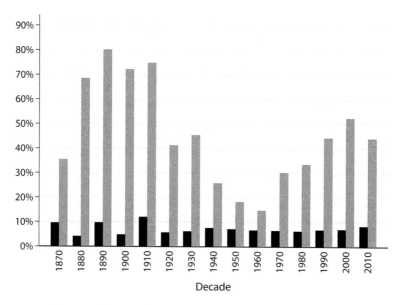

FIGURE 4.2 Percent of House districts with third-party and fusion candidates by decade, 1870–2016. This graph shows the percent of House districts with at least one fusion candidate (specifically, mixed party fusion candidate, in black) and one third-party candidate (in gray) by decade in general elections from 1870 to 2016. The graph shows that since the Civil War, fusion candidacies were always in much fewer House districts than third-party candidacies and, moreover, that the percent of House districts with fusion candidacies has remained relatively stable over the past century and a half. There has, in fact, not been a dramatic decline in the use of fusion as an electoral strategy since the nineteenth century.

Moreover, as Figure 4.2 shows, and contrary to the description presented in much of the literature, fusion candidacies did not decline dramatically around 1900. Quite the opposite, the percent of these candidacies in House races has remained relatively stable in the century and a half since 1870. Indeed, in the last three decades of the nineteenth century, fusion candidates ran in 7.9% of House districts. Since 1900, they have run in 7.5% of House districts.

There is, however, one significant change in the use of fusion as a campaign strategy. During the nineteenth century, New York State played only a minor role in fusion candidacies. Fusion candidacies began occurring more regularly in New York during the first decades of the twentieth century. But, then, two critical changes occurred. One, fusion began becoming a regular aspect of New York politics, beginning during the FDR administration. As the percentage of districts in New York with fusion candidates rose to virtually 100% by the 1940s, fusion had virtually disappeared throughout the rest of the country by the 1960s. Even though the percent of districts outside of New York with fusion candidates began increasing again around 1990, fusion today remains very much mostly a New York phenomenon.

While this domination of New York as the key fusion state seems to be a significant change, it is in many ways consistent with the history of fusion in post-Civil War America. For most House elections since 1870, fusion candidacies were concentrated in a small number of states. In the 2016 House elections, for example, there were fusion candidates in five states: Connecticut, New York, Oregon, South Carolina, and Vermont. During the largest fusion year since the Civil War, 1872, fusion candidacies were concentrated in nine states: Alabama, California, Georgia, Illinois, Indiana, Louisiana, Massachusetts, New York, and Pennsylvania. Of the ninety-seven districts with fusion candidates that year, eighty-one districts, or 84%, were in four states: Illinois, Indiana, New York, and Pennsylvania. Indeed, during the elections from 1870 to 2016, other than the 1896 election, there were never fusion House candidates running in more than twelve states.

In this way, since the Civil War, and even during periods when third-party scholars have described it as a widely used strategy, fusion has been mostly isolated to a small fraction of House districts in a small number of states. Except for three election years, when the percent of districts with fusion candidates spiked, the percent of districts with fusion candidates has been largely steady over the past century and a half. The only change is that, for approximately three decades from the 1960s through the 1980s, fusion became used almost exclusively by candidates in New York State. However, the number of states with fusion candidates has been gradually rising since the 2000 election. Thus, the use of fusion has already returned to levels surpassing that of the 1880s, the period when the Greenbacks were the strongest third party and which some scholars hail as the best period of widespread third-party support being driving by fusion.

Does Fusion Increase the Vote for Third-Party Candidates?

The three spike fusion years shown in Figure 4.1 suggest another problem with the fusion argument, when they are compared to the history of third-party voter support. During the first spike, in 1872, fusion candidates ran in around a third of House districts. Despite the large number of fusion candidacies—or maybe partially because of it—third-party candidates (that is, candidates nominated by a third party but not a major party) received only 3% of the vote. Already by 1874, the Liberal Republicans disappeared. The second fusion spike, 1896, was similarly unsuccessful for third parties. In the 1892 and 1894 elections, third parties had gained 9% and then 11% of the House vote. In 1896, the election in which the Populists co-nominated a large number of Democratic candidates, the third-party House vote dropped to 6%. By 1900, the Populist movement had effectively disappeared; the few Populist candidates remaining received far less than 1% of the total House vote that election. The 1916 fusion spike also followed the same pattern as the 1896 fusion spike. In 1912 and 1914,

88 Chapter Four

the third-party House vote was respectively 21% and 13%. In 1916, when the percentage of districts with fusion candidates spiked up to 18%, the vote for third-party candidates dropped to 5%. Indeed, 1916 could be considered the beginning of the century-long drought for third parties in American politics.

In all three of these cases, the widespread use of fusion was not related to significant vote gains by third parties. In the latter two cases, the general use of fusion coincides with a decline in third-party voter support. This history suggests that fusion might not dramatically increase the vote for third-party candidates, and its extensive use might even deflate it.

Indeed, a third prediction of the fusion argument is that fusion significantly increases the vote for third-party candidates. For fusion to help explain the decline of American third parties since the 1870s, this strategy would have to significantly improve the prospects of third parties. It does not. Third parties tend to run more candidates in fusion states than non-fusion states, and third-party candidates in fusion states tend to gain more votes than in non-fusion states. However, the third-party vote differences between fusion and non-fusion states are small.

Table 4.1 presents the results of the random effects logistic and linear regressions very similar to those shown in Table 3.1. The only difference between these two tables is that in Table 4.1 the data is extended back to 1870 and the impact of fusion is highlighted. For the logistic regression, the dependent variable is whether the district has at least one candidate nominated by a third party but not a major party. In other words, the question is whether fusion candidacies in a state increase the likelihood that candidates nominated by a third party but not a major party will run. For the linear regression, the dependent variable is the percent vote for candidates nominated by a third party but not a major party. Again, the focus is on whether third parties co-nominating major party candidates also benefits non-fusion third-party candidates in the same state.

A binary variable is used to measure fusion. If the district is in a state in which at least one House, senatorial, or gubernatorial candidate during that election was co-nominated by both a major and a third party, then the district is considered to be in a fusion state. This measure is used because it is consistent with a strategy third parties use when co-nominating major party candidates. By co-nominating a candidate in some races, the hope is that it will improve the prospects of their own candidates in other races.

The results suggest that third parties do indeed do better in fusion states, but that the gains are relatively small. The logistic regression suggests that third parties are more likely to run candidates in fusion than non-fusion states. The slope for this equation is 0.70 with a standard error of 0.048. Like with ballot access laws, this can be translated into probabilities. If one assumes that ballot access laws do not exist, the Democratic and Republican candidates received the same vote, and the various polarization scores are at their mean, then the model predicts that a district in a state without fusion candidates has a 0.28 probability of having at least one third-party candidate running in it; the confidence interval is 0.26 to 0.30. If that district were in a state with fusion

The Prohibition of Fusion **89**

TABLE 4.1 Impact of fusion on third-party success in House elections, 1870–2014

	Districts with a Third-Party Candidate	Percent Votes Received by Third-Party Candidates
Signature requirements	−0.06★★★	0.1★★★
(Percent of vote needed)	(0.006)	(0.015)
Previous vote	−0.08★★★	−0.17★★★
requirements	(0.006)	(0.016)
(Percent of vote needed)		
Fusion	0.70★★★	1.78★★★
(1 = Fusion candidates in	(0.048)	(0.156)
state)		
(0 = No fusion candidates)		
DW-NOMINATE,	1.93★★★	4.77★★★
Dimension 1	(0.121)	(0.387)
(Mean of state		
representatives)		
DW-NOMINATE,	1.70★★★	−2.28★★★
Dimension 1	(0.096)	(0.318)
(Representative)		
DW-NOMINATE,	0.79★★★	2.20★★★
Dimension 2	(0.097)	(0.306)
(Mean of state		
representatives)		
DW-NOMINATE,	−0.32★★★	0.28
Dimension 2	(0.063)	(0.209)
(Representative)		
Two-party margin	−0.01★★★	0.01★★★
	(0.001)	(0.002)
Minor party candidates		7.13★★★
		(0.102)
Constant	−.92★★★	−1.12★★★
	(0.068)	(0.196)
Wald chi-square	2230.08★★★	6583.49★★★
Number of cases	28669	28669
Number of groups	570	570
Overall R^2		0.18

$\star p \leq .05;\ \star\star p \leq .01;\ \star\star\star p \leq .001.$

candidates, the chance of there being at least one third-party candidate rises to 0.44 with a confidence interval of 0.42 to 0.47. In other words, all else being equal, the chances of a third-party candidate running in a fusion instead of a non-fusion state increases from 28% to 44%, or a 14% increase.

The linear regression also suggests that having fusion affects the vote. When third-party candidates run in states with fusion candidacies, their overall vote increases by 1.79%, or just under 2%. The confidence interval is from 1.48% to 2.10%. While statistically significant, a 2% increase in the vote would hardly

90 Chapter Four

explain the dramatic decline in third-party support by the 1950s even if the use of fusion had actually declined.

Examining the relationship between fusion and third-party success by election year provides an important caveat to this analysis. Figure 4.3 shows the percent of districts with third-party candidates in fusion states minus those in non-fusion states during each election from 1870 to 2016. The graph demonstrates that in fifty-nine of these seventy-four election years (80%), a higher percent of third-party candidates ran in fusion than non-fusion states. Overall, third parties ran in an average of 10% more districts in fusion than non-fusion states across these seventy-four elections.[3] The differences varied significantly from election to election but clearly lean in the direction of more third-party candidates running in states where third parties are also co-nominating major party candidates, with the greatest difference being in the 1920s to 1930s as well the 1950s to 1980s, when often third parties ran candidates in 20% to 30% more districts in fusion than non-fusion states.

The relationship between fusion candidacies and the percent vote for third-party candidates, however, is not as strong. Figure 4.4 shows how much greater

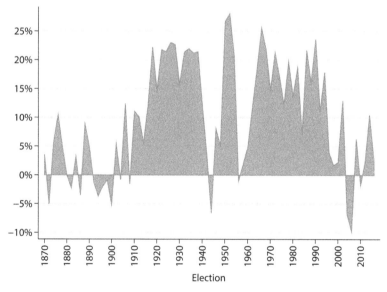

FIGURE 4.3 The percent of House districts with third-party candidates in fusion versus non-fusion states, 1870–2016. For each election year from 1870 to 2016, this graph shows the percent of House districts with third-party candidates in fusion states minus the percent of House districts with third-party candidates in non-fusion states. A fusion state is defined as one with at least one mixed party fusion candidate running for the House of Representatives, Senate, or governorship during that election year. The graph demonstrates that in most elections since 1900, third parties ran more candidates in states in which they also co-nominated major party candidates.

the percent vote for third-party candidates was in fusion states than non-fusion states. (That is, for the districts in which there was at least one third-party candidate, the graph shows the percent vote for third-party candidates in fusion states minus the percent vote for third-party candidates in non-fusion states.) The evidence is not only mixed; it also changes by period. For the first fifty years of the study, 1870 to 1918, the results varied significantly by election. In some years, third-party candidates received a higher percent of votes in fusion than non-fusion states while in other years the reverse was true. From 1926 until 1942, third-party candidates mostly received a lower percent of the vote in fusion states. From 1944 until 1996, third-party candidates in fusion states always received a higher percent of the vote overall than those in non-fusion states. Since 1998, the results have been once again mixed, as they were in the first fifty years of this study.

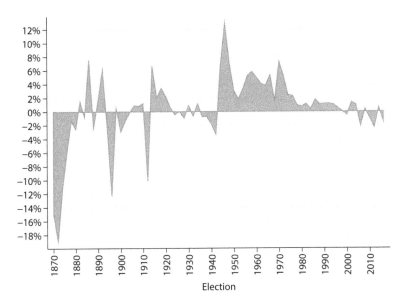

FIGURE 4.4 The percent vote for third-party candidates in fusion versus non-fusion states, 1870–2016. For each election year from 1870 to 2016, this graph shows the percent vote for third-party candidates in fusion states minus the percent vote for third-party candidates in non-fusion states. A fusion state is defined as one with at least one mixed party fusion candidate running for the House of Representatives, Senate, or governorship during that election year. The graph demonstrates that while third-party candidates gain more votes overall in fusion than non-fusion states—during this period, third-party candidates gained 2.5% more votes in fusion states—the relative impact varies dramatically by year. It is also worth noting that third parties received a much lower percent of the vote in fusion states in 1872 (when the Liberal Republicans co-nominated many Democratic candidates), 1896 (when Populists co-nominated many Democratic candidates), and 1912 (when the Progressive Party had its most successful election.)

92 Chapter Four

Nonetheless, overall, the impact of fusion on the third-party vote appears to be generally positive through most of the period studied. Third-party candidates did much worse in fusion states in the 1870s, but in most decades since, the percent vote for third-party candidates was higher in fusion than non-fusion states. Third-party candidates also fared particularly badly in 1896—another indication that co-nominating Democratic candidates was an unwise strategy for the Populists—as well as in 1912. But, overall, third-party candidates received 2.5% more votes in fusion than in non-fusion states from 1870 to 2016, almost the same increase predicted in the linear regression presented before. In other words, co-nominating major party candidates appears to modestly increase the vote for third-party candidates.

Thus, if fusion has any significant impact on third parties, it is probably that it helps them organize. As Figure 4.3 shows, for most of the past century, third parties ran candidates in a higher percent of House districts in fusion states than non-fusion states. However, there is a possible opposite explanation. It is quite possible, instead, that major party candidates become more open to being co-nominated by third parties in states where third parties are already well-organized and are an electoral threat. By being co-nominated by third parties, major party candidates avoid having third-party rivals on the ballot that can take away voter support. In this way, fusion might not be so much a strategy for strengthening third parties as it is a mechanism for co-opting them.

Conclusion

Proponents of the fusion argument for third-party decline make two main claims. The first is that when a third party and a major party co-nominate candidates, this significantly increases the vote for third-party candidates—that is, those not co-nominated by a major party. By co-nominating major party candidates, the argument goes, third parties gain advertisement as well as public legitimacy, which translates into voter support. The second claim is that fusion was once widely used in American electoral politics and has since largely disappeared, primarily because most states have banned the practice. The argument, in the end, is that if the co-nomination of candidates would return to the levels common in the nineteenth century, then third parties would again begin playing a critical role in American politics.

This argument has two significant problems. First, fusion was not widely used in the nineteenth century or at any other point after the Civil War, except for the 1872 and 1896 elections. Indeed, it was actually more commonly used in the 1910s than in most of the elections during the last three decades of the nineteenth century, and it is used in the same percent of House races today as it was in most elections in the 1870s and 1880s. The widespread prohibition of fusion around 1900 is also overstated, including with scholars claiming that

The Prohibition of Fusion **93**

states had banned fusion while candidates continued to be co-nominated by multiple parties.

Second, to the degree that fusion has any impact on the vote for third-party candidates, that impact is small. Most likely, all else being equal, third-party candidates gain around 2% more votes in fusion than non-fusion states. But even that 2% figure could be little more than an artifact of fusion being more likely in states in which third parties are already strong.

There is one other piece of evidence that contradicts the fusion argument for third-party decline. One of the implications of this argument is that if states throughout the country adopted fusion at the level of the late nineteenth century, then third parties would again play a critical role in American electoral politics. However, fusion is already widely used in New York State, and New York third-party politics is nothing like third-party politics in the late nineteenth and early twentieth century. In 1878, New York third parties received 17% of the vote. In 1912 and 1914, they received 27% and 13% of the vote. Since the 2000 election, New York third-party House candidates received an average of 2% of the vote. In other words, third parties in New York experienced roughly the same decline in third-party support as the rest of the country, despite the consistent use of fusion.

This does not necessarily mean that the WFP is running a wrong strategy by co-nominating major party candidates in New York and other states. Instead, it suggests that this is a strategy to follow when third parties are already so weak that they cannot mount a serious challenge against major parties anyway. What fusion seems to do, at best, is make third parties like interest groups. The standard strategy for political parties is to run candidates for office primarily in order to win seats, and then use those seats in order to affect policy in ways that makes it possible for the party to win more seats. I would argue that a secondary strategy might be to use running for office as a subversive strategy, to force policy changes by directly threatening to undermine electoral success for major party candidates. Fusion is a third strategy. There is little threat involved, and there is not even an attempt to win a seat. Instead, it is to make the claim that the party had something to do with the victory of the candidate—instead of money, it brings some votes—and then to use that claim to influence those politicians. The only threat is that the party might instead run independently during the next election if the major party politicians does not make enough concessions. Indeed, the WFP did not run a single non-fusion House candidate in the 2016 election.

Fusion likely does more to co-opt third parties than empower them. It is a mechanism major parties use to keep third parties from dividing the vote and undermining their electoral prospects. This might be why the three biggest fusion election years were moments of significant third-party defeat. 1872 was an election in which the Liberal Republicans may well have thrown away an opportunity by simply co-nominating many Democratic candidates instead of

94 Chapter Four

running their own. Instead of reshaping American electoral politics, the party collapsed rapidly. The fusion strategy of 1896 may well have destroyed the Populist parties as well, and the spike of fusion candidates in 1916 came as the last great third-party wave was ending. It is not clear whether fusion was more a cause or a symptom of third-party decline, but it certainly does not help explain why third parties nearly disappeared by the 1950s or why they are beginning to reemerge into American politics today.

Notes

1 From 1870 to 2016, there had been 258 candidates who were co-nominated by the Democratic and Republican parties. Of these, eighty candidates, or 31%, were also co-nominated by at least one third party.
2 If one is examining House races in which a candidate was nominated by both the Democratic and Republican parties, then these numbers are somewhat inflated for California because the California candidates were less likely to be also nominated by a third party than in New York and Pennsylvania. If one examines all candidates nominated by both major parties, including those nominated by a third party, then California had 171 (66%), New York had forty-eight (19%), Pennsylvania had thirty-two (12%), and Oregon had one. The figures are unchanged for the remaining states.
3 This 10% figure is slightly lower than the 14% estimation from the Monte Carlo simulation presented earlier. The reason for this difference is that, in the statistical simulation, the other independent variables were set to values that may have increased the prediction of how many candidates would run. Signature and previous vote requirements, for example, were set to zero. The 10% figure is the actual percent difference in third-party candidacies between fusion and non-fusion states without taking into consideration how other factors might have influenced whether third-party candidates ran.

5

DO PRIMARIES UNDERMINE THIRD PARTIES?

On February 19, 2009, a month after Barack Obama was inaugurated as president, CNBC reporter Rick Santelli burst into a televised tirade on the Chicago Mercantile Exchange against the Obama Administration plan for foreclosure relief. That diatribe, in which he argued for a "Chicago Tea Party" to protest moves to "subsidize the losers' mortgages," is generally considered the flashpoint that set off the Tea Party movement. Spread across Twitter and conservative blog sites, and then picked up by Fox News, Tea Party activists began organizing locally, with approximately 1,000 loosely connected local organizations emerging throughout the country (Skocpol and Williamson 2012, 7–8). The Tea Party has since had a substantial impact on American politics and especially on American conservatism and the Republican Party.

For our purposes, the important aspect of the Tea Party rise has been its electoral strategy. Despite its name, the Tea Party did not form into a third party. While there has been a very small number of third-party Tea Party candidates—Peg Dunmire, for example, ran for Congress as a Tea Party candidate in Florida in 2010—the main electoral strategy has been to promote candidates for the Republican nomination, to change the party from within. This strategy at times replaced Republican officeholders not deemed pure enough with more conservative politicians, and it also acted as a threat to those appearing too open to compromise with Democrats. In 2010, the Tea Party promoted former Florida House Speaker Marco Rubio for the Republican nomination for US Senate, defeating popular Republican governor Charlie Crist and then winning the general election. Similarly, in 2010, US Senator Bob Bennett was defeated by Tea Party-backed attorney Mike Lee in the Republican Party convention, which determined which candidates would advance to the Republican primary. Probably most famously, a little-known Tea Party Republican candidate, David Brat, defeated House majority leader Eric Cantor in the 2014

96 Chapter Five

Republican primary; effectively, a powerful and influential conservative was ousted from Congress to be replaced by an unknown and inexperienced but presumably more conservative Brat.

The Tea Party strategy of challenging the Republican Party from within could be considered an example of one of the most widely promoted arguments for third-party decline: the direct primary. The argument, in sum, is that when major parties began nominating their candidates through primary elections, opposition internalized within the Democratic and Republican parties. So, before the direct primary, the major parties selected nominees to run in the general election through closed-door conventions. Nominees were often selected by party bosses, and even when they were not, there was no direct way for groups outside the party to influence the process. For this reason, the only electoral option open to opposition groups was to run third-party candidates in general elections. Once states began enacting laws that required major parties to nominate candidates via primary election, the major parties lost control over the nomination process. Among other problems, they could not stop external groups from running candidates in their primaries. As the argument goes, primary elections were a better approach than running third-party candidates, and the absorption of these opposition groups by major parties helped lead to the decline in vote for third parties.

Was the introduction of the direct primary a key reason for the decline of American third parties over the twentieth century? My answer is no. The primary election argument for the decline of third parties has a fundamental flaw. Primary elections are inherently candidate-centered affairs, which generally require significant campaign resources. Unlike a general election, in which voters can distinguish candidates based on their party labels, voters would have to know which primary candidate represents which party faction by name identification alone. This effectively translates into an expensive, candidate-centered campaign for every single candidate, which would require an allocation of funds far beyond the resources of most third parties. So, for example, I would argue that the notion that in the 1910s the Progressives, the Socialists, or the Prohibitionists would have had a greater impact on policy by running candidates in the Democratic or Republican primaries misses a simple point. Most voters would likely have not known which candidates in each primary election was representing the Progressive, Socialist, or Prohibitionist movements.

Indeed, both Hirano and Snyder (2007) and Schraufnagel (2011) have shown empirical evidence that primaries were not a main reason why third parties have declined over the twentieth century. My evidence is more mixed but largely consistent with their findings. I found that while the enactment of primary laws may have reduced the number of House districts with third-party candidates by approximately 9%, that change had no impact on the vote for third-party candidates. Third parties continued to be strong in much of the United States after primaries had been introduced, and third parties have been gaining strength over the past few decades despite primary elections remaining a central characteristic of American electoral politics.

The Primary Election Explanation

The argument that primary elections undermined third parties contains an irony. Before primaries became mandatory in the early decades of the twentieth century, the candidate nominations by the Democratic and Republican parties were largely determined by party conventions. These conventions were often controlled by party bosses, and the nomination process was often corrupt. As the argument goes, one of the demands of the Progressive movement in the early decades of the twentieth century was for these nominations to be conducted in a more democratic manner through primary elections. State governments, mostly controlled by Democratic and Republican politicians, conceded on this reform, requiring the major parties to nominate their candidates via primary elections (Merriam 1909, 1–17; Ranney 1975). Primary elections, however, then led to opposition groups being absorbed by the major parties, undermining third parties, including the Progressive Party, which championed this reform.

The main thrust of the primary election explanation for third-party decline is the belief that primaries internalized opposition within the two major parties. Before the Democratic and Republican parties began nominating their candidates via primary elections (or "direct primaries," as they were often called in the literature), the only electoral avenue open to opposition groups was to form third parties and run against the major parties in the general election. With primaries, these groups could now run their candidates in primary elections and attempt to influence one of the major parties from inside. Since almost all elected positions were won by a Democrat or Republican, the argument goes, this approach significantly increased the chances of an opposition candidate actually winning that position.

Since it is an internal challenge, the primary election strategy also produces a greater pressure on a major party to shift its policy stands. The Tea Party insurgency in the Republican Party is a very good example of this; the always lingering threat of a primary challenge has clearly been one factor pushing Republican members of Congress to the right ideologically. On the Democratic side, this can be seen in the presidential primaries. In 2016, the challenge by Bernie Sanders forced the party into a greater discussion on income inequality, for example. Similarly, the insurgency by Howard Dean during the 2004 Democratic nomination brought the challenge to the Iraq War into the forefront of American politics.

On the surface, the primary election argument may also appear to have two empirical advantages to it. The first is that primary elections did become institutionalized in the United States around the time that third parties declined,

98 Chapter Five

in the early decades of the twentieth century. The second advantage is that it might explain why third parties are so much weaker in the United States than other major SMP systems, like Canada, India, and the UK. In these other countries, party nomination rules are largely determined by the party itself, and few of these parties ever nominate candidates via direct primary. In the United States, major parties are required by state law to nominate candidates using the direct primary, and the primaries for most elected positions are run by each state, not the party. For these reasons, in the United States, the major political parties have a much harder time controlling the nominations of their own parties, including trying to keep opposition candidates out.

A range of political scientists have made the primary election argument for third-party decline (Holcombe 1924, 316; Burnham 1981, 189; Epstein 1986, 129–32; Scarrow 1986, 638; Herrnson 1997, 25; Bibby and Maisel 2003, 62–63). One of the clearest versions of this argument is presented by Bibby and Maisel:

> One of the reasons for the unprecedented Democratic-Republican electoral dominance for over 145 years has been the direct primary system for nominating candidates to run for congressional and state offices. Primary elections, which allow voters to select party candidates directly, are a uniquely American institution. The pervasive use of this system in all fifty states has channeled dissent into the two major parties. In the United States, unlike in other nations, dissidents and insurgents do not need to go through the difficult and often frustrating exercise of forming an alternative party. Instead, they can work within the Republican or Democratic party by seeking to win major party nominations as a route to elective office. This "burrowing from within" strategy is much more likely to yield success than the third-party or independent candidate method.
>
> *(Bibby and Maisel 2003, 62–63)*

Leon Epstein makes a more nuanced version of the direct primary argument. Recognizing that the Populist movement had already largely disappeared before states began instituting the direct primary, he argued instead that third parties would have been much stronger had the mandatory primary for the major parties not existed:

> It is arguable, therefore, that the also distinctively American institution, the direct primary, is a cause of the distinctively American weakness of third parties. The reasoning is that third-party efforts are discouraged by the opportunity to capture the label of one or the other major party in a primary. At the start of any analysis, however, we must recognize that American two-partyism had been firmly established in the nineteenth

century, and that in 1896, before the adoption of the direct primaries, the Democratic party effectively absorbed most of the followers of the relatively new but substantial Populist party. The two-party alignment, though then highly sectionalized, seemed about as pervasive as it was to be after the institutionalization of the direct primary. Thus, to attribute to the direct primary an influence in deterring third-party development, it is necessary to argue that the twentieth century, more than the late nineteenth, would have provided other favorable political conditions for the growth of a new party if the direct primary had not existed.

(Epstein 1986, 131)

This argument that primary elections undermined third parties is generally attributed to V.O. Key's *American State Politics* (1956). In truth, while Key wrote a great deal about primary elections in this text, he had very little to say in it about third parties.[1] Nonetheless, the primary election explanation for third-party decline can be seen as an outgrowth of Key's research on primaries. Focusing on the two major parties, Key argued that the direct primary tends to shift political competition from being inter-party to intra-party; instead of the main competition being between the parties in the general election campaign, he argued, often the main political battle was in the primary election over who would be nominated. This, he argued further, is especially true in constituencies where one of the two major parties dominates, a situation that was very common in the period after the 1896 election. Since the party winning the general election was often a forgone conclusion, then the critical battle was always over who would win the nomination for the dominant party. As he described this logic:

> The more or less stable division of the electorate of a state between the Democratic and Republican parties fixes a framework within which intraparty politics operates. As the normal balance of electoral strength shifts to the advantage of one party, popular attention tends to center in the direct primary of that party, the arena of governing decisions in the politics of the states. Furthermore, as the decision of the nominating primary comes to be more certainly the final decision, the reality of the politics of the state comes to consist more largely in intraparty ballot of factions and personalities within the stronger party. This transfer of politics to the primary in its most complete development results in the formation of factions, more or less transitory, themselves organized and functioning somewhat after the manner of political parties in the usual sense.
>
> *(Key 1956, 104)*

A good example of this process, one could argue, was party politics in the South during the early decades of the twentieth century, a region that Key

100 Chapter Five

had studied in detail. As most of the southern states became almost completely dominated by the Democratic Party, Key argued, the Democratic nomination process instead of the general election became the main battle for electoral victory. As Key described in *Southern Politics*:

> The direct primary method of nomination, rather than the convention, was an inevitable consequence of the one-party system in the South. When single-party action determines the results of elections in advance, the logic of democracy requires a direct vote on the nominees rather than nomination through the convention system. When two parties compete, the question of convention versus direct primary nominations assumes a different significance than when the nominee of the same party invariably wins. The repression of competition between Democrats and Republican-Populist fusions in the southern states in the 1890's accelerated the demise of the convention as a nominating method. The direct primary, through statute or party rule, replaced the convention for most nominations, and it became, in reality, the election.
>
> *(V. O. Key 1949, 416–47)*

It is a small logical step to applying this argument to the decline of third parties—although, again, it is a step Key never seemed to take explicitly. Before the direct primary, opposition groups were effectively shut out of the major party nomination process and therefore had little option but to run third-party candidacies if they wanted any opportunity to affect policy via electoral politics. According to this argument, as the major parties began nominating their general election candidates via the direct primary, electoral competition became more internalized within the nomination process, which provided a better avenue for opposition groups. This pressure to run for nominations of major parties instead of running third-party candidates would have been even greater because after the 1896 election, most regions of the United States became dominated by one of the major parties. As one major party gains electoral strength over the other in a region, the ability of third parties to subvert a major party's electoral goals declines, and therefore so does its ability to push for change. In this situation, one might argue, an opposition group is better off running candidates for the larger party's nominations than attempting to take votes away from that party in the general election.

A question, though, is whether this logic can be applied past the South. As mentioned before, the primary election argument generally contains two steps: progressive opposition to major parties led state governments to instituting primary elections, and then primary elections internalized political competition in ways that undermined third parties, including those representing progressive ideals. In a thorough history of the rise of primary elections, Alan Ware (2002) has shown significant evidence that the first part of this argument is inaccurate.

Ware argued that this interpretation was heavily influenced by the work of Charles Merriam (1909), who was probably the main founder of political science as a field as well as V.O. Key's mentor at the University of Chicago. Merriam, Ware points out, was a progressive reformer before he became a scholar, and his classic text on primary elections, *Primary Elections* (Merriam 1909), was mostly a detailed analysis of the actual primary laws. Merriam, however, showed little evidence of a relationship between the progressive movement and the rise of the direct primary.

Ware was even more critical of Key's analysis. Ware argued that Key had generalized his analysis of southern primaries to the rest of the country, but that this generalization was inappropriate considering the differences between Jim Crow southern politics and the politics of the rest of the country at that time:

> [In] relation to nomination reform, there was an important respect in which Key developed a misleading argument. In what is probably his greatest work, *Southern Politics*, Key explained how the spread of the direct primary in that region after the early 1890s was associated with the collapse of party competition and the establishment of a new political order. However, later in two books published in the 1950s - *American State Politics* and the fourth edition of *Politics, Parties, and Pressure Groups* - he sought to link southern developments with those in the North. He argued that, just as in the South, where decline in party competition had prompted the rise of the direct primary [in Wisconsin and surrounding states where the Republicans ruled without serious challenge]... This is an ingenious argument, and, if it were true, it might explain how elected politicians, under pressure from mass electorates, came to be converted to support for the direct primary. In fact, there is little evidence to substantiate his claim about these midwestern states... By looking for a way of linking developments in the South, where his analysis may well have been correct, to those in the North, where he was not, Key inadvertently misled generations of scholars.
>
> *(Ware 2002, 17–18)*

While Ware emphasizes that his own research is about the rise of primaries in the North, and therefore he cannot speak specifically to whether Key was right about the South, he also writes that Key's analysis has not been universally accepted. Instead, it is one of the two major explanations for the rise of southern primaries. The other explanation focuses on race. For many scholars of southern politics, the primary elections were a method, along with Jim Crow laws and the resurrection of Civil War animosities, to eliminate black influence on southern politics (Ware 2002, 103).

Indeed, there is significant research that emphasizes the role of racial discrimination and the subjugation of black voters in the rise of primaries in

102 Chapter Five

the South (Alilunas 1940; Kousser 1974; Perman 2001; Walton, Puckett and Deskins 2012). On the one hand, these states created a set of impediments that significantly hindered the ability of blacks and poor whites from voting in the general election, including poll taxes that made voting expensive and literacy tests that were designed to be impossible to pass. On the other hand, the Democratic Party in these states also began nominating candidates via primary elections. These primaries were designed to make it virtually impossible for a candidate supported by black voters to win. One technique, instituted by many southern states, was to make these primaries white only. The second was to require a runoff election if no candidate received a majority vote. This way, if by some accident the vote among white supported candidates was divided enough that a black supported candidate received a plurality, the black supported candidate would have to run against the most popular white supported candidate in the runoff, and the latter would presumably win.

Thus, there are at least two ways that primaries might have helped cause the disappearance of third parties by the middle of the twentieth century. First and foremost, the very existence of primary elections could have led to electoral opposition being absorbed by the major parties. This, clearly, is the most widely held interpretation of how primaries undermined third parties. The second possibility is specific to the South from around 1900 to the mid-1960s. In cases when primaries coexist with significant voter suppression during the general election, running third parties in general elections becomes futile. The only option in this situation would be to run candidates in the dominant party's primary election.

The Impact of Primaries on Third Parties

In order to test this explanation for third-party decline, I examined the relationship between third-party strength and whether primaries were instituted for elections to the House of Representatives in the state that the district was in during the election in question. There are a number of sources of this data, including Merriam (1909), but I chose to use Table 2.1 from Boatright's *Congressional Primary Elections* (2014, 31) as my main source, since it is mostly a refinement of Merriam's work. However, these charts provided the year that each state legislature required primary elections for major party candidates for *all* elected offices, whereas the data for this study focuses on House elections. For this reason, if a state required primaries for elections to the House of Representatives before it expanded that requirement to all elected offices, I used the date for the House of Representatives requirement. The primary example of this change was Minnesota, which began requiring major parties to select their House candidates by primary in 1901 but did not expand that requirement to other offices until 1912 (Hein 1957). For this measure, the variable was coded "1" if that state had already instituted primary elections for major parties and "0" if it had not.

Figure 5.1 shows the relationship between the rise of primary elections and decline of third parties across the United States from 1870 to 2016. The percent of districts in which major party candidates had to be selected by direct primary is shown in relation to the left y-axis. As the line shows, the percent of House districts in states with mandatory primary elections rose rapidly from 1900, when there were no states with primary requirements for House elections, to 1918, when around 95% of major party candidates for the House of Representatives had to be nominated via direct primary. During the 1912 and 1914 elections, direct primary laws applied to 75% and then 86% of House districts, for example.

Figure 5.1 also shows the percent vote for third-party candidates in House races from 1870 to 2016, in relation to the right y-axis. It shows, as had been discussed in earlier chapters, three main waves of third-party support. The first wave, which is generally considered the Greenback Party era, lasted from around 1878 to 1882; the second, the Populist era, occurred from 1892 to 1896; and the third, the Progressive Party wave, occurred in the 1912 and 1914 elections. After the 1916 election, third parties became steadily weaker.

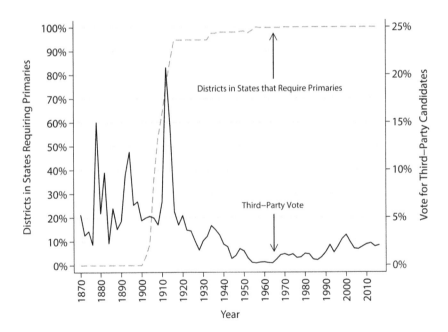

FIGURE 5.1 Rise of primaries and decline in third-party vote, 1870–2016. This graph shows the change in the percent of House districts in which major party candidates had to be nominated via primary elections (left axis) and the percent vote for third-party candidates in House races (right axis). The graph demonstrates that the great Progressive third-party wave in 1912 came *after* major party House candidates had to be nominated by primary election in three-quarters of all House districts.

104 Chapter Five

The critical thing this graph shows is that the rise of primary elections occurred between the second and third waves of third-party support. In other words, the enactment of most primary election laws *preceded* one of the biggest third-party waves in American history. Moreover, the Progressive Party, which was the main third party behind this wave, was not formed until 1912. Since the Progressive Party was formed after a large percent of states already had primary election laws, one cannot argue that this was simply a case of institutional inertia. Instead, the Progressives had a choice as they were forming in 1912 and preparing to run. Despite a clear option of running for major party nominations, presumably especially in the Republican primaries, this organization instead opted to run third-party candidates throughout much of the country.

The weak relationship between primary elections and third-party success is shown a different way in Table 5.1. This table presents the results of the random effects logistic and linear regressions very similar to those shown in Table 3.1 and Table 4.1. However, the data in Table 5.1 focuses on the election period when states were instituting primary elections, or from 1904 to 1924. The reason for this focus is that this is the point when there was variation across states and therefore districts in whether major parties nominated their candidates to the House of Representatives via party conventions or direct primaries. If primaries did indeed undermine third parties, then the evidence for it should appear during exactly this period, especially since this was the time when third parties were seeing their most rapid decline.

Table 5.1 suggests that the introduction of primaries had a relatively small impact on the percent of House districts with third-party candidates during this period. While the logistic regression in the left column suggests that there is a statistically significant relationship between requiring primary elections and the likelihood that third-party candidates would run, that impact of primaries on third-party candidacies was not consistent with the argument that primary elections undermined third parties. Instead, the slope for primaries in this equation, while statistically significant, is only -0.75 with a standard error of 0.122.

To further test the relationship between primaries and whether third-party candidates ran in the general election, I conducted a set of Monte Carlo simulations based on the results from the random effects logistic regression, as I had for the impact of ballot access laws on third-party candidacies in Chapter 3. The extent of this relationship between primary elections and third-party candidacies is shown graphically in Figure 5.2. In these simulations, all the independent variables except whether the state required primaries for major party nominations were held constant: ballot access laws were assumed to not exist, the state the district was in was assumed to have had no fusion candidates, the top two candidates in the district were assumed to receive an equal number of votes, and all the DW-NOMINATE scores were held at their mean. There were two runs of 1,000 simulations, once with the state having primaries and the other without. The left bar in Figure 5.2 shows the estimated probability

TABLE 5.1 Impact of primary elections on third-party success in House elections, 1904–1924

	Districts with a Third-Party Candidate	Percent Votes Received by Third-Party Candidates
Primary elections (1 = State requires it) (0 = No requirement)	−0.75★★★ (0.122)	0.46 (0.324)
Signature requirements (Percent of vote needed)	0.01 (0.014)	0.16★★★ (0.044)
Previous vote requirements (Percent of vote needed)	−0.04 (0.021)	0.01 (0.061)
Fusion (1 = Fusion candidates in state) (0 = No fusion candidates)	1.62★★★ (0.189)	1.75★★★ (0.411)
DW-NOMINATE, Dimension 1 (Mean of state representatives)	−2.68★★★ (0.489)	−4.32★★ (1.289)
DW-NOMINATE, Dimension 1 (Representative)	0.95★ (0.424)	−7.53★★★ (1.157)
DW-NOMINATE, Dimension 2 (Mean of state representatives)	−1.53★★★ (0.342)	2.22★ (0.894)
DW-NOMINATE, Dimension 2 (Representative)	0.56★ (0.225)	0.46 (0.611)
Two-party margin	−0.02★★★ (0.002)	0.001 (0.006)
Minor party candidates		8.36★★★ (0.338)
Constant	2.97★★★ (0.276)	2.53★ (0.780)
Wald Chi-Square	346.75★★★	957.63★★★
Number of cases	4,455	4,455
Number of groups	433	433
Overall R^2		0.22

★$p \leq 0.05$; ★★$p \leq 0.01$; ★★★ $p \leq 0.001$.

that a district would have at least one third-party candidate without a primary while the right bar shows that estimated probability if the state required primary elections for major party nominations. The error bars show the upper and lower bounds of each confidence interval.

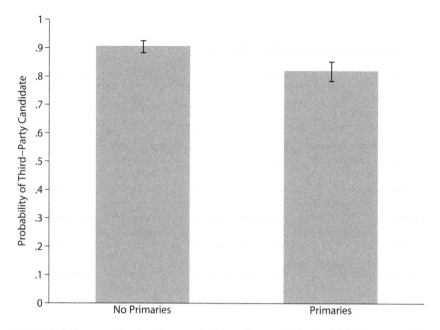

FIGURE 5.2 Impact of primaries on whether a House district had third-party candidates, 1904–1924. This figure provides a graphical representation of the results from the random effects logistic regression shown in Table 5.1. The graph shows the results of a Monte Carlo simulation based on that logit model in which all the independent variables were held constant except whether the state the district was in required major parties to nominate congressional candidates via primaries. The simulation also assumed that the district was in a state with no ballot access restricts or fusion candidates, that the top two candidates in the district received an equal number of votes, and that all the DW-NOMINATE scores were at their mean. The results show that, all other factors equal, districts in states with primary elections had a 9% less chance of having a third-party candidate on the ballot.

The graph shows that while the probability of there being a third-party candidate in a district declines when the state requires primary elections for major party nominations, that decline is not dramatic. For the period from 1904 to 1924, the model predicted that a district had a 0.91 probability of there being at least one third-party candidate running in the general election if there were no primary elections. If there were primary elections and all else was equal, the model predicted a 0.82 probability of at least one third-party candidate running. In other words, the chances of a third-party candidate running dropped by 9% when primaries were introduced. Instituting primary elections appears to have caused a real but relatively small decline in the percent of districts with third-party candidates.

The weakness of this relationship is shown another way in Figure 5.3. This graph shows both the rise of primary elections and the change in the percent of districts with third-party candidates from 1870 to 2016. Primary elections began to become mandatory for major party nominations to House elections in 1902 and then rose rapidly over the next two decades. By the 1912 election, primaries were mandatory in 75% of districts. By 1920, they were mandatory in 95% of districts. Looking at just this graph, one could generously argue that the institutionalization of primary elections might have driven the decline of third-party candidacies, provided that one stopped looking at data after the mid-1960s. Beginning in 1968, the percent of House districts with third-party candidates had risen steadily, even though primary elections are now a central aspect of elections to the House of Representatives. The narrative that primary elections led opposition groups to permanently abandon third-party runs in general elections simply does not fit the history of third parties over the past half century.

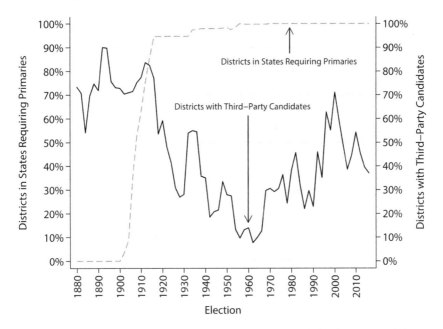

FIGURE 5.3 Percent of districts with primary elections and third-party candidates, 1880–2016. The graph shows the percent of House districts with mandatory primary elections for major party nominations to the US House of Representatives (dashed, gray line) and at least one third-party candidate (solid, black line). The graph suggests that primary elections and third-party candidacies followed two different patterns. While primary elections went from non-existent to almost universal in the period from 1900 to 1920, third-party candidacies declined rapidly after the 1914 election but then began to rise again in the 1970s.

108 Chapter Five

Moreover, the evidence shown in Table 5.1 also indicates that there is no relationship between primary elections and the vote for third parties. If the primary election explanation was correct, it would undermine third parties in two steps. In the first step, opposition groups would be more likely to run candidates for major party nominations instead of as third-party nominees in the general election. In the second, voters would cast their votes for major party candidates not only because there are fewer third-party candidates on the ballot but also because primary elections would make major party candidates more attractive as well as increase their public legitimacy, since they had been nominated through a process that at least seems more democratic. However, as the linear regression on the right column of Table 5.1 shows, there was no relationship between the percent vote for third-party candidates and whether a district was in a state requiring primary elections. The coefficient, 0.46, is not statistical significant—the standard error is 0.32—and moreover, it is positive instead of negative, suggesting that if there is any relationship at all between primary elections and the vote for third parties, it is extremely small and likely in the wrong direction.

Minnesota and Wisconsin

Another approach for examining the impact of primary elections on the third parties is to focus on specific states. Third-party strength has never been evenly distributed across the various states of the union, and as third parties declined over the twentieth century, the disappearance of these parties was not geographically consistent. Instead, by the 1940s, third-party activity became concentrated into five states (California, Minnesota, Pennsylvania, New York, and Wisconsin), and by the 1960s it became almost completely isolated to New York.

Minnesota and Wisconsin are important for a number of reasons, including because they sustained significant third-party activity in the 1930s and 1940s even as third parties had largely disappeared throughout most of the country. Figure 5.4 shows the percent vote for third-party House candidates in Minnesota and Wisconsin from 1870 to 2016 as well as the years that each instituted the direct primary for congressional elections: 1901 and 1903, respectively. As the graph demonstrates clearly, primaries had absolutely no impact on third-party support in these states.

Like much of the United States, third-party support in Minnesota rose in repeated waves until around 1920, including during the early 1880s, around 1894, and in the period from 1912 to 1916. From 1870 to 1920, Minnesota also had a composition of third parties common in many states. Like much of the country, the Prohibition Party ran consistently in Minnesota from the 1870s to the 1910s but rarely won more than a small percent of votes. Otherwise, third parties tended to come in small bursts. The Greenbacks ran in Minnesota

House races from 1876 to 1882, although it was often the Independent Republicans who gained the highest percent of the vote. The People's Party ran formidable campaigns in the state in 1892 and 1894, but like much of the country, it co-nominated Democratic candidates in all of its House districts in 1896 and then rapidly disappeared. Around 1912, there was another wave of third-party activity in Minnesota, including not only the Progressives but also the Public Ownership Party (1904 to 1912), which was a socialist party, and the Socialist Party itself (1914 and 1916), each of which received more votes in their respective active years than the Progressives in Minnesota.

Then, in 1920, a critical change occurred in Minnesota third-party politics: the rise of the Farmer-Labor Party. Also a left-wing party that tied together interests of small farmers with the working class, Farmer-Labor rose rapidly in Minnesota politics, not only receiving a much higher percent of the vote than its third-party predecessors but also winning scores of elected positions, including placing three governors, four US Senators, and even more members of the

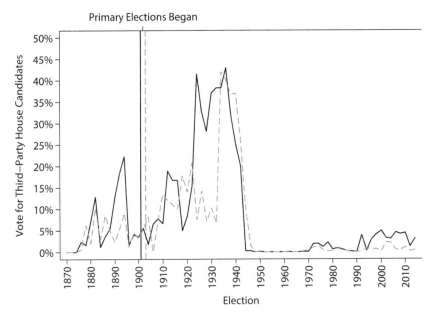

FIGURE 5.4 The impact of primary elections on third parties in Minnesota and Wisconsin, 1870–2016. The graph shows the percent vote for third-party House candidates in Minnesota (solid, black line) and Wisconsin (dashed, gray line) before and after Minnesota in 1901 and Wisconsin in 1903 began requiring that the Democratic and Republican parties nominate candidates to the House of Representatives via primaries. The graph demonstrates that significant third-party activity continued in both states decades after primaries became mandatory.

110 Chapter Five

House of Representatives. Then, in 1944, Farmer-Labor was absorbed into the Democratic Party and disappeared (Haynes 1984).

Wisconsin followed a similar pattern. Like in Minnesota, from the 1880s until 1932, the Prohibition Party was active in Wisconsin races. Other than 1882, when it received 6% of the House vote, the Prohibitionists never received more than 3% of the Wisconsin House vote, despite consistently running in a large percent of House districts in this state. Other parties came in waves. The People's Party was briefly active in Wisconsin in the late 1890s, receiving a high of 6% of the vote in 1894. By 1900, the main third party in Wisconsin was the Social Democrats, which received between 9% and 13% of the House vote from 1910 to 1916. Its successor, the Socialist Party, gained an even higher percent of the vote: 17% in 1918, 14% in 1920, and 22% in 1922. The Socialists were then replaced by the Wisconsin Progressives in 1934, which was formed as an alliance between the progressive wing of the Republican Party in Wisconsin, led by the adult children of Robert M. La Follette, Sr., and Wisconsin labor organizations. The Wisconsin Progressives received between 25% and 40% of the vote from 1934 to 1942. The party effectively disappeared by 1946.

Minnesota and Wisconsin both had longevity of third-party movements and even gaining third-party strength in the 1930s and 1940s while third parties were collapsing in almost every other state. What they also had in common is that in these states, ballot access laws, fusion, and primaries certainly did not play a role in the shift of third-party activity or support. The ballot access requirements for Minnesota, for example, were extremely high. In 1899, the state amended its constitution to make both its signature and previous vote requirements 10% of electors in the districts.[2] In 1915, Minnesota reduced both of these requirements to 5%.[3] While a significant drop from the previous requirement, these requirements were still much higher than most states at that time or even today. Yet, third parties remained very active in this state until 1944. Similarly, Minnesota third parties were not affected by a disappearance of fusion. Minnesota regularly had fusion candidates in House elections from 1890 to 1900, but not since. Nonetheless, third parties continued to thrive and even got stronger during the four decades after fusion stopped in this state.

Much the same was also true of Wisconsin. When Wisconsin instituted the Australian ballot in 1889, it created a relatively low signature requirement of 1% of every person who voted in the previous election.[4] But in 1913, it raised that requirement to one-sixth of the voters within the congressional district, or an extremely high 17%. Nonetheless, third parties continued to thrive in the state. Similarly, while a fusion candidate ran in every Wisconsin House district in 1874, there were only a small number of fusion House candidates in the decades that followed: one in 1884, two in 1888, one in 1894, and one in 1932. Running fusion candidates was clearly not a reason why Wisconsin third parties were stronger than in most states.

As Figure 5.4 clearly shows, Minnesota and Wisconsin third parties were also not hindered by mandatory primary elections for major party nominations. Indeed, they were among the earliest states to require the direct primary for elections to the US House of Representatives. Wisconsin was the first to pass a statewide direct primary law, in 1903. Minnesota's direct primary law, passed in 1901, was similar but less comprehensive, requiring nominations through primary election for the US House of Representatives, the state legislature, and all county and most city offices. Major party candidates for statewide offices were not selected by primary until 1912 (Hein 1957, 341–42).

Yet, third parties in these two states not only continued for four decades after primary elections became law. They gained strength. In the Wisconsin case, instead of internalizing political opposition with the major parties, the exact opposite happened. The progressive wing of the Republican Party, instead of simply running candidates for the Republican primary, completely left the party to join forces with labor organizations and run their own political party, the Wisconsin Progressives. Consistent with the more general analysis presented before, mandatory primary elections seemed to have no impact on third-party activities in these states.

Conclusion

Combined, what this all suggests is that while direct primaries became common and third parties collapsed around the same time, these two changes in American politics had little to do with each other. Third parties often remained strong even in states that were among the first to require the major parties to nominate their candidates via direct primary, and they were generally just as successful around 1912 in states with or without primary elections. Third parties were somewhat less likely to run in states with direct primaries, but the impact was relatively small and did not translate into a decline in the vote for third-party candidates. Primaries therefore did not play the central role in the decline of third parties during the middle of the twentieth century often attributed to them by third-party scholars.

But what of the Tea Party example given in the beginning of this chapter? Isn't the Tea Party strategy of running candidates in Republican primaries instead of as third-party candidates in the general election an example of how primaries have internalized electoral opposition? The answer is that it is not.

Within the literature on the Tea Party, one of the largest areas of debate is over whether it is a grassroots organization or simply a front for the political aspirations of an elite faction within the Republican Party. Democratic politicians, including Barack Obama and former House Speaker Nancy Pelosi, have referred to the Tea Party as "astroturf," implying that it is a fake network made to look like a grassroots movement to help push the agenda of right-wing Republican politicians. On the other hand, political scientist Ronald Libby (2014)

112 Chapter Five

has argued the opposite, that the Tea Party is a grassroots movement with some political elites playing a very small role in its success. Most political scientists who have conducted research on the Tea Party, however, have argued that it contains some combination of both characteristics (Skocpol and Williamson 2012; Fetner and King 2014; R.P. Formisano 2012). There is an element of a social movement in the Tea Party, but at the same time there are powerful interests within the Republican establishment that have used the movement to promote their own agenda. Skocpol and Williamson, for example, write the following:

> Indeed, one of the most important consequences of the widespread Tea Party agitations unleashed from the start of Obama's presidency was the populist boost given to professionally run and opulently funded right-wing advocacy organizations devoted to pushing ultra-free-market policies. Along with Republican Party operatives, who had long relied for popular outreach on independent-minded and separately organized Christian conservatives, national free-market advocacy operation would, via the Tea Party, enjoy new ties to grassroots activists willing to prioritize fiscal anti-government themes. One political action committee poured the old wine of GOP consultants and big-money funders into a new bottle labeled Tea Party Express (TPE), which allowed them to seem closely aligned with grassroots citizens. Other existing national organizations, such as FreedomWorks and Americans for Prosperity, suddenly saw fresh opportunities to push long-standing ideas about reducing taxes on business and the rich, gutting government regulations, and privatizing Social Security and Medicare.
>
> *(Skocpol and Williamson 2012, 9)*

In other words, the Tea Party was not an opposition group that forced its way into the Republican nomination process. The Tea Party was invited in and given lavish support by factions already well established in the Republican Party. In turn, these factions used their alliance with the Tea Party and its anti-establishment rhetoric to push the Republican Party even farther to the right ideologically. Thus, the Tea Party's promotion of candidates for the Republican nomination instead of creation of a third party does not suggest how primary elections have undermined third parties. Instead, it shows one of the many ways that major party actors can co-opt opposition movements and use their anti-establishment stance to promote their own political gain. The Tea Party can inform us about intra-party politics and possibly about the asymmetrical shift in American party politics, but it says nothing about how primaries affect third parties.

Nonetheless, the Tea Party does speak to one factor that may help explain the decline of American third parties: co-optation. The Tea Party did begin as a protest group, and it did spread in a grassroots manner, but it was also co-opted in dramatic speed by established, powerful groups. In the same way, there are characteristics of American third-party politics already discussed that fit within the co-optation framework. Duverger's Law is consistent with a theory about major parties co-opting smaller parties. Since the single-member district with plurality voting causes parties with similar ideologies to often divide their votes, there is a pressure on smaller parties to simply join the major parties, a pressure that is far weaker in proportional representation systems. Similarly, fusion, or the ability for a third party to simply co-nominate major party candidates, also produces a mechanism for third parties to be co-opted by major parties.

But if co-optation is such an important factor, then why did it become successful in the middle of the twentieth century as opposed to the late nineteenth century? Similarly, why would it have worked in the United States but not been a successful strategy in the UK or Canada? These questions will be explored in the next chapter.

Notes

1 Indeed, Key did not make this connection between primary elections and the decline of third parties in any of his major texts (Key 1949, 1964).
2 MN 1899 CH Sec. 2.
3 MN 1915 CH Sec. 336.
4 WI 1889 CH. 248 Sec. 4, Sec. 6.

6

CO-OPTATION AND THIRD-PARTY WAVES

Co-optation is one of the most common explanations for third-party decline (Rosenstone, Behr and Lazarus 1984, 43–44; Herrnson 1997, 30; Gillespie 2012, 18), and it is also part of the explanation for party realignments (Sundquist 1983, 28–29, 312–13), or when a large subgroup of Americans shift their party allegiance from one major party to another. As the argument is usually presented, whenever a third party starts becoming too popular and a threat to one of the major political parties, that party will co-opt the third party's issues and rhetoric. The major party may also try to co-opt the third-party organization as well. This collaboration could be through running fusion candidates—that is, having the third party co-nominate some of the major party's candidates—or having the third party simply become part of the major party. Ultimately, the third party is undermined by the major party "stealing" its issues and rhetoric and then its voter support. But, in the process, the major party adopts some of the third party's policy goals, and in this way the third party can influence the political process without winning any elected positions.

There certainly has been historical evidence for this co-optation of third parties. The most obvious example is the 1896 election (Hild 2007, 203), when Democratic presidential candidate William Jennings Bryan adopted the rhetoric of the Populist parties as his own at the same time that the Populist and People's parties co-nominated large numbers of Democratic Party candidates. The Populist movement as an electoral force collapsed rapidly after the 1896 election, but at the same time the Democratic Party began its gradual steps towards promoting progressive and pro-labor policies. Some have argued that the Greenback's demise was partially caused by co-optation (Summers 2004; Schwartz 2006, 119–44), and others, like Hirano and Snyder (2007), have argued that pro-labor parties were co-opted during the FDR era. Some, like

Rapoport and Stone (2008), have also argued that the Reform Party was co-opted by the Republican Party in 1994.

Can co-optation theory explain the long-term decline of third parties by the middle of the twentieth century? My answer is that it cannot. While the evidence that co-optation affects third parties is stronger than the argument that state election laws undermined third parties, the co-optation argument nonetheless has fundamental weaknesses. The biggest problem is that the long-term changes in third-party support are not consistent with the co-optation theory. In the world described by co-optation theory, third parties repeatedly rise to challenge major parties, but then the major parties respond through various strategies that win the voters back, including "stealing" the third party's issues and rhetoric. While one could argue that this argument fits the patterns of rising and declining third-party support from at least the Civil War until around 1920, it cannot explain the nearly complete disappearance of third parties by the middle of the twentieth century. Instead, starting around 1920, third parties stopped gaining waves of support, and then by the 1960s they stopped running candidates at all outside of New York State. In other words, in the late nineteenth century and early twentieth century, there were repeated waves of third-party support that one might argue were co-opted by the major parties. But by the middle of the twentieth century, there were no third-party challenges to co-opt in the first place.

The Co-optation Explanation

The co-optation argument is based on the assumption that the United States is fundamentally a two-party system. According to this argument, third-party activity occurs in waves, and these waves occur in steps. In the first step, a significant subset of the voting population is unhappy with the stance of the two major parties, and a third party articulates those concerns in a way that attracts these voters. The third party gains a significant portion of the vote. Then, recognizing this new threat, the major party co-opts the third party by stealing its issues and rhetoric, possibly by convincing that third party to join forces. In the final step, the major party gains a new set of supporters or attracts back former supports, and in the process, the third party is destroyed.

The co-optation thesis is consistent with the basic argument behind Duverger's Law, especially as it was articulated by Riker (1976). "Sophisticated voters," or those who think strategically, will generally support one of the two major parties in an SMP system. However, sometimes they become disillusioned with the major parties and then temporarily bolt to a third party. Once that disenchantment subsides, these voters return to the major party instead of splitting the vote in a way that increases the chances that the least liked major party will win. The co-optation argument simply adds one step. In this situation, recognizing the new threat, one or both major party shifts ideologically in

116 Chapter Six

order to attract those third-party voters. Placated, those voters return to voting for one of the two major parties, and that third party disappears.

The co-optation argument has been made by a range of third-party scholars. Rosenstone and his colleagues (Rosenstone, Behr and Lazarus 1984), for example, embraced the argument as one of their many explanations for why third parties are so weak in the United States. Gillespie similarly argued that one way that third parties are marginalized is the "Democratic and Republican appropriation—theft—of third-party positions on issues when they are seen as popular with voters" (Gillespie 2012, 18). Herrnson, using Ross Perot as an example, made a similar argument: "Strategic adjustments that rob minor party and independent movements of their platforms are common in American history. They enable the two major parties to absorb, protest, and help maintain the existence of the two-party system" (Herrnson 1997, 30).

While the co-optation argument has been widely cited in the third-party literature, it is often only one of many explanations given by these scholars. These authors, including Rosenstone and his colleagues, do not specify how co-optation might relate to other explanations but instead simply include it in a long list of reasons for third-party weakness. There are two important exceptions. Rapoport and Stone (2008) present a theory of third-party challenge that treats co-optation as the central reason for third-party weakness. They also tested their theory on the 1992 Perot campaign. Hirano and Snyder (2007) have also argued that the key to third-party decline was co-optation. Instead of a repeated pattern of challenge and co-optation, however, they argue that the co-optation of Left parties by the Democrats during the New Deal era not only suppressed third-party challenges then but effectively destroyed these third parties for the decades that followed. Since they are the strongest co-optation arguments with the best empirical evidence, I will focus on them.

The "Sting like a Bee" Explanation

Probably the most thorough of the standard version of the co-optation argument was made by Rapoport and Stone in *Three's a Crowd* (2008), where they elevate co-optation to a general theory of third-party behavior. The gist of the argument is that whenever a third party becomes too successful, which they define as receiving at least 5% of the vote in a presidential election (Rapoport and Stone 2008, 5), one of the major parties co-opts their issues and rhetoric. For them, this is not simply one other factor affecting third parties but both the central way that third-party efforts are undermined and that third parties have an impact on policy:

> The key to understanding how third parties produce change is another widely observed regularity: successful third parties do not last long. In fact, the historian Richard Hofstadter (1955, 97) put it succinctly, "Third

Co-optation and Third-Party Waves **117**

parties are like bees; once they have stung, they die." He might have said, "Because they sting, they die." The sting and subsequent demise of the party is what we label the "dynamic of third parties." The dynamic applies to "successful" third parties-candidates and movements that have sufficient electoral clout to "sting" the political system. Change occurs because the successful third party presents the minor parties with an opportunity to appeal to the third party's constituency in subsequent elections. One or both major parties changes its positions to bid for the third party's constituency, and former third-party supporters migrate into the party that makes the successful appeal. The third party then dies because its constituency has been co-opted by a major party and because it can no longer attract significant support.

(Rapoport and Stone 2008, 5)

In this way, American third parties can be classified into two types. One type, like the Prohibition Party, have a small backing. Since they do not threaten the major parties, they can be safely ignored, which makes it possible for them to survive for decades. Indeed, the Prohibition Party is one of the longest lasting political parties in American history (Andersen 2013), partially because it was never strong enough to drag many votes away from Democrats or Republicans. The more successful third parties rise quickly but then become serious threats to the major parties. In this case, the major parties steal the third party's issues and voters, and the third party quickly disappears. Thus, the Greenback, Populist, and Progressive third-party waves can be explained as the process of challenge and co-optation. For Rapoport and Stone, this is a fundamental process of third parties, explaining both their short lives and why they are so weak.

But, there is a problem if we are trying to explain the long-term decline of third parties. In co-optation theory, major parties do not stop third parties from initially rising; they instead destroy these parties once they have already gained some public support. In the world envisioned by co-optation theory, third parties repeatedly rise to challenge major parties, but then the major parties respond through various strategies that win the voters back, including "stealing" the third party's issues and rhetoric. As Figure 6.1 shows, however, while this description is largely consistent with the movement of third-party support in the late nineteenth to early twentieth century, it is not consistent with third-party support over the past century. From 1870 until 1920, third-party support often came in waves. The most successful third parties did rapidly gain a significant percent of the vote only to disappear within the next few election cycles, a process that could be explained with the co-optation theory. In sharp contrast, since 1920, there have been no such waves of third-party support. Instead, voter support for third parties has been largely flat and often very close to, if not below, 1%. The co-optation theory might explain why the Greenbacks declined in the 1880s, Populists declined in the 1890s, and

118 Chapter Six

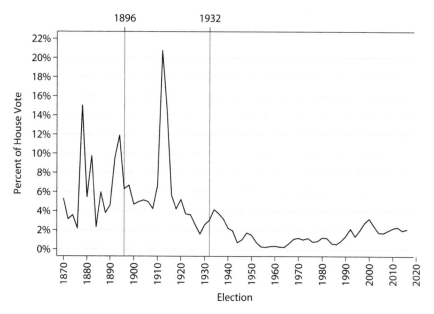

FIGURE 6.1 Percent House vote for third parties and predicted co-optation years, 1870–2016. This graph shows the percent vote for third-party candidates in elections to the US House of Representatives as well as the two elections some scholars believe that third parties had been co-opted. The graph suggests that while support for third parties (notably the Populist and People's parties) declined after the Democratic-Populist fusion of 1896, the graph also suggests that third parties were already in decline by the time Franklin Delano Roosevelt won the presidency in 1932.

Progressives disappeared in the 1910s, but it has a much harder time explaining why new third-party waves did not occur at all for a century since the end of the Progressive Era.

This issue is shown another way in Figure 6.2. It shows electoral threat to the two major parties measured a different way than Rapoport and Stone's approach. For Rapoport and Stone (2008, 5), the critical question is whether the third-party presidential candidate had received at least 5% of the vote. The limitation of this approach is that while 5% or even 10% of the vote for a single candidate at the top of the ticket might suggest a threat to Democratic and Republican presidential candidates and might even suggest an opportunity for new issues for these parties to adopt, it is also not a real threat to the candidates of the major parties running for any other office. The Reform Party, Rapoport and Stone's main empirical case, is a good example of this. Ross Perot certainly had a dramatic impact on the 1992 and 1996 presidential races, and the Republicans in 1994 may have co-opted Perot's primary issues.[1] But, other than Perot and Jesse Ventura's successful 1998 bid to become governor of Minnesota, there is little evidence that the Reform Party was any threat to the major parties.[2]

Another approach would be to measure what percent of elections *could have been* subverted by third-party candidates, with subversion in this case meaning that the third-party candidates caused the candidate who would have won the election without a third-party challenge to lose. This subversion could happen two ways. One, a major party candidate who would have won without a third-party challenge lost because third-party candidates took enough votes away that the other major party candidate got the plurality. Two, the third-party candidate got the most votes and won the election. In either case, the total third-party vote would be greater than the vote difference between the Democratic and Republican parties. Therefore, if the total vote for third-party candidates in a House race is greater than the absolute value of the total vote for the Democratic candidate minus the total vote for the Republican candidate, the race is considered to be potentially subverted by the third party.[3]

The emphasis in this measure is potential third-party subversion, not actually undermining the election prospects of a major party candidate. It is almost impossible, especially without survey data, to determine whether an election was actually subverted by third-party candidates, since this would require knowledge of voters' intentions had there been only two major party candidates. Nonetheless, this measure of potential subversion can be used to compare elections to the same body across time as well as elections to different types of offices, and it can be used to compare third-party threats across countries.

As Figure 6.2 shows, the percent of House races that have been potentially subverted by third-party candidates declined dramatically around 1920 and has remained low for nearly the last century. In the decades from 1870 to 1918, between 9% and 25% of House races were potentially subverted by third parties. That figure dropped to 4% and 6%, respectively, during the 1920s and 1930s. For the decades from the 1940s to the 2010s (that is, 2010 to 2016), less than 3% and often less than 1% of House races were potentially subverted by third-party candidates. Put more generally, from 1870 to 1918, an average of 16% of House races were potentially subverted by third parties; in comparison, from 1920 to 2016, 2% of House races were potentially subverted in this way.

In other words, the "sting like a bee" explanation cannot explain the long-term decline of third parties, since these waves completely disappeared after around 1920, and moreover, third parties stopped being an electoral threat to the major parties. Co-optation theory, as it is described by Rapoport and Stone, does not predict a complete stop of third-party activity, nor does it predict that new parties will not emerge. Instead, once the third-party vote rises to a point that major parties see a threat or opportunity, one of those parties steals the third party's issues and rhetoric and often takes other steps to co-opt it. What this version of co-optation theory cannot explain is why third parties have stopped rising in the first place.

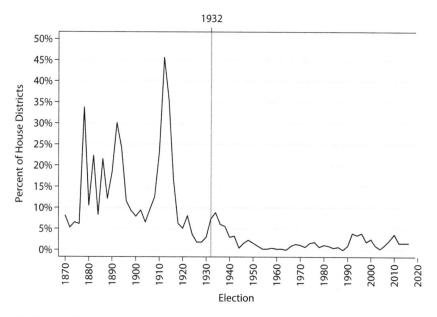

FIGURE 6.2 Percent potential third-party electoral subversion, 1870–2016. This graph shows the percent of House races in which third-party candidates might have caused a major party candidate to lose the race. For each district, potential electoral subversion is defined as when the combined vote for third-party candidates is greater than the vote margin between the Democratic and Republican candidates. The graph shows that third-party candidates were potentially undermining a significant percent of House races from the late 1870s until 1916. From 1918 until the late 1938, this figure dropped to under 10% of districts each election. From 1940 until today, fewer than 5% and often fewer than 1% of House races were potentially subverted by third-party candidates.

The New Deal Explanation

Another version of this theory, promoted by Hirano and Snyder (2007), is that the Democratic Party co-opted pro-labor third parties during the New Deal and then kept these parties from reemerging by maintaining pro-labor policies ever since. They argue that

> We find considerable evidence consistent with the co-optation argument. More specifically, we find that the large and seemingly permanent decline in left-oriented third-party voting was linked to the large and sustained leftward shift of the Democratic Party during and following the New Deal.
>
> *(Hirano and Snyder 2007, 3)*

They similarly state a few pages later that

this is the first paper to argue and provide quantitative evidence that the overall decline in third-party electoral support in late twentieth century was facilitated by the Democratic Party's adoption of a left-wing position during and following the New Deal.

(Hirano and Snyder 2007, 14)

There are two main differences between this paper and much of the third-party literature. The first is that it is a quantitative analysis that tests various explanations. They find, as have I and others (Collet and Wattenberg 1999; Stratmann 2005; Burden 2007; Tamas and Hindman, 2014), that state election laws have had little impact on third-party success and do not explain their decline over the twentieth century. Instead, they argue that the primary cause of third-party decline is the co-optation of left-wing parties by the Democratic Party during the New Deal. Second, unlike much of the co-optation literature, they explicitly address the issue of why third-party challenges stopped by the middle of the century. For them, the Democratic Party did not simply steal third-party issues. Instead, by permanently shifting to the left, the Democratic Party effectively took away the major fuel for left-wing third parties. Also showing that much of the rise and fall of third-party vote from the Civil War until 1930 was support for left-wing parties (Greenbacks, Populists, Progressives, Socialists, and the like), they argue further that the disappearance of third-party movements was largely produced by the disappearance of these left-wing parties.

Hirano and Snyder also directly address one of the critical measurement issues with co-optation theory. Unlike the percent of signatures needed to get onto a ballot or the number of fusion candidates in a state, it is very much a question of interpretation whether third-party issues had been co-opted. While 1896 is an obvious example of the Democrats trying to co-opt the Populist movement—the People's Party did co-nominate many Democratic candidates, and William Jennings Bryan clearly adopted Populist rhetoric—other major elections are not as clear cut. Hirano and Snyder present additional evidence of Democratic co-optation during this period. (1) They cite historical analyses claiming that the Democrats during the FDR period had co-opted issue stands from the progressive movement; (2) they demonstrated that labor unions that had been funding pro-labor third parties shifted their financial support to the Democratic Party; and (3) they showed evidence that politicians who had run as third-party candidates began running for office as Democratic candidates.

But Hirano and Snyder's argument does have limitations. The first is their emphasis that third-party support began its decline in the 1930s. As they wrote:

Figure 1 shows the decline in third-party electoral competition clearly.... The pattern in the figure shows a clear decline in third-party electoral support starting around 1930. The third-party vote share dropped from an average of about 6% to an average of around 3%.

(Hirano and Snyder 2007, 2)

122 Chapter Six

Contrary to Hirano and Snyder's claim, I would argue that the decline in voter support for third parties began *before* FDR came to office. This can be demonstrated in Figure 6.1, which shows the total percent vote for third-party House candidates from 1870 to 2016. During this 144 year period, there were four peaks in the vote for third-party candidates: 1878 (15%), 1882 (10%), 1894 (11%), and 1912 (21%). From 1916 to 1920, this figure ranged from 4% to 5.5%, and then starting in 1922 the percent vote for third-party House candidates was less than 4% every year except 1932 (4.15%). In truth, even these numbers in the 1920s and 1930s are inflated because of the strength of the Wisconsin Progressives and Minnesota Farmer-Labor Party. If one removes these two states, then the percent vote for third-party House candidates was less than 3% from 1922 until the 2000 election.

Figure 6.3 presents this point from a slightly different angle. It shows the shifting mean of the percent vote for third-party House candidates from 1880 to 2016. In this case, the shifting mean would be the average percent vote for third-party candidates that election and the previous four elections, or one decade. (Thus, the figure for 1930 was the average third-party vote for 1922, 1924, 1926, 1928, and 1930.) In each election from 1880 to 1922, this figure was between 5% and 10%. In 1924, the figure began dropping steadily. By 1932, it was 2.7%, even though it was the average of the third-party vote for all the elections from 1924 to 1932. It then remained relatively stable throughout the 1930s and only began dropping again in the late 1940s.

I would argue that even their own data, as presented in Figure 1 of their article (Hirano and Snyder 2007, 2), suggests that third-party support was already declining in the 1920s. From the 1870s to the 1910s, the vote share for third-party candidates each decade, as they calculated it, was between 0.6 and 0.12, with significant variation from decade to decade. From the 1910s to the 1920s, this figure dropped from over 0.11 to 0.04. After rising slightly in the 1930s, it began dropping again and reached a low point in the 1950s.

Hirano and Snyder do emphasize that they are focusing on the decline of Left third parties, not all third parties, and include the Greenbacks, Populists, Progressives, and Socialists in their list. But if one focuses on the main Left parties active in the early decades of the twentieth century, the Progressives and the Socialists, the evidence points even more towards the decline starting in the 1920s, not the 1930s. (The Greenbacks and Populists respectively disappeared by 1890 and 1900, both more than thirty years before the 1932 election.) As Figure 6.4 shows, the Progressives rose rapidly in 1910, had significant electoral gains again in 1914, and then had virtually disappeared by 1916. As the graph also shows, the Socialists also mostly declined by the middle of the 1920s. After a significant jump in support in the 1910s, peaking at 6.7% of the House vote in 1912, the Socialists vote dropped to just over 2% in 1920, jumped to 4% in 1922, and then bottomed out in 1924, receiving

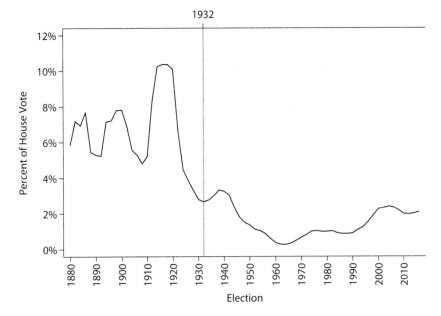

FIGURE 6.3 Shifting mean of percent House vote for third-party candidates and 1932 election. This graph shows a smoothed version of the percent vote for third-party candidates in elections to the US House of Representatives, in order to minimize the impact of individual elections and emphasize long-term trends. For each election from 1880 to 2016, a shifting mean (in this case, the average percent vote during the election in question and the previous four elections) was calculated. The graph shows that the vote for third-party House candidates began to decline at least a decade before Roosevelt won the White House in 1932 and continued to decrease steadily into the 1960s.

only 1% of the House vote. The Socialists then received less than 1% of the vote starting in 1926 with very little change through the 1930s. In 1940, that support dropped to less than 0.01%.[4]

There is another issue. Hirano and Snyder argued that the Democrats not only co-opted Left parties with the New Deal but maintained that co-optation for decades afterwards by continuing to support pro-labor policies. But, they provide neither statistical nor historical evidence to support the argument that the New Deal co-optation would hold for generations. They also did not respond to obvious counterexamples. For example, in 1947, Congress passed the anti-union Taft-Hartley Act, which significantly curtailed the activity of labor unions and dramatically weakened the labor movement. While promoted by Republicans, who temporarily controlled the House and the Senate after a dramatic seat swing during the 1946 election, the override of President Truman's veto included 106 Democratic votes in the House of Representatives. Only

124 Chapter Six

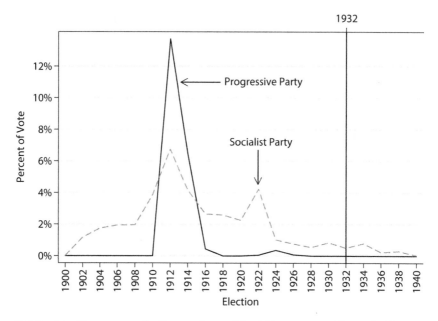

FIGURE 6.4 Percent vote for Progressive and Socialist party candidates, 1900–1940. This graph shows the percent House vote for third-party candidates nominated by the two main pro-labor third parties in the early decades of the twentieth century: the Progressive and the Socialist parties. The graph shows that voter support for these two parties had already dropped dramatically before the Democratic Party was swept into power in 1932.

seventy-one House Democrats voted against it. Why was a vote by a majority of congressional Democrats for a bill that dramatically harmed the union movement not enough to end the co-optation of pro-union third parties? In a standard co-optation framework, a rational strategic move by at least part of the labor movement would be to form another third party and challenge the Democrats from the left, to pressure the party into supporting pro-union policies again. No such third-party challenge occurred.

Indeed, there are a range of moves by the Democratic Party over the decades after the New Deal that could have led to the reemergence of Left third parties. Starting with the Truman Administration, the Democrats repeatedly failed to pass universal health care until 2010, even when they controlled both houses of Congress and the White House. The Reagan Revolution, including its anti-union policies, passed Congress even though the Democrats controlled the House of Representatives. Then, Bill Clinton actively shifted Democratic Party politics to the right, including promoting international trade deals opposed by unions. None of this led to the reemergence of pro-union third parties. It is hard to imagine that the co-optation of Left third parties was so

Co-optation and Third-Party Waves   **125**

thorough in the 1930s that the labor movement became so satisfied with the Democrats that they had no interest in forming new third parties, despite Democratic support for unions often being spotty at best.

So how does one reconcile the evidence of co-optation with this evidence against the co-optation argument? The standard narrative in the third-party literature is that every time a third party begins rising in popularity and threatens to create a multiparty system in the United States, the major parties co-opt their issues and destroy them. The implication is that if the major parties simply stopped "stealing" third-party issues, these parties would be not only vibrant today, but the United States would have evolved into a multiparty system. But what if the causal arrows are reversed? What if, instead of co-optation making third parties weak, that weak third parties make co-optation possible? This would explain both the evidence for co-optation and the evidence that Left third parties began declining before, not after, the New Deal. It would also explain why Left third parties did not reemerge once the Democrats became less steadfast in their support of unions. As they were getting weaker in the 1920s, they became easier to co-opt. By the 1950s, they were so weak that this co-optation was no longer necessary.

Minnesota's Farmer-Labor Party is a good example of this. Arguably the most successful labor party in American history, it was built on an association of unions and farmer organizations, and it gradually gained power in Minnesota after it was established in 1918. In the 1930s, once the Great Depression had begun, Farmer-Labor began winning elections, including winning the state governorship several times as well as sending a number of its nominees to the US Senate and House. Farmer-Labor was not co-opted by the Democratic Party during its gradual rise or when it began actually winning large numbers of elected positions in Minnesota. Instead, once the party began to falter in the early 1940s, it accepted a merger with the Democratic Party to become the Democratic-Farmer-Labor (DFL) Party. To this day, the Minnesota branch of the Democratic Party retains the DFL name (Haynes 1984).

This argument that the weakness of third parties opens the door to co-optation also helps explain why major parties in other SMP countries have not been able to co-opt smaller parties. To the best of my knowledge, co-optation theorists have never presented evidence that major parties in other liberal democracies, including other countries with SMP systems, do not try to "steal" issues from smaller parties. Instead, the key difference was probably that labor movements in most western democracies were stronger and more unified than in the United States. The UK is an obvious example. The Labour Party was rising around the same time that the Progressives and Socialists were reaching their strongest point in the United States. But, there was little chance that the Liberal Party in the 1920s could simply change a few issue stances and alter their rhetoric enough to stop Labour from continuing its climb into the center of UK politics. Having a much weaker and more divided labor movement, once

126 Chapter Six

the Democratic Party made significant steps to promote pro-labor policies in the 1930s, the Left parties in the United States had little option but to accept whatever deal the Democrats would offer them. Co-optation, in this sense, was more a symptom than a cause.

Conclusion

In this chapter, I reviewed the co-optation argument for third-party decline and argued that it does a poor job of explaining the disappearance of third parties starting around 1920. Co-optation, as it is usually presented in the third-party literature, is a potentially good explanation for the decline of specific third parties or a particular wave of third-party support. It also fits closely with the historical evidence for at least one election: 1896, when William Jennings Bryan ran as both a Democrat and Populist. But the co-optation argument, as it is usually presented, predicts a rise of third-party support, a reaction by one or both major parties, and then a shift of the support for third-party candidates back to one of the major parties. After 1916, there was never a large wave of support for any national third party below the presidential level, and therefore there were never third parties that threatened most major party candidates. Over the past century, there have been no significant third-party movements to co-opt.

There is also an issue with the co-optation theory from a comparative politics perspective. The key to the argument is that when third parties become too popular, one of the major parties will steal its issues, which leads voters to shift their vote to that major party and the third party to collapse. One has to wonder, why does this co-optation strategy work only in the United States? If major parties can simply co-opt the issues of threatening third parties, then why has this not happened in other SMP countries, or even countries with proportional representation systems? Indeed, co-optation is a strategy that any major party in any SMP system could employ. Yet, as was effectively demonstrated in Chapter 2, third parties have not been eliminated through co-optation in the other major SMP systems.

It is also worth pointing out, almost as an aside, that while the rapid rise and fall of some third parties is consistent with co-optation theory, co-optation is not the only possible explanation for this phenomenon. New parties, especially those that rise rapidly, can self-destruct. There are a few interrelated reasons why. The first is that they are not yet institutionalized. The internal rule structures can be very weak, for example, and this can increase the chances of factionalization within the party translating into an intra-party civil war on the rules or directions itself. The second is that third parties are generally run by activists instead of seasoned, experienced politicians. Lacking the type of competencies that develop over a career in party politics, these activists can often employ self-destructive strategies.

The collapse of the Reform Party is a good example of this. It was caused by a fight for power between Perot's old allies, who wanted to retain control, and the rising importance of Jesse Ventura, who had won the governorship of Minnesota. In order to fight off Ventura, Perot's allies gave Pat Buchanan the blueprints on how the take over the party—a classic case of drinking cyanide in order fight a cold. During the 2000 election, Buchanan took over and then decimated the party. The Republicans may have co-opted Perot's signature issues, as some scholars argue, but the destruction of this party occurred because of conflicts internal to the party.

But there is another, broader way that co-optation could lead to the demise of third parties. The main fuel for political parties outside of the political system and challenging the established parties is discontent. One way to remove that threat is to placate the public. Producing jobs, outlawing child labor, increasing minimum wages, promoting worker safety, providing retirees Social Security, and making education free and higher education affordable: these are all methods for increasing the basic satisfaction of a mass public that might otherwise be attracted to candidates and parties that challenge the legitimacy of the established parties. This can also be seen as a form of co-optation, and it is broadly consistent with the main points of Rapoport and Stone and well as Hirano and Snyder. It is also consistent with the most important change in America politics over the twentieth century: the decline and reemergence of political polarization.

Notes

1 Even here, though, the case is not clear cut. Rapoport and Stone emphasize that Perot had run on reforming government and passing a balanced budget constitutional amendment. However, Ronald Reagan also ran on a balanced budget constitutional amendment years before—see YouTube, "Reagan Calls for a Balanced Budget Amendment", www.youtube.com/watch?v=paZZzFOSYNw, (Retrieved January 25, 2017)—and calling for government reform is hardly a dramatic shift in policy.
2 Indeed, United We Stand, Perot's movement behind his 1992 bid, ran no candidates other than Perot himself. The Reform Party was created in 1995, after the Republicans gained control over Congress. It ran House candidates in 5% of districts in 1996, 7% of districts in 1998, and 8% of districts in 2000, the year that the party imploded. In comparison, the Libertarians ran House candidates in 35%, 36%, and 55% of districts in 1996, 1998, and 2000, respectively. In 1996, the median vote for Reform Party House candidates was 3%. That figure was around 1% in 1998 and 2000.
3 In cases in which there is a single major party candidate, including one co-nominated by both the Democratic and Republican parties, the major party margin of victory is calculated as 100%. In rare cases in which there is a candidate co-nominated by both the Democratic and Republican parties being challenged by a candidate nominated by only one of these major parties, then the major party margin of victory is the vote difference between these two candidates. In cases of multimember at-large districts, which usually produce multiple Democratic candidates and Republican

128 Chapter Six

candidates, the equation is the absolute value of the total vote for all Democratic candidates minus the total vote for all Republican candidates.

4 One may also suggest the Farmer-Labor Party as an example of a Left party that was also potentially threatening the Democratic Party around the time that FDR took power. In every election from 1926 to 1942, Farmer-Labor received more votes nationally than the Socialists, and in 1932 it received 3% of House votes, six times that of the Socialists. However, despite calling itself a national movement, Farmer-Labor was heavily concentrated in Minnesota, where it had become so successful that it was temporarily the most dominant party in the state. Other than Minnesota, there were only three Farmer-Labor candidates in 1932: one in Colorado, who received one-third of a percent of the vote, and two in Illinois, who received 1.6% and 0.8% of the vote. In 1944, Farmer-Labor was co-opted by the Democratic Party, creating the Democratic-Farmer Labor Party, which is still the Minnesota branch of the Democratic Party. That co-optation was largely a reaction to the reemergence of the Republican Party and the weakening of Farmer-Labor, not the New Deal.

7

THE DECLINE AND RISE OF POLITICAL POLARIZATION

Thus far, I have reviewed five of the most widely cited theories about why third parties had declined and nearly disappeared from American politics by the middle of the twentieth century. In Chapter 2, I argued that while there is significant evidence in favor of Duverger's Law, or the argument that SMP electoral systems reduce the number of effective political parties, this theory cannot explain why third parties are weaker in the United States than other SMP systems or why American third parties began to decline rapidly after 1920. In Chapter 3, I showed that while ballot access laws had gotten more difficult over the twentieth century, these laws had very little impact on the number of House districts each election with third-party candidates or the percent vote received by third-party House candidates in each district. I explored the argument that the prohibition of fusion undermined third parties in Chapter 4, and I showed that, in fact, fusion had never been a widely used strategy by third parties and that therefore its prohibition was not a significant reason for the near disappearance of these parties. In Chapter 5, I demonstrated that there was little relationship between the institutionalization of primaries and the decline of third parties. Finally, in Chapter 6, I argued that while there is strong evidence that major parties attempt to co-opt the most successful third parties and that this likely led to the demise of specific parties, it cannot explain why third parties largely stopped challenging the major parties by 1950.

These results suggest that co-optation and changes in election laws had little impact on the long-term decline of American third parties, not only as individual factors but also as combined influences. The impact of ballot access laws on the vote are close to zero, for example. Similarly, the use of fusion is roughly the same today as it was the late nineteenth century except for the 1872 and 1896 elections, which suggests that it had little impact on overall third-party success. Mathematically speaking, a non-change in the use of fusion combined

130 Chapter Seven

with the small impact of ballot access laws similarly adds to almost no consequence on the long-term health of third parties.

This lack of a combined impact by these various factors is suggested a different way in Chapter 5. Minnesota and Wisconsin had no significant history of fusion candidacies, very high ballot access laws, and among the earliest primaries for House candidates outside the South. Yet, in the 1940s, when third parties had all but disappeared in the rest of the country, Minnesota and Wisconsin third parties not only thrived but often dominated politics in their respective states. Minnesota and Wisconsin third parties were the last holdouts before the nearly complete disappearance of third parties by the 1950s, but their respective demises had nothing to do with state election laws or co-optation.

Indeed, there have been a wide range of explanations for third-party decline presented by political scientists over the past half century, and as I have shown thus far, most are poor predictors of when and where third parties have declined. These traditional arguments similarly do not provide an explanation as to why third-party activity and voter support has risen since the late 1960s.

There is, however, a possible explanation for the changing activity of and support for third parties over the past century that has not been explored within the third-party literature: political polarization. Political scientists have shown considerable evidence that American politics were very polarized through most of its history but then became much less so during the middle decades of the twentieth century. However, starting in the late-1960s, polarization has emerged again. It has steadily gained more intensity over the past few decades.

In other words, levels of third-party activity and political polarization have followed roughly the same pattern over the past 170 years. When polarization was high in the late nineteenth and early twentieth century, third parties were very active. As polarization began declining during the Progressive Era, third parties began disappearing. Once polarization levels began rising again in the late 1960s and especially the 1980s, so did third-party activity. As political divisions continued to widen between Democratic and Republican politicians and as American politics became steadily more conflictual, third parties also continued to be more visible and active.

Indeed, for a range of reasons that I will elaborate in the following, high political polarization leads to a political environment much more conducive for third party success. Polarization is closely related to a higher level of discontent, for example, and in almost any representative democracy, when the population becomes disenchanted with the conditions of their lives or with the major political parties, they become more likely to support fringe parties, often including those holding extremist views (Williams 2006; Van Kessel 2015). Similarly, a more polarized politics reduces the options for voters when they are dissatisfied with the performance of a major party. In a more polarized setting, for example, Republican identifiers are unlikely to vote for Democratic House

The Decline and Rise of Political Polarization **131**

candidates even when they are very unhappy with a Republican president. Third-party candidates become a much more viable option in this case.

As I will demonstrate as follows, the decline of third parties in the middle of the twentieth century and their reemergence since the 1970s is closely related to the fall and rise of political polarization over the same period. The primary reason for the decline of third parties in the middle of the twentieth century, I argue, is that the United States became much less polarized politically. Effectively, the political disenchantment and contention that fuels third-party activity and support declined considerably during this period. However, this period of low polarization was temporary. As polarization began increasing again over the past half century, third-party activity and support also began increasing. The rising contentiousness of American politics is not simply dividing Democratic and Republican politicians and making governing far more difficult. It is also producing fuel for a reemergence of third parties.

Polarization

Political polarization is a situation in which members of or citizens identifying with each major political party hold ideological views that are distinct from those of the other major party (Baldassarri and Gelman 2008; Hetherington 2009). In other words, if most Democrats hold virtually all the same views on major issues in opposition to the views held by most Republicans, then they would be considered to be highly polarized. In sharp contrast, if there is a great deal of overlap between the two groups, including with much agreement on major issues by many Democrats and Republicans, then this would be a situation of low polarization. Thus, in the less polarized period in the middle of the twentieth century, it was not uncommon for politicians to define themselves as liberal Republicans or conservative Democrats, and there were a large number of moderates who saw themselves as distinct from their more ideologically extreme colleagues. Today, however, liberal Republicans and conservative Democrats are virtually non-existent. Not only is there very little ideological overlap between Republican and Democratic politicians, but Republican politicians have become much more conservative than they were even a few decades ago, and Democrats have become steadily more progressive on economic and social issues.

Indeed, one of the most important research findings in political science has been this rise of polarization in American politics over the past few decades. Likely the first critical evidence of this development came from Keith Poole and Howard Rosenthal (1997), who developed the DW-NOMINATE system, which uses virtually all the roll call votes for the US House of Representatives and Senate to estimate the ideological position of all members of Congress.[1] Poole and Rosenthal had two main findings. First, at any given moment in US political history there were only one or two dimensions of these ideological positions.

132 Chapter Seven

The first dimension is generally interpreted as the member of Congress's support for government intervention in the economy, or liberal-conservative in the modern era. The second dimension reflects the member of Congress's views on race issues at various periods in American history, including slavery before the Civil War and civil rights from the 1940s to the 1970s. Since 1980, the second dimension seems to have little importance; the critical difference has become between liberal and conservative, as these terms are currently defined.

The more important finding, for our purposes, is that the level of polarization has shifted significantly since the Civil War. During the late decades of the nineteenth century and early decades of the twentieth century, members of Congress were deeply divided on the economic issues, or the first dimension. However, that polarization began declining around 1910 and then dropped dramatically from 1920 to 1940. The ideological distinction between Democrats and Republicans became much less clear. But, since around the late 1960s, that polarization has risen again, especially after the 1980 election, when Ronald Reagan won the presidency in a landslide (Poole and Rosenthal 1997).

Others have shown evidence of this change outside of Congress as well. Kevin Quinn and Andrew Martin (2002) have developed a similar measure of the Supreme Court that showed the very same change in polarization in the votes of justices. A range of other studies (Abramowitz and Saunders 1998; Hetherington 2001; Jacobson 2005) have shown that the political beliefs among Republican and Democratic voters have become more distinct over the past few decades. Since then, there have been other indicators of this rising polarization over the past few decades, such as the heightened rhetoric between Democratic and Republican members of Congress (including in the US Senate, which had been until recently an institution with norms of civility among members), extreme gridlock, government shutdowns, and the unwillingness of Republican senators to consider judicial appointments by a Democratic president.

Nonetheless, there is significant debate among scholars about the nature of this polarization. As Marc Hetherington (2009) argues convincingly, there is widespread agreement within the literature that the political elite has become much more polarized over the past few decades. There is much more disagreement, however, over the question of whether the public is also more polarized ideologically. On the one hand, Abramowitz and Saunders (2008) argue that Americans have become dramatically more ideologically polarized since the 1970s, especially among the well-educated and politically engaged segment of the American public. On the other hand, Morris Fiorina (2005) famously argues in *Culture Wars* that, contrary to popular perception, there is actually not a great ideological polarization within the public or ideological distance between voters in red states and blue states.

Instead, Fiorina argues that the major public change over the past few decades has been "sorting." Conservative Americans have not become more conservative; they are simply more likely to support the Republican Party today

The Decline and Rise of Political Polarization **133**

than a few decades ago. The same is true for liberal support of the Democratic Party. One reason for this sorting, Fiorina and his coauthors argue, is that the parties have become clearer in their ideological stands, making it easier for voters to choose the party that more reflects their views. Fiorina and Abrams (2009), for example, present a number of cases in which the two parties diverged on key issues (e.g., abortion, environmental protection, Civil Rights) and then segments of the public for whom those issues were particularly salient switched to the party closest to their positions. This argument remains hotly debated. While many political scientists agree with Fiorina that the primary cause of polarization is sorting (Baldassarri and Gelman 2008; Hetherington 2009), others (Abramowitz and Saunders 2008) argue that sorting alone cannot fully explain these divisions within the mass public. As Abramowitz summarized his thoughts in the preface of *The Disappearing Center*:

> Polarization in Washington reflects polarization within the public, especially within the politically engaged segment of the public. It is the politically engaged segment of the public—the attentive, informed, and active citizens—that most closely reflects the ideals of democratic citizenship, and it is the politically engaged segment of the public that is most partisan and ideologically polarized. In contrast, it is among the least attentive, least informed, and least active members of the public that partisanship is weakest and moderation thrives. Far from turning Americans off on politics, polarization has served to energize the public by clarifying the stakes in elections.
>
> *(Abramowitz 2009, x)*

Yet another explanation is that polarized behavior, including the decline of voters willing to vote for both Democratic and Republican candidates, is that certain dividing issue have become more salient. As Hetherington and Weiler have argued in *Authoritarianism and Polarization in American Politics*:

> The polarization in voter behavior and evaluations of partisan players is hard to square with the lack of polarization on issues. We argue that the key to solving this puzzle is accounting for the things that divide ordinary Americans today. In our view, the issue is less one of distance than it is of salience, intensity, and nature of issues. To that end, it is worth noting that we find evidence of increasngly deep sorting on several hot-button, gut-level considerations. When people are divided along lines such as these, it becomes much harder for them to view the other political party as an acceptable alternative to theirs, a position that will yield increasingly favorable evaluations of politicians whom people perceive share their beliefs and increasingly negative evaluations of politicians whom they perceive do not.
>
> *(Hetherington and Weiler 2009, 28)*

134 Chapter Seven

Finally, McCarty, Poole, and Rosenthal (2016) present a different explanation for rising polarization: income inequality. They demonstrate that political polarization in Congress is closely related to several measures of income inequality, including the Gini coefficient and the proportion of income going to the top 1% of all income earners. Indeed, income inequality has been measured to have been very high in the period from the Civil War to around 1920, dropped considerably beginning around 1920 and especially after the New Deal and Second World War, and then began rising again around 1970; it follows the same pattern as political polarization and third-party activity.

McCarty, Poole, and Rosenthal do not argue that income inequality is simply driving political polarization. Instead, they see it as a process in which income inequality drives up polarization and then polarization increases income inequality. As they summarize this aspect of their argument:

> We characterize the relationships as a "dance"—that is, relationships with give-and-take and back-and-forth, where causality runs both ways. On the one hand, economic inequality feeds directly into political polarization. People at the top devote time and resources to supporting a political party strongly opposed to redistribution. People at the bottom would have an opposite response. Polarized parties, on the other hand, might generate policies that increase inequality through at least two channels. If the Republicans move sharply to the right, they can use their majority (as has been argued for the tax bills of the first administrations of Ronald Reagan and George W. Bush) to reduce redistribution. If they are not in the majority, they can use the power of the minority in American politics to block changes to the status quo. In other words, polarization in the context of American political institutions now means that the political process cannot be used to redress inequality that may arise from nonpolitical changes in technology, lifestyle, and compensation practices.
>
> *(McCarty, Poole and Rosenthal 2016, 3–4)*

How Polarization Affects Third Parties

In sum, there are a range of explanations for the rise of polarization in American politics. However, regardless of what drove its change over the twentieth century, polarization tends to produce an environment more conducive for third-party activity. Indeed, there are a number of ways that polarization can increase the activity of and support for third parties.

The first problem is that, as voters become more spread out ideologically, as happens if the public becomes more polarized in the way that Abramowitz describes, then it becomes more difficult for two giant, umbrella parties to keep their voter bases satisfied. No matter what ideological stance the party takes, it can alienate a larger percentage of its voter base. If a party moves too far towards its extreme, then it can lose supporters to the other major party, which could take a more moderate position. It could also lose those moderate voters to a new party, assuming that such an organization could enter the electoral arena. Conversely, if it moves too close to the center, and if new parties can enter the electoral arena, then it might lose supporters to another party that presents more extreme positions.

Similarly, as the voting population becomes more polarized, they will also likely begin seeing the opposite party as completely unacceptable and even a threat. In this scenario, the opportunity for third parties emerges when these voters become dissatisfied with the party that they usually support. Political scientists have long identified retrospective voting (Downs 1957; Fiorina 1981), or the tendency for voters who are dissatisfied with the state of the country to vote against whatever party happens to be in power. Dissatisfaction with the party holding the presidency has been shown to cause significant increases in the vote for congressional candidates of the other major party, for example (Tufte 1975). But, what happens when voters become dissatisfied with one of the major parties but also consider the other major party unacceptable? Under these circumstances, third-party candidates become a better protest option. Indeed, during the late nineteenth century in the South, support for third-party candidates was often very high. In 1882 and 1894, third parties in states that were in the former Confederacy received respectively 26% and 25% of the vote. One reason for these high numbers, by third-party standards, may well have been the very low support for the Republican Party there; for most southern voters at the time, the Republicans were not a viable option, even if they were dissatisfied with the Democratic Party.

Polarization also drives anger and discontent. As the public moves farther towards two opposite poles or becomes divided on particular issues that it finds very salient, the legitimacy of the other side as well as the legitimacy of compromise with that other side declines. The normal workings of governance thereby loses legitimacy as well. This produces circumstances unfavorable to the major parties regardless of their reactions. If members of Congress in this situation reach compromises, as one must do to produce results in a legislative body, then they can be seen as caving in, which might produce deep dissatisfaction within their base of support. If they do not compromise, the effectiveness of government drops and the level of contention rises, which then can fuel dissatisfaction with both major parties and a decline in trust in government. Either situation increases the number of dissatisfied voters who might consider supporting third-party candidates.

This problem with polarization occurs for the major parties even if the process is elite driven and partisan polarization is mostly a case of sorting. In a non-polarized political environment, the conflict between the parties is relatively civil and conducted in a manner that does not challenge the legitimacy of each party or the major institutions of government. Government appearing to do its job to solve problems does not create incentives for third-party activity or support. However, as gridlock increases and political conflict intensifies, the

136 Chapter Seven

basic trust in the system can decline considerably. As trust declines, the incentive for supporting third-party candidates rises (Hetherington 1999).

Finally, if McCarty, Poole, and Rosenthal (2016) are correct that partisan polarization is closely related to income inequality, then we can see another reason that polarization would be closely related to third-party activity and support. Voting for third-party candidates in a two-party system always requires a rejection of the major two parties, and it is often related to low satisfaction with the political system in general. Stagnating or declining economic conditions would be one fuel for exactly this dissatisfaction. This framework would produce a simple explanation for the decline and reemergence of third parties. As income inequality began dropping around the 1920s, partially due to reforms during the Progressive Era, political polarization declined, as did anger towards and lack of trust in the government. After the Democrats responded to the Great Depression with the New Deal reforms and standards of living rose and continued to rise into the 1950s and 1960s, any incentive for supporting third parties would have declined further for two reasons: standards of living were high enough for the new middle class to produce no incentive for supporting third parties, and the decline of polarization reduced the amount of severely contentious politics. However, starting in the 1970s, as income inequality began rising again, standards of living stagnated and even dropped at the same time that very contentious, polarized politics between the two major parties began rising again. While these changes have not as of yet produced the levels of third-party activity that were common before the 1920s, they have led to a reemergence of these parties and a steady increase in their voter support.

Political polarization therefore produces a very different answer to the decline and rise of third parties than is common within the third-party literature. The third-party literature generally assumes, implicitly implies, and sometimes explicitly states that the reason third parties are weak is that the American political system is rigged against them. Third parties would have been just as strong in the 1950s as the 1890s had it not been for repressive state election laws, for example. Thus, Gillespie (2012) has referred to the American two-party system as "forced." But another possibility is that third parties become more successful when political contention is high. When the public is very polarized politically, it becomes much harder for two giant, umbrella organization to satisfy most voters. A higher percent of the most politically engaged get involved, and third parties begin running candidates in higher numbers. At the same time, voters deeply dissatisfied with the two major parties become more open to choosing third-party candidates. For this reason, when American politics became less polarized in the middle of the twentieth century, the fuel that drives third parties largely disappeared. This also suggests that third-party weakness is not permanent. When polarization is high, as it is again today, the probability of third parties having an impact on the political system becomes much better than when polarization is low.

The Relationship Between Polarization and Third-Party Activity

Figure 7.1 shows how partisan polarization and third-party activity has changed on the aggregate from 1880 to 2014. For this graph, polarization is measured as the distance between the mean DW-NOMINATE score for Democratic members of the House of Representatives and the mean DW-NOMINATE score for Republican members of that institution during each House session. Third-party activity is measured as the percent of district-level races to the House of Representatives that include at least one third-party candidate.[2]

Figure 7.1 shows that the aggregate pattern of change for partisan polarization and third-party activity largely match each other. Polarization was very high through the late nineteenth century until around 1922, when it began dropping. That drop continued until around 1936, when it reached its bottom.

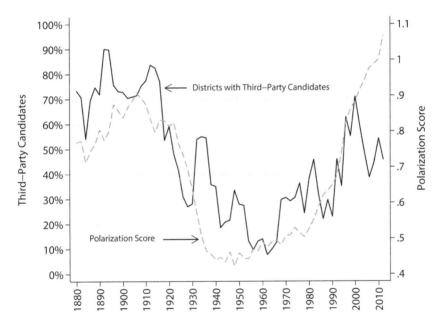

FIGURE 7.1 Partisan polarization and third-party activity, 1880–2014. This graph shows the relationship between partisan polarization and third-party activity. Polarization (shown as a dashed, gray line) is measured each term as the absolute value of the mean of DW-NOMINATE scores, first dimension, for Democratic members of the House of Representatives minus the same score for Republican representatives. Third-party activity (shown as a solid, black line) is measured as the percent of House districts each election that have at least one third-party candidate. The graph demonstrates that, on the aggregate, polarization and third-party activity follow roughly the same pattern over the past century.

138 Chapter Seven

Partisan polarization began climbing again in 1970, and that climb sped up after the 1980 election. This estimate of partisan polarization is now higher than it was in its early twentieth-century peak in 1906. Third-party activity has followed roughly the same pattern, beginning its drop in the 1920s and reaching its bottom in the 1950s and 1960s. Starting in 1968, it also began to rise, reaching a peak in 2000, when 70% of House races had at least one third-party candidate on the ballot, the highest level since 1916, the last election of the Progressive third-party wave. Since 2002, third-party candidates have run in 40%–55% of House districts.

This relationship between third-party activity and partisan polarization can also be shown at the individual district level. Table 7.1 presents the results of the random effects logistic and linear regressions identical to that shown in Table 4.1 in the chapter on fusion. The key independent variables are the

TABLE 7.1 Impact of polarization on third-party success in House elections, 1870–2014

	Districts with a Third-Party Candidate	Percent Votes Received by Third-Party Candidates
DW-NOMINATE, Dimension 1	1.93★★★	4.77★★★
(Mean of state representatives)	(0.121)	(0.387)
DW-NOMINATE, Dimension 1	1.70★★★	−2.28★★★
(Representative)	(0.096)	(0.318)
DW-NOMINATE, Dimension 2	0.79★★★	2.20★★★
(Mean of state representatives)	(0.097)	(0.306)
DW-NOMINATE, Dimension 2	−0.32★★★	0.28
(Representative)	(0.063)	(0.209)
Signature requirements	−0.06★★★	0.1★★★
(Percent of vote needed)	(0.006)	(0.015)
Previous vote requirements	−0.08★★★	−0.17★★★
(Percent of vote needed)	(0.006)	(0.016)
Fusion	0.70★★★	1.78★★★
(1 = Fusion candidates in state)	(0.048)	(0.156)
(0 = No fusion candidates)		
Two-party margin	−0.01★★★	0.01★★★
	(0.001)	(0.002)
Minor party candidates		7.13★★★
		(0.102)
Constant	−0.92★★★	−1.12★★★
	(0.068)	(0.196)
Wald Chi-Square	2230.08★★★	6583.49★★★
Number of cases	28669	28669
Number of groups	570	570
Overall R^2		0.18

★$p \leq 0.05$; ★★$p \leq 0.01$; ★★★$p \leq 0.001$.

The Decline and Rise of Political Polarization **139**

absolute value of the DW-NOMINATE scores for individual members of the House of Representatives from 1870 to 2014. I included both the first and second dimension of these scores.

Moreover, for each dimension, I include both the score of the member of Congress representing the district and the mean score for all representatives in the state. The latter is important because, despite discussion of political parties nationalizing over the twentieth century (Klinghard 2010), third parties have in many ways remained state organizations over the past 140 years. The distribution of third-party House candidates is not random across districts. Instead, they tend to cluster in specific states, although there is regularly a smattering of third-party candidates in states without large third-party activity. In other words, when they organize, they organize by state, and therefore the level of polarization within the state will likely have a greater impact on whether third parties become active than what is occurring within a particular district. For this reason, the equations include four DW-NOMINATE scores: dimension one (or the economic dimension) for the representative of the district, the average score of dimension one in the state, dimension two for the representative of the district, and the average score of dimension two in the state.[3]

As Table 7.1 shows, for the period from 1870 to 2016, third-party candidates were more likely to run for office in locations where the members of Congress were farther ideologically to the left or right. As is shown in the results of the random effects logistic regression, in the left column of this table, the less moderate the members of Congress (and presumably their constituents), the more likely that third-party candidates would run for office. Not unexpectedly, the relationship is stronger for the economic DW-NOMINATE dimension than the second DW-NOMINATE dimension. For the mean absolute value of the DW-NOMINATE economic dimension scores for each state, the slope is 1.93 with a standard error of 0.12, and for the absolute value of the DW-NOMINATE economic dimension score for the individual member of Congress, the slope is 1.70 with a standard error less than 0.10.

The strength of this relationship between the first DW-NOMINATE dimension and third-party candidacies is shown in Figure 7.2. Since the results of logistic regressions cannot be interpreted in the direct manner that one can analyze linear regressions, I ran a set of Monte Carlo simulations based on the results from the random effects logistic regression shown on Table 7.1 and then presented those results in this graphic. This is the same approach that I used for analyzing the impact of ballot access laws on third-party activity, except with the focus on the ideological scale. In these simulations, I held all the independent variables constant except the DW-NOMINATE first dimension: ballot access laws were treated as non-existent; there were no fusion candidates in the state; the DW-NOMINATE second dimension variables were held at zero, or ideologically moderate; and the top two major party candidates in the district received an equal number of votes. Since DW-NOMINATE scores are

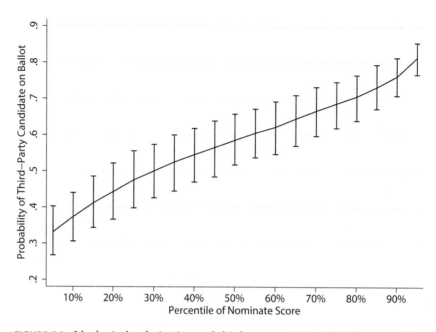

FIGURE 7.2 Ideological polarization and third-party activity. This figure provides a graphical representation of the results from the random effects logistic regression shown in Table 7.1. The graph shows the results of a Monte Carlo simulation based on that logit model in which all the independent variables except two were held constant: the absolute value of dimension one of the DW-NOMINATE score for the member of Congress in that district, and mean absolute values of dimension one of the DW-NOMINATE scores for all members of Congress in that state. For each run (represented on the graph with each vertical error bar), DW-NOMINATE scores were held constant at the same percentile. The graph shows that the farther the ideological position of these members was from zero, the greater the likelihood that third-party candidates would be running in that district.

estimates of politicians' position in ideological space, that estimate is useful for understanding their ideological position vis-à-vis other members of Congress, but it is not a concrete concept like the percent of the vote a party needs to remain on the ballot. For this reason, instead of using the actual absolute value of the DW-NOMINATE estimate, I ran the simulation by percentiles. In this way, one can judge the relationship by showing the likelihood that a third-party candidate would run in a district based on how moderate or ideologically extreme that district or state is.

As the graph shows, third parties were most likely to run in states or districts in which their representatives had the most extreme DW-NOMINATE scores. Those in the fifth percentile—that is the districts and states with representatives

The Decline and Rise of Political Polarization **141**

that are the least polarized—the model predicts a 0.33 likelihood that there would be at least one third-party candidate running. At the ninety-fifth percentile—that is, the districts and states with representatives that are most polarized—the model predicts a 0.81 likelihood of a third-party candidate running. In this way, DW-NOMINATE scores are a strong predictor of how active third parties have been in different regions and at different times.

Two important points are worth adding here. The first is that DW-NOMINATE scores are comparisons not only of members of Congress during a single congress but across time as well. It was not just that members of Congress began voting more consistently with members of their own party in the middle of the century. It was also that members of Congress became more moderate (that is, relative to each other) during this period. The mean absolute value of the DW-NOMINATE scores also decreased around the 1950s, and it also began rising again starting in the 1970s.

Furthermore, that level of moderation almost definitely reflects, at least to some degree, the ideology of these members' constituents. One does not win elections in most rural parts of the Rocky Mountain states, for example, by running on decreasing military spending, restricting gun ownership, expanding the welfare state, and funding abortions. As discussed before, it is not clear whether the public has become more ideologically divided or if the changes over the past few decades are largely a case of sorting. Nonetheless, lacking survey data to measure the ideological positions of each House district since 1870, in this case DW-NOMINATE can act as a proxy measure of the underlying state and district. The conclusion one can reach, then, is that the farther a district moves to the left or right ideologically, the more likely third-party candidates are to run in that district. Moreover, as these districts became more moderate during the middle of the twentieth century, the less likely third-party candidates were to run.

The Relationship Between Polarization and Third-Party Support

One more important point needs to be added. If one looks at the linear regression (in the right column of Table 7.1), one can see that there is also a significant relationship between the first dimension of the DW-NOMINATE scores and the vote for third-party candidates. For every one point increase in the average score for a House state delegation—that is, a move from a very moderate to a very polarized district—third parties are predicted to receive a boost of 4.77% of the vote. However, at the same time, for every one point increase in that score for the individual House member representing that district, the third-party vote is predicted to decrease by 2.28%. Therefore, if the representative of that district and the entire state's House representatives moved from moderation to far on the left or right, the net increase in the vote for third-party candidates would be around 2.5%.

For third parties, an average increase of two and a half percentage points is not insignificant. But, at the same time, it does not explain the shift from peak waves like 1894 and 1912 to decades of third parties receiving less than 3% of the House vote. Indeed, this is a rather odd set of findings: polarization can dramatically increase third-party activity, yet its impact on the vote is minimal.

An explanation for these findings is presented in Figure 7.3. The graph is based on the exact same regression model shown in Table 7.1, except that they are run independently for each decade from 1890 to 2010. Each bar on the graph shows the slope for a single independent variable: the statewide DW-NOMINATE first dimension. For example, the bar for the decade from 1890 to 1898 is a positive 8.8%. This means that, all other factors held equal, a change from 0, or very moderate, to 1, or very polarized, would increase the vote for third-party candidates by an average of 8.8%.

This graph shows two important findings about the relationship between polarization and the vote for third-party candidates. First, it suggests that when

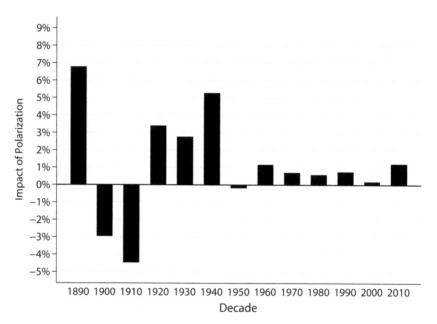

FIGURE 7.3 Impact of polarization on the vote for third-party candidates by decade, 1890–2014. Each bar in this graph shows how much the polarization of a state's House delegation increases the percent vote for third-party House candidates by decade. More specifically, it is the coefficient for the first independent variable in the regression equation in Table 7.1 (DW-NOMINATE, dimension 1, mean of state representatives) when the equation is run separately for each decade. The graph demonstrates that the impact of polarization levels on the third-party vote was significantly higher before the 1950s than after.

The Decline and Rise of Political Polarization **143**

there is a relationship between polarization and the third-party vote, it is not always the voters in the most polarized states who vote for third parties. Instead, it suggests that during some periods (notably the first two decades of the twentieth century), it might be the opposite, that the voters in the more moderate areas abandon the major parties for third-party candidates. So, the 1910s was a period of both very high polarization as well as very active third parties. 1912 was arguably the largest third-party wave of the 146 year period studied. Yet, for that decade, the coefficient for the statewide economic DW-NOMINATE dimension is a −4.8%, meaning that, all else being equal, third parties gained 5% more votes in moderate than polarized states. This is not inconsistent with the history of third-party movements at the time. The Progressives in particular were battling the conservative wing of the Republican Party, which was led most of this time by the reactionary Speaker of the House Joseph Cannon. The results suggest that as the Republican Party split between its reactionary and progressive wings, third-party support rose most in the less polarized areas of the country.

The graph further suggests that the impact of polarization on the third-party vote changed dramatically around 1950. In absolute terms, from 1890 to 1948, the average impact of a one point change in the DW-NOMINATE scores for a state delegation—that is, moving from one extreme to another—would increase the vote for third-party candidates by 5.4%. From 1950 until today, that impact dropped to under 1%, or 0.88%. In other words, polarization tends to galvanize third parties into running candidates for office, and before the 1950s it would also translate in a significant increase in the vote for third-party candidates. But, beginning around 1950, the impact of polarization on the third-party vote became muted. Even as polarization has risen steadily over the past few decades, and even though this polarization has both increased the amount of conflict in American politics and helped lead to third parties running more candidates, this process has not translated into a similar increase in the vote for the third-party candidates on the House ballot.

In other words, during the first half century after the Civil War, partisan polarization was likely the primary drive behind the waves of third-party activity and support. As polarization dropped starting around the 1920s, so did the activity of and support for third-party candidates. However, once polarization began rising again, so did third-party activity, but polarization did not have the same significant impact on the third-party vote that it had in the late eighteenth and early twentieth century. Something fundamental had changed that muted this relationship.

Conclusion

This chapter presented the argument that partisan polarization increases third-party activity and support. Polarized politics produce, or reflect, high levels of

144 Chapter Seven

contention, and they create political battles that can decrease trust in both the major parties as well as the government itself. Polarization can similarly make it harder for two large parties to satisfy a wide tent of potential supporters. Indeed, at moments of high polarization, representatives of the major parties might be tasked with the unrealistic dual expectations of never compromising with the other major party and yet getting policy results. In this situation, dissatisfied voters might simply not see switching their vote between the two major parties as a realistic option, and this would lead them to being more open to supporting third-party candidates. Finally, when polarization causes or is a consequence of some other reason for significant dissatisfaction, like dropping standards of living, then one can expect a close relationship between levels of partisan polarization and third-party activity.

The previous analysis also shows that polarization and third-party activity as well as support are related. Three key findings are presented. The first is that political polarization is a significant driver of third-party activity. As the House of Representatives (and, it seems, American politics in general) became less polarized around 1920, the percent of House district-level races with third-party candidates also declined. Conversely, as polarization began rising again in the 1970s, so did the number of candidates running. Second, polarization also increases the vote for third-party candidates, when there is at least one third-party candidate on the ballot. It is not always the most polarized regions that have this increase in support for third parties; sometimes high polarization drives up the vote for third-party candidates in more moderate states, such as appeared to have happened in the first two decades of the twentieth century. Third, the impact of polarization on the third-party vote decreased over the twentieth century. This change was not gradual. Instead, polarization seemed to have a large impact on the third-party vote until around 1950, and then that impact suddenly dropped dramatically.

Thus, the findings in this chapter show that, indeed, there has been a relationship between polarization and third-party success over the past century and a half. However, while they provide us an answer as to why third parties declined by the middle of the twentieth century and began rebounding around 1970, they also leave us with a dilemma. What changed around 1950? Why did polarization suddenly have a much lower impact on the third-party vote than in the earlier decades of the twentieth century?

The most likely cause of this change was the rise of candidate-centered campaigning, one of the most important changes in American politics over the twentieth century. Scholars of American politics often argue that campaigns in the late nineteenth and early twentieth century were party-centered. They focused on rallying the party base, and since modern communication technology had not been invented yet, they were largely conducted through local newspapers and through rallies. The rise of radio and television, and a host of other related factors, ushered in a new form of campaigning by the 1960s that focused more on the candidate. For a range of reasons, this change produced an environment that was extremely difficult for third parties to compete in, a topic I will explore in more detail in the next chapter.

Notes

1 For a short but detailed introduction to the logic and statistics behind DW-NOMINATE, see Phil Everson, Jim Wiseman, and Rick Valelly, "NOMINATE and American Political History: A Primer" at www.swarthmore.edu/SocSci/rvalell1/documents/Nominate_000.pdf (Retrieved June 20, 2016).
2 All DW-NOMINATE data downloaded from www.voteview.com/ (Retrieved September 10, 2016).
3 The Pearson's correlation between dimension one for the individual representative and the state was 0.41, and the correlation between dimension two for the individual representative and the state was 0.57. Thus, there was no threat of confidence intervals expanding due to multicollinearity.

8

THE EVOLUTION OF PARTY RESOURCES

One of the most widely cited and obvious disadvantages for third parties vis-à-vis the major parties is lack of resources (Rosenstone, Behr and Lazarus 1984, 27–39; Herrnson 1997, 25–28). The major parties and their candidates are able to amass far greater campaign finances than their third-party competitors, and since American campaign finance laws are lax about not just how much money can be raised but also how much can be spent, third-party advertisement efforts are generally overwhelmed by the Democratic and Republican parties. The major parties are similarly able to attract talented, seasoned politicians to run for office as well as hire competent, trained staff to help them guide their campaigns (Rosenstone, Behr and Lazarus 1984, 30–33). Herrnson described this advantage as follows:

> The career paths of the politically ambitious are extremely important in explaining the weakness of and short-term existence of most minor party movements in the United States. Budding politicians learn early in their careers that the Democratic and Republican parties can provide them with useful contacts, expertise, financial assistance, and an orderly path of entry into electoral politics. Minor parties and independent candidacies simply do not offer most of these benefits. As a result, the two parties tend to attract the most talented among those interested in public service. A large part of the parties' hegemony can be attributed to their advantages in candidate recruitment.
>
> *(Herrnson 1997, 29)*

Major parties also have another dramatic resource advantage over their third-party competitors: media access (Clarke and Evans 1983, 60–62; Graber 1983, 262–70; Rosenstone, Behr and Lazarus 1984, 33–37; Bibby and Maisel 2003,

69–70; Gillespie 2012, 19–21). While third-party candidates are generally ignored by major media outlets, politicians representing the Democratic and Republican parties are almost continuously guests and even paid contributors on widely seen news programs. Unable to gain significant resources like money, third parties also have trouble reaching voters because they are ignored by the free media.

But why do the major parties have such an overwhelming resource advantage over third parties in the United States? I argue that resources have a cybernetic character to them; they can be like self-feeding loops. If a party cannot gain resources, it cannot use those resources to gain public exposure or win seats. Unable to gain public exposure or win seats, the party is then unable to gain resources it needs to compete in the future. In other words, by winning most of the elected positions in the US government, the Democratic and Republican parties are able to use their roles in government to monopolize other critical resources needed to keep winning those positions. In sharp contrast, third parties are trapped in a vicious cycle. Unlikely to win seats, they are unable to raise campaign funds or attract competent politicians, which makes them less able to attract voter support. Similarly, unable to gain voter support, they are not considered important news topics and therefore ignored by the news media, which also makes it very difficult for them to gain voter support.

This cyclical nature of resources also helps explain the difference of third parties between the United States and other SMP countries. All single-member district systems magnify the percent of seats that the largest parties receive, making it very hard for smaller parties to win legislative elections unless their public support is geographically concentrated. Winning elected positions translates into resources for political parties, including increased legitimacy, public exposure, influence on policy, ability to raise more funding, and incentives for strong candidates and competent staff to join the party. Since smaller parties in single-member district systems win fewer seats, they also gain fewer resources, which translates into them having more trouble competing against the largest parties in the future, which again leads to winning fewer seats. This cyclical process is even more extreme in the United States, since campaigns are privately funded. For big donors, financing is a strategic decision (Jacobson and Kernell 1981, 35–48), and contributing to a party unlikely to win seats and influence policy is a bad investment. So, while smaller parties in Canada or Australia can receive government funding simply for gaining a certain percent of the vote, in the United States third parties are dependent on raising money from contributors with no strategic interest in funding candidates with little chance of winning.

This nonetheless leaves an important question unanswered. The major parties have always had a significant resource advantage over third parties. How then do resources explain a *decline* in third-party support during the twentieth century? As Rosenstone, Behr, and Lazarus demonstrate in detail (1984,

148 Chapter Eight

27–39), this resource disadvantage for third parties is not a new phenomenon. It can be traced back long before even the Civil War—that is, during the entire period starting with the Jacksonian Era, when modern, mass parties were formed. In other words, a significant major party resource advantage is roughly a constant in American politics. Like the SMP electoral system, it can explain why third parties have always been weaker than major parties, but it cannot explain why the vote for third parties started dropping dramatically around 1920 and nearly disappeared by the 1950s.

I would argue that what had changed was not the amount of resources per se but the types of resources that are most important. The difference is the political environment. Over the twentieth century and especially since the 1960s, political campaigns have changed dramatically, and these changes have altered what resources are most important for electoral combat. This has been caused by several interrelated developments over this period: (1) a revolution in communication technology, especially the rise of television and radio, which created an expensive approach to campaigning; (2) a reduction in the number of political news sources, which has caused alternative news outlets to largely disappear and allow major news organizations to virtually shut out most third-party candidates; and (3) the rise of candidate-centered campaigning, which also dramatically increased the cost of campaigning at the same time that it increased the need for competent, professionally run campaigns. All of these changes created a heightened need for the types of resources that are most difficult for third parties to acquire, like money.

But, as with partisan polarization, circumstances continue to change. 2016 was likely a key election for third parties. The rising importance of the internet and social media has increased the possibility of raising large sums of money from small donors, who unlike interest groups do not treat campaign donations as a technique for increasing access for lobbying (Jacobson and Kernell 1981, 37–38). At the same time, the internet has significantly reduced the cost of campaigning. Moreover, while the critical change in the news media from the late nineteenth to mid-twentieth century was from fragmentation to centralization, the internet has again fragmented control over news, increasing the possibility of third parties to reach voters via free media. One can expect that third parties will always have a significant resource disadvantage vis-à-vis major parties, but the extent of this disadvantage may also be declining.

Rise of Candidate-Centered Campaigning

The high cost of running for office is closely related to the rise of candidate-centered campaigning. From the late nineteenth century, when third parties were vibrant, to the late twentieth century, electoral campaigning in the United States changed dramatically. The most common summary of that change, possibly introduced by Stephen and Barbara Salmore (1985), is the argument that a century ago, campaigning was mostly party-centered and by the late 1960s, it became candidate-centered. In party-centered campaigning, individual candidates are of little consequence, and instead the party is promoted as a team. This approach focuses heavily on emphasizing party differences and on promoting turnout amount party supporters. However, after the Second World War—most congressional election scholars would argue that the change came in the 1960s (Aldrich 1995, 252–73)—candidates for national offices began campaigning using a different approach. Attributes of individual candidates became strongly emphasized, often with their party affiliation deemphasized if not ignored completely. Candidates focused on their own records or policy positions instead of their party's ideology, and they highlighted personal characteristics that they believed would increase their voter support, especially as credible, authentic, and likeable people prepared to serve the public (Arbour 2014).

The rise of this type of campaigning is one of the most widely cited and thoroughly researched changes in American electoral politics (Epstein 1986, 272–75; Wattenberg 1991; Carson and Roberts 2005; Parker 2008). It is also closely related to the rise of the incumbency effect, another phenomenon well-established within the political science literature and intensely studied by electoral behavior and congressional scholars (Jacobson and Carson 2016, 35–76). Candidate-centered campaigning is not only a fundamental difference between how elections are run today as compared to a century ago, when third parties were much stronger. They are also a way that electoral campaigns in the United States are different from those in other single-member district countries, like Canada and Great Britain.

A common explanation for the rise of candidate-centered campaigning is the change of communication technology, especially the introduction of radio and television, over the twentieth century. The proliferation of television and radio created a new way for candidates to communicate directly with voters. It also created a method that was particularly suited for advertising a candidate as an individual. Through a television screen, a candidate could speak directly, if briefly, to voters and show the candidate in very personalized ways, including acting as elected officials, listening to voters, attending church, and spending time with their families. These technologies proved much more powerful than campaigning techniques common during the party-centered period, like rallies and party run newspapers, since they could reach voters in a very direct and personal matter and, in the case of radio and direct mail, could be used to target the voters the candidate needs for victory. As Andrea Louise Campbell (2007, 70) summarized this argument:

> Moreover, technological change made candidate-centered elections possible. Before, when election campaigns were not only party-dominated but also labor-intensive, the parties, through their strong grassroots organizations, supplied the manpower. Candidate-centered campaigns are,

150 Chapter Eight

by contrast, technology-intensive. Advances in mass communications and other technologies facilitated the polling, advertising, fund raising, and travel necessary for the modern candidate (Aldrich 1995, 272). Television made possible direct communication with voters; no longer would candidates have to rely on party workers to be their face to the public.

Others have argued that these technological changes cannot alone explain the rise of candidate-centered campaigning in the United States. Comparing them to the more party-centered campaigns of Western Europe, Leon Epstein (1986, 273–74) summarized this argument as follows:

> [The] increased political role of financial resources cannot itself account for the American development of candidate-centered politics as a substitute for party politics. No more than the technological methods on which the money is spent does the cash economy of late-twentieth-century campaigns stand as a peculiarly American phenomenon. To be sure, American candidate-centered politics thrive on primarily financial resources, but the candidate-centered campaigning itself can hardly have been produced by the cash economy of modern politics when the same economy elsewhere has not led to similar campaigning. Other more distinctively American circumstances must help account for our candidate campaigns.

One of those distinctively American circumstances was the direct primary. Before the primaries, state party organizations and often party bosses would determine which candidates would be allowed to run, and there was a high premium put on these candidates being loyal supporters of the state party organization. With primaries, candidates could be independent agents running their own campaigns as they saw fit. They could build campaign organizations to win primary elections, and then use those organizations semi-independently from the party to campaign for the general election (Herrnson 1997, 26; Jacobson and Carson 2016, 27). Indeed, as Hirano and Snyder (2011) point out, it is "conventional wisdom" within the comparative politics literature that institutions that promote intra-party competition, like primaries, tend to lead to campaigns that are more candidate-centered than party-centered.

Ultimately, candidate-centered campaigns produced a very difficult environment for third parties to compete in. Candidate-centered campaigning works against the basic strategy of third parties, which is almost always party-centered below the presidential level. For third parties in the United States, the most common strategy is to attract voters who are discontent with the two major parties, which is facilitated by attacking and distinguishing itself from those parties. Candidate-centered campaigning produces a way for major party politicians to insulate themselves from the perceived failings of their respective parties as well as avoid controversial issues, blunting these third-party attacks. Maybe more significantly, candidate-centered campaigning requires significantly more resources than party-centered campaigns. To run candidate-centered campaigns, candidates have to build their own campaign operations and run more professionalized campaigns, including hiring consultants and professionally trained staff. In the modern media age, this also means paying for significant advertisement that builds the third-party candidates positive name recognition and distinguishing that candidate from the major party candidates.

Strategic Politicians

The rise of candidate-centered campaigning not only changed the amount of money needed to run electoral campaigns. It also changed the calculus of both politicians considering running for office and interest groups planning to contribute to campaigns. Much of the literature on strategic behavior in campaigns builds off of the work of Gary Jacobson and Samuel Kernell (1981), who summarize their argument with the equation:

$$U = PB - R$$

in which U is the utility of the target office, P is the probability of winning that office, B is the value of that office, and R is the risk taken on by trying to win that office. In other words, a politician's decision to run for office is based on a combination of how good of a position it is, how likely the politician is to win the seat, and how risky it is to run for that office. For example, while a state senator might have great ambitions of winning a seat in the House of Representatives, the senator will be hesitant to run against a popular incumbent because the senator will likely lose that election as well as forfeit the state senate seat in order to run. In other words, the P is low while the R is high. However, if the incumbent decides to retire, or if the incumbent's party is suffering at the national level, then the probability of winning increases, and this state senator becomes more likely to run. Conversely, for someone without a political position, running for Congress might come with very few risks, in which case it can be worth running for an elected position even if the probability of winning is very low.

This framework can be applied to a range of phenomenon related to American elections. First, it leads to the prediction that high quality candidates are most likely to run as challengers or for open seats if they believe there is a reasonable chance of actually winning the seat. If an incumbent is very secure, people building a political career are unlikely to waste resources and especially risk damage to their careers by challenging that incumbent. In this situation, the incumbent often goes unchallenged and therefore wins by default, or the party finds a "sacrificial lamb" to run against the incumbent. These candidates

152 Chapter Eight

are virtually always very inexperienced and running either because of a delusional belief that they might win or an idealistic belief in supporting the party.

The professional staff needed to run a campaign also follows this logic. Experienced campaign consultants will likely work for strong candidates for two main reasons. They want to be paid, and stronger candidates are more likely to be able to raise funds. They also want to work for a candidate with a serious chance of winning, since winning the election is a critical form of capital for them. Weaker candidates are unlikely to attract competent consultants and staff to work for them, since these campaign professionals have little to gain from working with a candidate with little ability to raise money and chance of winning.

Campaign funding also follows the same logic. Jacobson and Kernell argue that there are two types of interest group funders. The first type is attempting to gain favor so that they can lobby sitting members of Congress. In this case, they will fund the likely winner, even if that candidate will win easily and does not need to the money. A second type has a more ideological motivation; they are trying to elect politicians who will promote their agenda. In this case, the interest group will focus its funding on close races, in which it has the best chance of increasing the number of officeholders that hold similar views. Jacobson and Kernell contrast this with small, private donations, in which people are mostly focused on promoting what they consider to be the public good (Jacobson and Kernell 1981, 35–43).

This strategic logic can be applied to third parties, except that the impact is much more extreme. Once third parties collapsed by the end of the 1940s, there became little incentive for rational political actors to provide any of these resources to their candidates. (1) Experienced politicians would not run for third parties since the chances of winning are so slim that it would do little more than damage their political careers. Therefore, with a few notable exceptions, third parties will have trouble running any candidates, and those who do will likely have little experience and do it mostly out of a sense of duty. (2) Professional staff are unlikely to work with these candidates since they cannot pay them and are very unlikely win. (3) Major donors are unlikely to fund these campaigns, since their contributions are unlikely to translate into any impact on policy or increase in access to the policymaking process. The only way to raise money is from small donations, although even in this case third parties have little method for reaching most potential donors.[1]

Figure 8.1 shows the funding aspect of this argument for the 2014 elections to the House of Representatives. In 2014, the mean spending of incumbents running for reelection was $1.46 million. When it was an open seat, major party candidates spent an average of $1.20 million. In sharp contrast, the mean spending by major party challengers running against an incumbent was $423,000. In other words, on average and as one would predict with a strategic politician framework, major party challengers spent less than a third of the

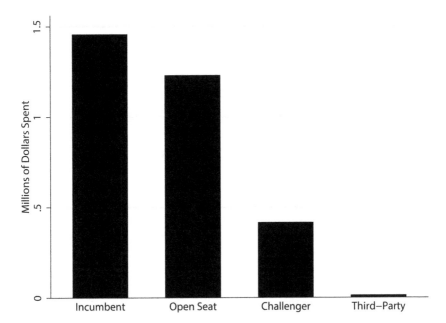

FIGURE 8.1 Campaign spending by types of House candidates, 2014. This graph shows the amount of money spent in millions of dollars by major party House candidates (incumbents seeking reelection, challengers against incumbents, and candidates seeking open seats) and third-party House candidates in 2014. The data includes only those candidates who submitted a campaign finance report to the Federal Election Commission. The data demonstrates, consistent with the strategic politician thesis, that incumbents spent far more than challengers. It also demonstrates that third-party House candidates spent only a small fraction of the money that major party candidates spent.

money as incumbents, despite most challengers' need to spend much more in order to gain comparable name recognition.[2]

In comparison to this, spending by third-party candidates was a pittance compared to major party candidates. While the mean spending of all major party candidates was $823,000, the average spending of third-party candidates was $14,000. Ironically, because these figures include only the spending of candidates who submitted reports to the Federal Election Commission, they almost definitely inflate the spending of third-party candidates. The FEC does not require candidates to report their spending unless it exceeds $5,000. While 94% of all major party candidates reported their campaign donations and expenditures to the FEC—the exceptions were all challengers or candidates running for an open seat—only 16% of third-party candidates submitted these reports. Even if one were to assume that every third-party candidate who did not report expenditures to the FEC had spent $5,000, the maximum allowed

154 Chapter Eight

by law, then their average spending would have been only $6,400. In other words, even the most generous reading of these figures would lead to the conclusion that in the 2014 elections to the House of Representatives, the average major party candidate spent approximately 125 times as much money as the average third-party House candidate.[3]

This analysis suggests that American third parties face a severe resource disadvantage in comparison to the Democratic and Republican parties not just because of the significant amount spent on American elections but also because of the strategic behavior of those who provide parties and candidates key resources. Third parties in the late twentieth and early twenty-first century are not in a position to gain significant campaign resources. They are caught in a trap in which any individuals who might provide them resources has no interest to do so. Viable candidates are unlikely to run on a third-party ticket since their chances of winning are virtually non-existent. Professional political staff and consultants are unlikely to work for a third-party candidate for the same reason. Interest groups are also similarly unlikely to fund these organizations, even if the party presents a platform that is ideologically close to that of the interest group. Third parties are therefore stuck in a vicious cycle of not being able to build resources because they are seen as unable to win, and unable to increase their voter support because they cannot raise resources.

Media Access

Lacking the resources to pay for running ads on expensive television and radio programs, third parties are hurt further by their inability to gain news coverage. Third parties face the same vicious cycle in news coverage that they do when trying to secure other resources. Journalists and editors do not see them as viable candidates or important political players, and since third parties are at best supported by a minority of voters, editors also do not consider them a topic most readers would be interested in. Not being able to gain news coverage, combined with a lack of money for advertisement, makes it extremely difficult for third parties to gain public support, which then reinforces the decision by news organizations to ignore these parties.

Quoting an unpublished paper by Paul Bass, Rosenstone, Behr, and Lazarus (1984, 35) also argue that newspaper editors consider third parties unnewsworthy because they are unlikely to win, a decision that ironically makes them less likely to win. Bibby and Maisel similarly argue that news editors do not consider third-party candidates realistic contenders, since their public support is so low. For this reason, newspapers generally ignore third parties, and when they do cover them, they treat them as illegitimate (Bibby and Maisel 2003, 69).

This problem, however, was not a constant over American history. It is instead a consequence of significant changes in the news industry. Nineteenth-century newspapers were highly partisan. They were often closely allied to if not run

The Evolution of Party Resources **155**

outright by political parties. As Gerald Baldasty (1992) argued, the first two steps of a new political party in the nineteenth century was to organize governing committees and then start a new newspaper, and the editors were often party leaders. As he also wrote:

> The single most important link between party and electorate... was the partisan newspaper. Newspapers *alone* were not sufficient; even the best newspaper could not sell a poor candidate. But political newspapers, as a link between party and electorate, were vital. They helped the party mobilize voters and were an extremely efficient way to reach a dispersed rural population. Political parties did not have a paid staff to send out to court voters, and even if they had, travel was slow and difficult. Farmers, laborers, merchants, and other voters simply could not attend many party meetings or rallies. But the newspaper took the party's views, arguments, and candidates to them.
>
> *(Baldasty 1992, 14. Italicized in original text)*

In terms of third parties, he added:

> Newspapers were ideal for organizing grass-roots political support, particularly for new political parties or groups supporting a certain candidate or program. The Antimasons, a third-party movement in the late 1820s and early 1830s, relied extensively on the press simply because they had few other means to reach the public. The first New York State Antimasonic convention, in 1829, concluded with a report that stressed: "Free presses constitute the means upon which the country must rely to uproot and overthrow Free Masonry. They enlighten and stimulate public opinion."
>
> *(Baldasty 1992, 15)*

Baldasty argues further that while the primary funding of newspapers in the Jacksonian era came from political parties, sometimes through patronage, by the end of that century it was shifting to advertisement. This shift hurt third parties partially because the content changed to attracting a wide audience instead of promoting a political agenda and party candidates. But that change also undermined the fragmented nature of newspaper coverage. As Ben Bagdikian (2000, 118) argued, the rise of advertisement as a key source of newspaper revenue also fueled the destruction of smaller papers. Because publishing a newspaper is a combination of fixed costs (e.g., the printing presses) and variable costs (e.g., the amount of paper), the cost per paper declines as the amount of circulation rises. Papers with wider circulation could charge each reader less, and it could charge advertisers less per reader as well. For larger advertising clients, this created a strong incentive to advertise with the paper with the largest circulation, creating further revenue for these papers and allowing them to cut the

156 Chapter Eight

cost to each reader even more. For papers with smaller circulation, this meant having a more expensive product with less ad revenue that often translated into financial loss and eventually bankruptcy. He wrote:

> Before mass advertising, however, papers succeeded solely because they pleased their readers. Readers were clustered in terms of their serious political and social ideas—some were conservative, some liberal, some radical—and they had religious or regional loyalties. Each paper tended to focus a great deal of its information on the preferences of its readers. Because papers were physically smaller, lacking mass advertising, they were cheaper to print... Because newspapers were cheaper to print, newspaper businesses could be started more easily, either when new communities arose or when existing papers did not satisfy the interests of some significant group in the community. The result was a wider spectrum of political and social ideas than the public gets from contemporary newspapers.
> *(Bagdikian 2000, 125)*

Not only did this change lead to the eliminations of newspapers that were more likely to promote third parties. It also undermined the fragmented nature of American news—a structure that produced something akin to John Stuart Mill's notion of a "marketplace of ideas"—and replaced it with the notion that the goal of journalism is objectivity, which included being "fair and balanced." Newspapers shifted to a focus on who, what, when, where, why, and how as well, and they began employing the technique of showing "both sides" of an issue, which during policy debates generally meant comparing and contrasting the Democratic and Republican sides of an issue. Election coverage, instead of focusing on policy differences, highlighted the horse race, which had the great advantage for news organizations of being exciting and avoiding offending potential readers or viewers. In this framework, it was easy to ignore third parties, since they were clearly not winning the contest and could be simply dismissed as external to the legitimate debate between Democratic and Republican politicians (Mindich 1998).

The rise of radio and television added further to this problem for third parties. Television news on the major networks began in the late 1940s and gradually evolved into a half an hour program on each of the three networks: ABC, NBC, and CBS. Extremely limited time combined with the desire to reach a mass audience made it easy for these programs to focus on only the two largest parties and the most important political figures, especially the president. The need for visuals added to this problem, especially since for most of this period the movement of televisions crews was slow, as was the transporting of newsreels to the network headquarters. This institutional problem increased the amount of news coverage of the president and congressional leaders, since it was much easier to have news crews stationed at these two locations in Washington and use whatever stories they found and film they produced (Epstein 1972). This combination of factors made it extremely difficult for third parties to gain any national exposure.

Thus, for various reasons, the movement of news outlets from newspapers associated with political parties to commercially driven outlets severely hurt third parties. While a new party could simply produce its own newspaper in the nineteenth century, the evolution to commercial news outlets driven by advertisement gradually led to the general exclusion of third parties. Indeed, the problem for third parties may have become primarily that, as far as editors were concerned, stories about them would not increase readership or viewership. Once third parties largely disappeared by the 1950s, they were not interesting enough to give news coverage, and lacking both news coverage and the money needed to advertise, they were unable to build the public awareness needed to gain news coverage.

Duverger's Law

This still leaves open the question of why third parties are so much weaker in the United States than in other SMP countries. Answering this question, I believe, requires a revisit to Duverger's Law.

As outlined in Chapter 2, Duverger (1954, 203–28) argued that SMP favors a two-party system because (1) the mechanics of translating votes to seats in single-member district systems is heavily biased towards larger parties except when third-party support is regionally concentrated, (2) voters gravitate towards the two strongest candidates in each district to avoid wasting their votes, and (3) parties in SMP systems are more likely to form electoral coalitions in order to avoid spoiling the vote. In other words, the theory provides a universal statement about SMP systems. Indeed, as I showed in Chapter 2 and has been demonstrated elsewhere, the top two parties generally receive more votes and win more seats in SMP than PR systems.

But, there are limitation's in the ability of Duverger's Law to explain differences across electoral systems. (1) As I showed in Chapter 2, there is significant evidence at the district level that voters in SMP systems often vote for third parties even when Duverger would argue that they are wasting their votes. (2) As Cox (1997) and others have shown, the effective number of parties appears to be more closely related to the district magnitude, or the number of elected positions per legislative district, than on whether there is a threat of vote wasting. As I showed in Chapter 2, for example, at the district level the vote for third-party candidates is just as high in Australia as in Canada, India, and the UK even though the former employs preferential voting, which effectively eliminates the threat of spoiling the vote. (3) The second proposition of Duverger's Law predicts only that voters would gravitate to the top two candidates in any electoral district and that political parties would join forces in order to

158 Chapter Eight

avoid vote wasting. It does not explain why SMP systems become dominated by two major parties. As Michael Gallagher discussed:

> Many writers have pointed out that the logic of Duverger's argument applies within each constituency but that it is unclear why, even if the number of viable parties per constituency usually have a maximum value of 2, these should be the same parties in every constituency. Why will we not find parties A and B are dominant in one constituency, A and C in another, and D and E in a third? Even if each constituency tends toward two-party competition, why should the country as a whole have two-party competition?
>
> *(Gallagher 2005, 547)*

I argue that there is a fourth way, along with the three explanations given by Duverger, that SMP reduces the number of effective parties in a country. This added explanation not only strengths Duverger's Law by providing answers to all of the issues mentioned before. It also helps explain why American third parties are much weaker today than a century ago.

Specifically, the logic presented previously about the cyclical nature of party resources can be applied to our understanding of how electoral systems affect political parties. Duverger's first proposition is that the simple mechanics of SMP tends to reduce the vote for smaller parties. This argument is self-evident and easily demonstrated. While a party receiving 10% of the vote in PR system would likely win around 10% of the seats, a party receiving 10% of the vote in an SMP system would likely win no seats unless that vote was concentrated in a small number of districts. Generally speaking, winning seats also translates into gaining other resources, including public exposure, greater ability to raise funds, the legitimacy of being part of a governing body, and whatever funds the government provides for parties with elected positions. The more seats a party wins, the more resources it is capable of acquiring, which it can then use to win further seats. In other words, since single-member district systems tend to allocate seats to fewer parties, they effectively distribute political resources in a way that makes it easier for those fewer parties to remain in a dominant electoral position.

This framework therefore leads to the conclusion that electoral systems help determine how many effective parties there are in a political system by influencing how party resources are distributed. It also affects the strategic behavior of political actors. In a proportional representation system with a low minimum vote threshold, a small party could be a good investment for donors, since there is a good chance that it could receive the 2% or 3% of the vote needed to enter the parliament. Strong, ambitious candidates are more likely to join the party and competent political consultants are more likely to work for the party and its candidates for the same reason. However, as the threshold for getting seats into

The Evolution of Party Resources **159**

the parliament gets tougher, the probability of smaller parties winning seats declines, which make them a worse investment. Strategic political actors are less likely to commit resources to these parties, which makes them even less likely to win many votes. Since lower district magnitudes effectively translate into higher thresholds, smaller parties become an even less attractive investment in countries with single-member districts unless support for those parties is geographically concentrated.

This framework also provides an answer to some of the criticisms of Duverger's Law. One, it can explain why the critical factor in determining the number of parties is district magnitude, not whether there is a threat of wasting votes. Two, it can explain why SMP systems lead to not only fewer effective parties but also greater voter support for the largest parties even while there is ample evidence that voters are supposedly wasting vote. Three, it explains why SMP leads to two dominant parties, not simply the vote gravitating to the top two candidates in each district irrespective of what party nominated them. Effectively, single-member district systems tend to inflate the size of the victory for a small number of parties—the percent of seats they win tends to be greater than the percent vote they receive—which leads to greater resources for these parties and makes them a better investment for strategic politicians, which increases their resources further.

This difference also helps explain why third parties are so much weaker in the United States than in other major single-member district countries. There are two critical differences between elections in the United States and these other countries. The first is that while American campaigns have become much more candidate-centered, campaigns in these countries remain very much party-centered, most likely since they are parliamentary systems. The second is that campaign finance laws are much stronger in these countries than the United States. In Australia, any candidate or party that receives at least 4% of the first preferences in parliamentary elections is awarded public funding, calculated as a figure based on the Consumer Price Index multipled by the number of first preferences received. There are no caps on private funding or campaign spending, which can lead to significant spending by the major parties, but at least parties that meet the minimum threshhold are provided with funding. In the United Kingdom, there are no limitations in how much funding a candidate or party can raise. However, the amount spent on campaigns is capped, a policy that has been in place since the Corrupt and Illegal Practices Prevention Act 1883. And in Canada, there is both public funding and spending caps. Until 2015, when direct public funding was eliminated, federal political parties that received at least 2% of all votes or 5% of votes in districts in which they had candidates received a subsidy based on the number of votes received. Parties meeting these vote limits also receive a reimbursement that subsidizes 50% of their spending during that election. Canada also allows private funding, but that funding is heavily subsidized via tax credits. At the same time, Canada

160 Chapter Eight

significantly limits the amount that parties and individual candidates can spend on electoral campaigns, capping spending for parliamentary seats at levels far lower than races to the House of Representatives in the United States.[4]

In effect, these differences increase the impact of strategic political behavior, as proposed by Jacobson and Kernell, in the United States vis-à-vis these other single-member district countries. In countries in which smaller parties are provided campaign funding by the government, the impact of ambitious politicians gravitating towards and donors shifting money to the strongest parties is reduced. The same is true when the amount being spent on campaigns is limited either directly by law or indirectly, such as by having shorter campaign seasons. Indeed, these boosts can put smaller parties into a strong enough position that they can become a better choice for strong candidates and investment for donors. However, in the United States, where there is effectively no public funding of campaigns at the federal level below presidential elections and where campaign spending is extremely high, there are no incentives for strategic politicians to commit resources in third parties. The impact of single-member districts is therefore more extreme in the United States than Australia, Canada, and the UK.

This difference across these four single-member district systems is shown in Figure 8.2. It shows descriptively the relationship between the vote for and the spending by third-party candidates[5] across four single-member district systems: Australia, Canada, the UK, and the United States.[6] In order to compare spending across countries with different currencies, I calculated it as a percent of total spending within each district. The results shown in this graph suggest that the critical difference across these countries is not whether voters were threatened with the possibility of wasting their votes and possibly helping the less liked of the two top candidates. Instead, it was the amount of money spent by third-party candidates in comparison to the top two candidates. In Australia, 25% of campaign spending was done by third parties and their candidates. In Canada and the UK, that figure was respectively 37% and 28%. In the United States, third-party candidates spent one quarter of 1% of campaign spending to the House of Representatives in 2010. The vote for third-party candidates followed the same pattern. In Australia, Canada, and the UK, third-party candidates received between 20% and 24% of the vote. In the United States, they received just under 2% of the vote. Money, not a fear of spoiling the vote, appears to have been the critical difference.

This relationship is shown more clearly in Table 8.1. This table shows a linear regression of percent vote for third-party candidates on three variables: percent campaign spending by third-party candidates, whether the district was in a country with an SMP electoral system and thus created a threat of vote wasting, and whether there was at least one third-party candidate in the district.[7] The table demonstrates that both campaign spending and the type of electoral system reduce the vote for third-party candidates. However, the impact

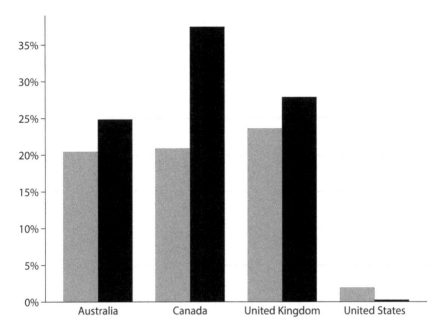

FIGURE 8.2 Mean percent district-level vote and expenditures for third parties across SMD systems. This graph shows the average district-level vote for (gray bars) and the average percent campaign expenditure of (black bars) third-party candidates in three SMP system elections (Canada in 2011, the UK in 2010, and the United States in 2010) as well as the 2013 elections in Australia, which uses preferential voting for its lower house of Parliament. The graph shows that both campaign spending by and the vote for third-party candidates is much higher in Australia, Canada, and the UK than in the United States. It suggests that the key difference among these countries is not whether voters might split their votes but how many campaign resources third parties have.

of campaign spending is much greater. For every 1% increase in the spending by third-party candidates, they received an increase of around a one-third of a percent of the vote, or 0.38. The confidence interval was a rather tight 0.36 to 0.40. In comparison, having an SMP instead of an alternative electoral system reduced the vote for third-party candidates by 1.67%. While a real difference, a reduction in the vote of one and three-quarters percent hardly explains the difference between the United States and other single-member district systems.[8]

The partial correlations, shown in this table as well, also suggest that campaign finance plays a greater role than whether voters might want to avoid spoiling their votes. The r-squared for the entire equation is 0.62, which means that these three variables explain 62% of the variation in third-party vote. The partial correlation for campaign expenditures by third parties is 0.67; squared, this figure is 0.44, meaning that 44% of that variation is explained by money.

162 Chapter Eight

TABLE 8.1 Regression of third-party vote on campaign expenditures and electoral system in Australia (2013), Canada (2009), the United Kingdom (2010), and United States (2010)

	Coefficients	Confidence Intervals	Partial Correlation
Percent of expenditures by third-party candidates	0.38★★★ (0.01)	0.36 to 0.40	0.67
Electoral system (1 = single-member plurality) (0 = alternative)	−1.67★★ (0.69)	2.81 to −0.54	−0.07
At least one third-party candidate	−9.25★★★ (0.60)	−10.42 to −8.08	−0.37
Constant	10.91★★★ (0.61)	9.71 to 12.10	
F	847.90★★★		
Number of cases	1543		
R^2	0.62		

★$p \leq 0.05$; ★★$p \leq 0.01$; ★★★$p \leq 0.001$.

The partial correlation for having an SMP system is 0.07; squared, this figure is 0.005. In other words, the threat of vote spoiling explains approximately half a percent of the variation in the third-party vote in elections within these four countries. Both may be having an impact, but the amount of campaign spending is likely having a much greater impact.

The evidence presented in this table is a snapshot that shows a strong relationship between the vote for third-party candidates and the distribution of money across four countries with single-member district elections. I would argue that this addition to Duverger's Law also helps explain long-term patterns in different countries. An obvious example is the Liberal Democratic Party in the UK. This party, then called the Liberal Party, was a prime example Duverger used to illustrate his argument about the strategic behavior of voters and parties, as I had discussed in Chapter 2. The electors, however, did not desert the Liberal Party, as Duverger predicted. Quite the opposite, the Liberals gradually climbed into being a formidable third strongest party in the United Kingdom. While the party received 9% of the vote in the 1945 and 1950 elections, that public support collapsed to under 3% in the election of 1951, the year Duverger's *Party Politics* was first published. From there, public support for the Liberal Party climbed gradually. In the February 1974 election, it received 19% of the vote. In 1983, when it ran as an alliance with the Social Democratic Party, it received over 25% of the vote. That support dropped into the mid-teens in the 1990s, but in the 2005 and 2010 general elections the party, now calling themselves the Liberal Democrats, received 22% and 23% of the vote

The Evolution of Party Resources **163**

and became a coalition partner with the Conservatives in 2010. In 2015, that public support dropped back down to 8%, although this appears to have much more to do with anger over joining that coalition government than with voters wanting to avoid wasting their votes.

While this description is not consistent with Duverger's argument that avoiding spoiling the vote would lead to the demise of third parties in SMP systems, it is consistent with a cybernetic understanding of party resources. The Liberals in the UK had advantages that third parties in the United States cannot muster. The Liberal Party has a much longer history in British politics than any American third party and thereby has a much better brand. It is also in a setting in which resource differences across parties are not as stark as in the United States, a factor combined with a more party-centered than candidate-centered approach to campaigning, which helps reduce the impact of resource disparities between larger and smaller parties. Beyond all this, the reemergence of the Liberal Party into UK politics was a gradual process, one that is consistent with there being a cyclical relationship between winning seats and acquiring resources.

What this all suggests is that the United States is a particularly difficult environment for smaller parties, and that it became even more difficult with the rise of candidate-centered campaigning. The single-member district electoral system allocates more seats to the two largest parties, which then translates into these parties gaining a greater share of resources needed to compete in future elections. But since campaign spending is both less regulated and more private in the United States than in other stable democracies with single-member district systems, the impact of this cyclical process is more extreme. There is no good strategic reason for interest groups to fund campaigns that have little chance of winning, which effectively starves third parties of basic campaign resources. This problem became much more extreme with the rise of candidate-centered campaigning in the 1960s, which helped lead to American third parties competing with severe resource disadvantages.

The Internet and Social Media

Thus, a second critical impediment for American third parties in the second half of the twentieth century and the beginning of the twenty-first century is resource disparity. Third-party candidates are inexperienced, especially compared to incumbents and other political professionals running on major party tickets, and these candidates raise a tiny fraction of the campaign funds that major party candidates acquire each election cycle. Third parties have also been largely shutout of mainstream political news coverage, which overwhelmingly focuses on Democratic and Republican candidates and officeholders. The rise of candidate-centered campaigning over modern communication technology and the consolidation of news outlets put third parties into a much more difficult campaign environment than they were in a century ago.

164 Chapter Eight

But that environment continues to shift. Like the decline and reemergence of political polarization discussed in Chapter 7, the nature of party resources is also changing rapidly. The rise of the internet and especially social media has created circumstances in which third parties can become much more capable of competing against the major parties. Indeed, a key indicator that third-party activity will continue to rise is fundamental change in political communication.

The first critical crack in the argument that Americans are predisposed to vote against third parties was Ross Perot's impressive run for the presidency in the 1992 election. Superficially a third-party candidate—he was more of an independent candidate who built a third party in name with little effort put into running other candidates—his support rose rapidly after he announced that he would seek the presidency if voters put him on all the ballots in all fifty states.[9] There were a number of factors that suggest that it was a good year for a third-party candidate to run for president. The economy was in a recession. The level of polarization was rising steadily. And like the 2016 election, the median percent vote for third-party House candidates (that is, when there was at least one third-party candidate on the ballot) spiked in 1990 election, reaching its highest level since the last great third-party wave of the 1910s.

But, for our purposes here, there is one critical aspect of the Perot phenomenon that is often mentioned as a historical fact but otherwise ignored. *The Perot campaign was launched on CNN.* CNN, then and now, follows a strategy consistent with that of the nightly news programs of the major networks, focusing on winning a large audience through excitement and avoiding topics that might drive viewers away. But, unlike the half hour nightly news programs on the major networks, it is also a format that requires producers to fill twenty-four hours each day with news content (Küng 2000, 23–44). It is within this context, unimaginable before the rise of cable television, that Larry King Live gave Ross Perot an hour of free media coverage. Before cable, the primary television news outlets had half hour formats with little space for anything but the primary news of the day. Perot would likely have been given no air time, and therefore Perot would not have been able to gain the public exposure needed to launch a serious attempt at the White House.

The Perot phenomenon was an early stage of the major changes in communication technology that are affecting news media in ways that have similarities to news of the late nineteenth century. A critical step was the spread of cable television, especially the rise of Fox News as well as liberal media programs like the Daily Show with Jon Stewart. Unlike CNN, these were more targeted programs with niche audiences. While Fox is closely tied to the Republican Party and is certainly not an outlet that would promote third-party candidates, it does reflect a change towards a more fragmented and partisan news media.

The most important change, though, is the rise of the internet and social media. The World Wide Web, of course, emerged in the 1990s, and social media began with the launching of Facebook in 2004. The internet has

The Evolution of Party Resources **165**

dramatically increased the variety of news outlets, and this fragmentation has changed the economics of news. Part of this change has been that traditional news sources, including major newspapers, have been losing revenue, partially because of rising competition and partially because people are reading news online instead of purchasing newspapers. But this fragmentation also means that revenue is gained by developing a niche, not by attempting to attract all readers or viewers. Instead of taking neutral stances to avoid offending a wide audience, many news sources present more ideologically laced content with the intent of attracting a smaller but more loyal audience. As Anderson, Downie, and Schudson (2016) described this change:

> What does increased news fragmentation mean, in simple terms? It means that the news outlets of the future will be forced to rely on patronage of smaller and smaller audiences with well-defined interests and reasons for consuming this journalistic content. And this need—to forsake a mass audience and the mass advertising that came with it—will mean an in- creasingly fragmented world of journalistic production.
>
> *(Anderson, Downie and Schudson 2016, 144)*

They continue a few pages later:

> A lot of future-of-news commentators speak as if digital fragmentation were universally bad. It certainly sounds terrible--fragmentation implies the shattering of something whole. But what the fragmentation of news audiences also does is that it creates new communities, and new freedoms to learn about the issues that concern them directly. Perhaps the Internet really has shattered the large community conversation that existed in the era of monopoly local newspapers and three big networks. But we shouldn't forget that that "large conversation" also reflected the narrow interests of a specific group of people and often excluded many other points of view. Now these less powerful communities can be created out of the very process of fragmentation itself, and with this can come new freedoms to engage in politics in a new way.
>
> *(Anderson, Downie and Schudson 2016, 146)*

The way readers access news items over the internet also increases that frag- mentation dramatically. Unlike traditional newspapers, in which editors were guessing what topics readers would find most interesting, internet news sites measure and directly make profit by the number of viewers who click on an article link. If a news outlet can attract a subset in the population to click on a news item—or even better, share the article or video across social media— then the outlet earns revenue. During the 2016 primary elections, these out- lets discovered that having "Bernie Sanders" in titles of news items increased

166 Chapter Eight

the amount of clicks received[10] and, moreover, that "Bernie fans" had a high tendency to share these items, creating an incentive for these organizations to produce more material on Sanders. While major news outlets were providing him much less coverage than Clinton,[11] newer media sources were increasing his coverage. In other words, news fragmentation over the internet and social media has effectively eliminated the ability of news editors at major newspapers or news networks to act as gatekeepers blocking coverage of insurgent and third-party candidates.[12]

The internet also increases the ability of insurgent candidates to fund campaigns from large numbers of small donations. This ability to raise funds via digital communication technology was spearheaded by Howard Dean during the 2004 Democratic primary election and then advanced considerably by the Obama primary campaign in 2008 (Stromer-Galley 2004, 75–78, 110–112). But, the true show of the power of this approach was the 2016 primary election campaign by Bernie Sanders. Refusing to take corporate donations, Sanders raised $228 million during the 2016 election cycle.[13] The approach proved to be particularly effective for insurgent candidates, since the idealistic challenge against the mainstream by these candidates seems to galvanize loyal followers willing to help fund campaigns with small donations.

Finally, the internet and other technological changes have significantly reduced the cost of advertisement, provided that campaigns can convince followers to share those ads across social media. The technology now exists that virtually anyone can film a commercial with an inexpensive camera, edit it using tools like Microsoft Movie Maker, and then post it on a website or distribute it via email. While these commercials would likely not be of the quality of those created by media companies, and while television remains the easiest way to reach many voters, this drop in costs suggests that third parties are no longer completely shut out from reaching potential voters.

Combined, this suggests that changes in communication technology that damaged third parties in the mid- to late twentieth century are now changing in a direction more favorable for these parties. The fragmented news media of the nineteenth century that allowed for third-party outlets was replaced by smaller numbers of commercially run news outlets, a situation that led to third parties being all but shut out. While still very much commercial, news is fragmenting again, and as the Sanders campaign has demonstrated, internet news sites will post articles even about a self-proclaimed Democratic Socialist if it can increase the number of readers—or more specifically, the number of clicks on a link. While large donors will surely remain important in American campaign politics, the internet has produced an alternate route for raising funds, and it has also created an alternative, cheaper method for advertising.

This all suggests further that American electoral politics is in the midst of significant change and that circumstances for third parties are improving rapidly. The major parties will likely retain significant resource advantages over

The Evolution of Party Resources **167**

third parties. Indeed, the fact that they win the vast majority of elected positions and will likely continue to do so virtually insures that they will retain the bulk of the political resources needed for effective electoral competition. But, third parties need not match major parties in acquiring resources. They simply need to challenge and disrupt. One of the major questions left open, then, is whether third parties will take advantage of these changes, including finding innovative approaches to running insurgent candidacies and peeling voters away from the two major parties.

Notes

1 Following Jacobson and Kernell's argument, and especially after the Supreme Court ruling in *Citizens United v. FEC*, it is also possible that rich individuals or well-funded organizations would promote a third party through an independent media campaign because they see it as a public good. However, to date, there is little evidence of this type of independent spending in favor of third parties.
2 Campaign spending data downloaded from Federal Election Commission, "Summary Data Files, House and Senate Candidates", www.fec.gov/finance/disclosure/ftpsum.shtml. (Retrieved August 2016.)
3 This lack of funds is also true of the Libertarian Party, despite its pro-business ideology. In 2014, the mean receipts for Democratic and Republican House candidates was $1.1 million. For Libertarian House candidates, it was $12,000. In other words, the average major party war chest was almost 100 times greater than the money available to the average Libertarian Party candidate. Like with other third parties, that $12,000 figure is exaggerated, since 20% of Libertarian candidates did not even file with the FEC, which implies that they had contributions of less than $5,000.
4 "Campaign Finance: United Kingdom". Library of Congress. www.loc.gov/law/help/campaign-finance/uk.php (accessed December 30, 2016). "Regulation of Campaign Finance and Free Advertising: Canada". Library of Congress. www.loc.gov/law/help/campaign-finance-regulation/canada.php" (accessed December 30, 2016); Campaign Finance: Australia". Library of Congress. www.loc.gov/law/help/campaign-finance/australia.php (accessed December 30, 2016).
5 Like in the related analysis in Chapter 2, third-party candidate is defined here as any candidate who was nominated by a political party and did not receive the most or second most votes in a district. For Australia, a "vote" means their first preference.
6 India was removed from this aspect of the study because the campaign spending data was not available.
7 I chose to use OLS regression instead of a Tobit analysis, despite the zero lower bound, for two reasons. First, I considered it important to measure the impact of simply not having a third-party candidate instead of assuming that there could somehow be negative third-party candidates or negative spending. Second, for this analysis, the r-squared and partial r's were helpful information in comparing the relative importance of money and electoral systems. For Tobit, the pseudo r-square is largely meaningless.
8 The election results for each district in each country were gathered from the following sources: for Canada, Parliament of Canada, "History of Federal Ridings Since 1867", www.lop.parl.gc.ca/About/Parliament/FederalRidingsHistory/hfer.asp?Language=E&Search=Gres&genElection=41&ridProvince=0&submit1=Search; for India, Election Commision of India, "Election Commission of India, General Elections, 2009 (15th Lok Sabha), 25-Constituency Wise Detailed Result", http://eci.nic.in/eci_main/archiveofge2009/Stats/VOLI/25_ConstituencyWiseDetailedResult.

168 Chapter Eight

pdf; for the UK, file "Results(XLS)" for UK Parliament general election on May 6, 2010 at The Electoral Commission, "Election data", www.electoralcommission.org.uk/our-work/our-research/electoral-data; for Australia, file "First Preferences by Candidate by Voting Type" at Australian Electoral Commission, "House of Representatives Downloads", http://results.aec.gov.au/17496/Website/HouseDownloadsMenu-17496-csv.htm. Expenditures for each candidate were calculated by adding expenditures by that candidate with expenditures by the party nationally divided by the number of constituencies in which that party ran a candidate. Expenditures were calculated as a percent spending within each district. Expenditures for each country were gathered from the following sources. Australia party expenditures: http://periodicdisclosures.aec.gov.au/SummaryParty.aspx; Australia candidate expenditures: Australian Election Commission, "Election Returns Locator Service", http://electiondisclosures.aec.gov.au/; Canada party expenditures: Elections Canada, "Registered Party Financial Transactions Return", www.elections.ca/WPAPPS/WPF/EN/PP/SelectParties?act=C2&returntype=1&period=0; Canada candidate expenditures: Elections Canada, "Candidate's Electoral Campaign Return", www.elections.ca/WPAPPS/WPF/EN/CC/SelectDistricts?act=C2&eventid=34&returntype=1&option=3; UK party expenditures: The Electoral Commission, "Political Parties' Annual Accounts", www.electoralcommission.org.uk/find-information-by-subject/political-parties-campaigning-and-donations/political-parties-annual-accounts; UK candidate expenditures: The Electoral Commission, "Candidate Spending and Donations at Elections", www.electoralcommission.org.uk/find-information-by-subject/political-parties-campaigning-and-donations/candidate-spending-and-donations-at-elections. (All data retrieved April 20, 2015.)

9 Ballotpedia. "Ballot Access for Presidential Candidates." https://ballotpedia.org/Ballot_access_for_presidential_candidates#Ross_Perot.2C_1992 (Retrieved January 21, 2017).

10 Timothy B. Lee, "How the Internet is Disrupting Politics", Vox, March 14, 2016, www.vox.com/2016/3/14/11211204/sanders-trump-disrupting-politics.

11 Thomas E. Patterson, "Pre-Primary News Coverage of the 2016 Presidential Race: Trump's Rise, Sanders' Emergence, Clinton's Struggle", Shorenstein Center on Media, Politics and Public Policy, Harvard Kennedy School, June 13, 2016, https://shorensteincenter.org/pre-primary-news-coverage-2016-trump-clinton-sanders/#_ftnref22.

12 To be clear, the issue at hand is not the rise of the internet or the invention of the World Wide Web in 1989. It is instead how politicians are learning to use this technology to circumvent traditional barriers to entry. As Stromer-Galley (2014) makes clear, the starting point of these changes was the Howard Dean primary campaign in 2004, and key advances were since made by the Obama campaigns in 2008 and 2012. What the Sanders campaign demonstrated in 2016 is that these techniques can be used by an outsider campaign as well, and they can be used to sidestep traditional gatekeepers. My argument is that it would be a small, logical step for third parties to imitate the Sanders campaign.

13 Center for Responsive Politics. "Bernie Sanders (D)". www.opensecrets.org/pres16/candidate.php?id=N00000528 (Retrieved December 29, 2016).

CONCLUSION

A Reemergence of Third Parties?

Over the past half century or more, political scientists have given a wide range of explanations as to why third parties are weaker in the United States than most democracies, even those with similar electoral systems. Ballot access laws are too difficult (Herrnson, 1997, 24–5; Winger 1997, 164; Rosenstone, Behr and Lazarus 1984, 19–21; Bibby and Maisel 2003, 70; Gillespie 2012, 25–8). The prohibition of fusion damaged third parties (Argersinger 1980; Scarrow 1986; Winger 1997, 164; Disch 2002; Gillespie 2012, 28–30). Primaries undermined third parties by internalizing opposition into the major parties (Epstein 1986, 129–32; Herrnson 1997, 25; Bibby and Maisel 2003, 62–3). Major parties simply co-opt any popular policy stands that third parties promote (Rosenstone, Behr and Lazarus 1984, 43–4; Herrnson 1997, 30; Rapoport and Stone 2008; Gillespie 2012, 18). The Electoral College creates standards that third parties cannot meet (Rosenstone, Behr and Lazarus 1984, 17; Herrnson 1997, 24; Bibby and Maisel 2003, 62; Gillespie 2012, 23–5). Some third-party scholars even argue that Americans are predisposed to support only two parties (Herrnson 1997, 22–3; Romance 1998; Bibby and Maisel 2003, 58–60). Indeed, third-party scholars have presented a long list of explanations for the decline of third parties that strongly imply that these parties cannot reemerge as significant players in American politics.

But, as I have argued before, many of the explanations for third-party decline that have gained wide circulation among political scientists and even within the public debate are not supported by empirical evidence. For example, the evidence I have shown previously, and evidence presented elsewhere (Collet and Wattenberg 1999; Stratman 2005; Burden 2007; Tamas and Hindman 2014), strongly suggests that while ballot access laws have gotten more difficult over the twentieth century, they have had little impact on the ability of third parties to get onto the ballot or attract votes. Similarly, there is little evidence that fusion was widely used in the late nineteenth century, except for the 1872 and 1896 elections,

170 Conclusion

and therefore its prohibition by most states could not have been a primary reason for the decline of third parties. Similarly, the evidence shown here and elsewhere (Hirano and Snyder 2007) suggests that the decline of third parties was largely unrelated to the introduction of primary elections for major party candidates.

The problem with this literature goes beyond the paucity of empirical testing, which has just begun to change over the past decade or so (e.g., Hirano and Snyder 2007; Schraufnagel 2011). Much of the literature on third parties violates one of the most basic tenants of scientific research, Occam's razor, or the notion that simple explanations are generally better than complicated ones. When Rosenstone, Behr, and Lazarus (1984) presented a list of over twenty reasons why American third parties are so weak, for example, they circumvented the difficult work of determining what the key factors are and what factors are more peripheral. While they never argued this explicitly, it also led to the rather safe conclusion that the status quo, weak third parties, was both inevitable and permanent. With few, mostly recent exceptions (e.g., Collet and Wattenberg 1999; Burden 2007; Hirano and Snyder 2007; Schraufnagel 2011), third-party scholars barely challenged each other's theories on why third parties declined and instead either promoted their own theories without questioning others or presented them all as if they were a single narrative.

Indeed, many of these explanations suffer from a fundamental flaw. As a group they produce sweeping statements about third-party weakness that seem to assume that these changes are largely permanent. They therefore have no explanations as to why third-party activity has been rising over the past half century as well as why voters are much more likely to vote for third-party House candidates, when there is at least one such candidate on the ballot, today than a few decades ago.

I believe that a more dynamic explanation is also more realistic. For sure, the United States is a structurally difficult political system in which to build a successful third party. One is more likely to have success in a more proportional system like Denmark or even across the border in Canada. Nonetheless, through much of the nineteenth century and during the first two decades of the twentieth century, third parties played an important, disruptive role in American politics. Around 1920, circumstances changed dramatically against third parties, and over the next few decades these parties largely disappeared. However, those circumstances were not permanent. As history continues to push forward, the factors that undermined third parties in the middle of the twentieth century are becoming less pronounced, and these parties now have a growing opportunity to climb their way back into American politics.

A Different Explanation

In this book, I have argued that there are two factors that have the greatest influence on third parties: polarization and resources. First, I argued that the most important driver of third-party activity since the Civil War has been the level of political polarization. As American politics became less polarized in the middle of the twentieth century, third parties largely disappeared across the country. As polarization levels began rising in the 1970s and especially after 1980, third parties again became more active in American politics. Second, while the vote for third-party candidates on the ballot has risen considerably over the past few decades, third parties have not been able to muster the waves of voter support more common in elections from 1870 to 1918. I argue that this is because of the type of resources parties need to run modern electoral campaigns. While parties could function more like social movements in the nineteenth and early twentieth century, electoral campaigns by the late twentieth century were waged over modern communication technology, requiring third parties to raise significant amounts of money or gain free media attention. They were not in a strong position to gain either. However, as both Bernie Sanders and Donald Trump have demonstrated during the 2016 primary elections, the internet and social media have created new ways to communicate with voters and raise funding from small donors that circumvent the near complete monopoly the Democratic and Republican Party establishments had over these resources.

This argument can be made more general by considering that American third parties focus primarily on electoral disruption and are therefore engaging in a form of contentious politics (Tilly and Tarrow 2015). They therefore have characteristics analogous to social movements (Tarrow 1998) and can be understood to need three main things to be successful.

1 The third party needs to be able to tap into *discontent* that a subset of the public has with the government and established parties. People need a reason to not vote for one of the dominant parties and instead vote for an alternative. That discontent might be because of the performance of and lack of trust with the government (Hetherington 1999), for example, or it might be because each major party presents itself ideologically in a way that leads segments of the population to feel ignored. In this way, moments of discontent, which often happen during economic downturns, are generally better times for third-party challenges than moments of economic and social tranquility.

Polarization may also be related to levels of discontent, either because voter discontent (such as because of a declining standard of living) is driving polarization or because a polarized political elite increases discontent, possibly because of the highly conflictual nature of political rhetoric or because the government becomes less capable or willing to produce policy output that benefits the mass public. When each major party is questioning the legitimacy of its opponent, for example, this makes it easier for third parties to question the legitimacy of both.

172 Conclusion

2 Third parties need to frame themselves as a clear alternative to the major parties. This *distinctiveness* is not simply about how each third party presents itself. It also has to do with the major parties. If each major party takes clear ideological positions, it becomes much easier for a smaller party to choose an alternative stand that challenges the major parties. But, if each major party has muddied positions, such as if its politicians are not ideologically consistent, then it becomes much harder for a third party to show itself as an alternative.

Elite polarization can increase this distinctiveness. When there is a lack of partisan polarization, the respective positions of each major party can be confused by their ideological overlap. Slippery distinctions can be hard to challenge, especially if they are defended by each party presenting itself as working pragmatically with their main opponents. As the parties become more polarized, they produce increased clarity that is easier for third parties to distinguish themselves from, and easier to attack. Ironically, the usual argument by third-party activists that there is not, to quote George Wallace (Yesnowitz 2008), a "dime's worth of difference" between the two parties can only work when both parties clearly hold a policy or ideological stance that a subgroup in the population finds abhorrent. Generally speaking, significant differences and negative, intense conflict between the two major parties help third parties.

3 Third parties need to be able to mobilize *resources* to compete against the major parties. The distribution of resources among parties can also vary greatly across countries as well as across time. If a nation provides significant financial support for parties that had received a small percentage of the vote during the previous election, for example, then it becomes easier for third parties to compete than if they have to raise all their funds through private donations. This also relates to how campaigns communicate with the public. If campaigning can be done in an inexpensive manner, such as through local newspapers and public rallies, then third parties have a greater opportunity to challenge the major parties. However, if campaigns advertise themselves primarily on television and radio, requiring both the ability to attract free media and pay for campaign commercials, then third parties can have a much harder time competing. One can also apply this logic to the organizations onto which these parties are built. A social-democratic party is much easier to build onto a thriving and unified workers' movement with powerful unions than a fractured workers' movement with weak unions.

These three factors, I would argue, go a long way to explaining why third parties are weaker in the United States than other countries, why third parties nearly disappeared starting around 1920, and why they have as of yet not recovered fully from that decline. These factors also lead to the conclusion that current political changes, including the unexpected election of Donald Trump, are dramatically improving the prospects for third parties.

The Decline of Third Parties

While third parties had always been weaker in the United States than most other democracies with SMP electoral systems, they nonetheless played an important role in American electoral politics since mass political parties first emerged in the 1830s. During the half century that followed the Civil War until around the First World War, repeated waves of third-party activity and support disrupted elections and sometimes pushed the major parties towards policy reform. However, beginning around 1920, third parties quickly disappeared. The last great wave of third-party support ended in 1916, and by 1946 there were very few third-party candidates running for office outside New York State. Of those few that ran for seats for the House of Representatives, most received very few votes. In the 1960 election, for example, there were third-party candidates in only 14% of House districts. In those districts, the median aggregate percent vote for third-party candidates was one-third of 1%.

What changed around the 1920s and 1930s? Most likely, progressive and pro-labor reforms by the Second World War helped create an environment that was very difficult for third parties to succeed in. The first was the reforms pushed for by the Progressive Movement, including significant policy steps to reduce corruption in government. The progressive reforms already removed many of the primary issues that were likely fueling discontent among American voters at the time. The New Deal reforms took even larger steps, including adopting policies that significantly improved the economic conditions of many Americans. These reforms, subsequently combined with the post-World War II boom of the American economy, ushered in a period of much greater economic security that lasted until at least the 1970s. In this larger sense, the progressive and pro-worker third parties of the early twentieth century had gained major portions of the policy changes they had been promoting, effectively removing reasons for the discontent that helped fuel their voter support.

At the same time, this period also ushered in a decline in political polarization among politicians within the major parties, which as McCarty, Poole, and Rosenthal (2016) demonstrate, closely matches the rise of greater income equality. This drop in polarization is key. The ideological distinctions between Democratic and Republican became fuzzier. Despite initial Republican attempts to reverse the New Deal, eventually the Keynesian framework became largely accepted by most of the political elite. The most liberal Republicans were often farther left ideologically than the most conservative Democrats, for example. This produced several important changes that hurt third parties even more. The first is that this less conflictual political environment was less apt to fuel public discontent, including because the government became more capable of addressing policy concerns that affected the public. The second is that this lower polarization also made party distinctions less clear, making it harder for third parties to challenge the major parties.

174 Conclusion

This decline of party unity opened the door and may have been a primary reason for another change that hurt third parties: the rise of candidate-centered campaigning. Especially in races for seats in the House of Representatives, candidates began running more as individuals with personal attributes each constituency might support than as proponents of their respective political parties (Salmore and Salmore 1985; Aldrich 1995). In swing districts, it was not unlikely for candidates to downplay or even hide their partisanship. This strategy created an effective approach for incumbents to increase their chances of retaining their seats, and it also helped the parties win votes even in districts where the party was otherwise less likely to gain voter support. A significant hurdle for major party challengers, this new strategy was even harder for third parties, which gain votes by distinguishing themselves from and fueling discontent against the major parties. Major party candidates could easily insulate themselves from this type of attack by distinguishing themselves from their party, focusing on local concerns, and even pretending to be "outsiders" with no connection to politics in Washington.

This problem becomes even more severe when one considers resources (Parker 2008). As the twentieth century developed, campaigns began to compete over modern communication technology, especially radio and television. While earlier campaigns could be waged with little money and function more like social movements, this approach required resources third parties have a very hard time acquiring. This included not only raising money to run campaign commercials. It also meant gaining free media access. At the time, national television news was controlled by a small number of outlets that could easily act as gatekeepers that excluded third parties from nightly news programs. Similarly, these modern campaigns required trained staff to perform tasks like surveying voters, targeting likely supporters, and designing advertisements. There was little reason for trained political professionals to help third-party candidates, not only because of the lack of money to hire them, but also because there was little reason to believe that any of these candidates could win.

The middle of the twentieth century was therefore a period not conducive for third-party challenges. Progressive reforms and then the New Deal provided most Americans a better living and reasons for optimism, and the postwar boom that stretched into the 1960s reduced further discontent related to economic well-being. The decline of partisan polarization translated into a muddy period that made challenging major parties very difficult. The nature of campaigning produced a style that was not conducive to the oppositional politics of third parties, and it required resources far out of reach for most third parties and their candidates.

However, these changes that led to the decline of third parties in the 1920s were not permanent. If in fact third parties had been undermined by changes in state election laws in the late nineteenth and early twentieth century, as many third-party scholars have argued, then there would be little possibility that these parties would be able to regain an influence in American politics without a substantial and unlikely change of those laws. However, as I have shown in Chapters 3–5, there is little evidence that the rise of ballot access laws, prohibition of fusion, or institutionalization of primary elections had a significant impact on third parties or caused their demise around 1920. Instead, the factors that had changed to the detriment of third parties are continuing to change and, in fact, beginning to parallel aspects of American politics in the early decades of the twentieth century.

A Rebirth of Third Parties

Starting in the 1970s and especially over the past decade, these three factors began to change in a direction that was more positive for third parties. First, the polarization of the political elite, which had declined dramatically in the United States by the middle of the twentieth century, began rising again in the 1970s (Poole and Rosenthal 1997). This rise continued further after the Reagan Revolution began in 1980, the Republicans swept control over Congress in 1994, and further still during the Obama administration. The intensity of partisan polarization is clearly increasing even further during the Trump presidency. As contention rose in Washington between Democrats and Republicans, so did gridlock, to the point that a Republican-controlled Senate refused to even consider a replacement to the Supreme Court by a Democratic president in 2016. That polarization was echoed in the larger public, partially because of sorting (Fiorina 2005).

A second factor, closely related to the rise of political polarization, has been the return of income inequality (McCarty, Poole and Rosenthal 2016). A primary drive behind the decline of third parties in the 1920s and 1930s was likely the decline in discontent related to increased income equality and the emergence of the American middle class. But, this economic improvement was also temporary. Starting around the 1970s, income inequality began rising again in the United States, and the standard of living for the middle class began stagnating, if not dropping. These changes may be related to an unravelling of social welfare policies as well as global changes that push economies towards inequality. If the progressive reforms and other economic changes in the middle of the twentieth century effectively helped co-opt potential supporters of third parties, then the reversal of those middle-class gains would make anti-establishment candidates like Donald Trump and Bernie Sanders more attractive and help fuel third-party challenges.

As partisan polarization has risen over the past few decades, so has third-party activity. As I showed in Chapter 7, as polarization has increased over the past few decades, so has the percent of House districts with third-party candidates, and third-party candidacies have been most likely in districts and states with politicians farthest to the extreme on these polarization scales. The vote

176 Conclusion

for third-party candidates has also risen considerably over the past few decades, when there was a third-party candidate on the ballot.

Nonetheless, the percent vote for third-party candidates has not been as high as it was a century ago, when there were repeated waves of voter support for third-party movements. Why? I argue that this is because of the changes in resources. In the late eighteenth and early nineteenth century, parties could run more like social movements; without modern communication technology and with a more fragmented and localized print media, money was a less important resource and access to at least some newspaper outlets was far easier. As the number of newspapers declined (Bagdikian 2000) and radio and television became more important to campaigning (Salmore and Salmore 1985), third parties began finding it more difficult to gain free media access at the same time that they were unable to raise the money to run commercials. Third parties were easily excluded and largely ignored unless they could be treated as novelties.

However, over the past few decades, critical advances in communication technology has been changing what resources parties and campaigns can raise and how they communicate with voters. This change started primarily with the rise of cable television and the cable news networks, which began the process of undermining this gatekeeping monopoly.

But the critical change in communication technology is the one that effectively began revolutionizing American campaign politics in 2016. Indeed, the 2016 presidential election may be a critical year for American third parties. The underlying storm of American politics has been developing since the late 1960s. The evidence of a return to highly contentious politics (and with it, insurgencies by third parties) has been mounting slowly but largely unnoticed by political scientists until recently. The nature and results of the 2016 election were a product of these changes, and these results will likely fuel third-party challenges.

2016 Election and Beyond

2016 was an important year for third-party candidates at both the presidential and House level, and it was a very good year for insurgent and outsider candidates, especially Donald Trump. For third parties, 2016 is particularly important because of its relationship to the underlying factors discussed before.

During the 2016 election, the vote for House third-party candidates spiked. As Figure C.1 shows, the median total percent vote for third-party House candidates has been rising steadily since the 1960s. From 1952 to 1960, the median total percent vote for third-party House candidates was between a third and a half of a percent. This figure then began rising in the late 1960s and then jumped to 4.5% in 1990, the House election right before Ross Perot's presidential run. Starting in 2008, this figure was consistently over 3% of the vote, and then jumped again to 4.5% in 2016. It is now at the highest level since 1914.

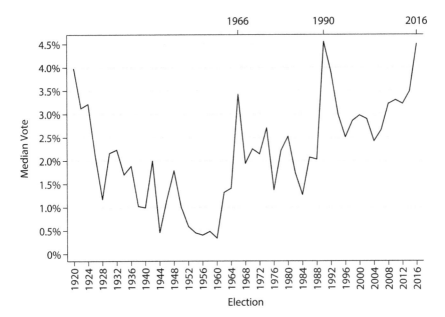

FIGURE C.1 Median percent vote for third-party House candidates, 1920–2016. The graph shows the median total percent vote for third-party candidates in each House district each election *if there was at least one third-party candidate on the ballot*. The graph demonstrates that the median vote for third-party House candidates declined steadily from 1920 to 1960 and then began rising again. That vote, which spiked during the 2016 election, has been higher over the past three elections than any equivalent period since the 1910s.

Third-party candidates also had increased success at the presidential level. Over the past half century, successful third-party and independent presidential candidates have been high profile individuals who were able to use their celebrity to attract significant attention to themselves, like billionaire Ross Perot, consumer activist Ralph Nader, and segregationist George Wallace. In 2016, the third-party candidates were largely unknown by the general public, yet received a significant increase in votes in comparison to the previous presidential election. The most successful was Libertarian presidential candidate Gary Johnson, who received around 3% of the vote nationally. This was by far the most successful presidential election for the Libertarian Party. In 2012, with Johnson as their nominee, they received 1% of the vote, and in each of the presidential elections dating back to 1972, when the party was founded, they received less than half a percent of the vote. Evan McMullin, a largely unknown, anti-Trump independent candidate, similarly received a whopping 21% of the presidential vote in Utah in 2016.

Support for third-party and independent presidential candidates was also more concentrated in the Midwest and West. As a percent of the vote, these

178 Conclusion

candidates received 25% in Utah, 12% in Idaho, 11% in New Mexico, 8% in Alaska, Colorado, Washington, and North Dakota, and 7% in Kansas, Hawaii, Minnesota, Montana, and Oregon. Of those states in which at least 6% of the vote went to third-party candidates, only Maine is east of the Mississippi River.

At the presidential level, third parties may also have been a decisive factor, both because the third-party vote had increased since the previous elections and because the vote for the two major party candidates was extremely close in critical states. In thirteen states, the vote for third-party candidates was greater than the margin of victory. Of these, only two (Arizona and Utah) had voted for Mitt Romney in 2012. Trump won both of these states in 2016. Seven other states (Colorado, Maine at-large, Michigan, Minnesota, Nevada, New Hampshire, New Mexico, and Virginia) were won by Obama and Clinton in 2012 and 2016. The remaining four states had been won by Obama in 2012 and then by Trump in 2016: Florida, Michigan, Pennsylvania, and Wisconsin. In Michigan, the third-party vote was seventeen times higher than Trump's margin of victory, and in Wisconsin it was five times higher. If Clinton had received the votes of one out of every twenty Stein or Johnson voter in Michigan and one out of every five Johnson or Stein voter in Wisconsin, she would have won these states. Indeed, Clinton could have won both these states simply by getting the votes that had gone to Stein. In Pennsylvania, the combined vote for Johnson and Stein was two and a half (2.6) times as great as Trump's margin of victory. To win this state, assuming that turnout remained the same, Clinton would have had to have gotten all the Stein votes and beat Trump 59% to 41% among Johnson supporters. This suggests that, had these third-party candidates not been on the ballot, the results could have been much closer in Pennsylvania, forcing a recount.

The critical factor for third parties in 2016, though, is not the vote gain. Instead, 2016 is important because it suggests exactly the changes that the evidence presented before leads to and because the outcome will like push those changes further. All three critical factors have shifted considerably in 2016 and will likely shift further during the highly contentious Trump presidency. The level of discontent rose dramatically during the 2016 election, to the point of violence, with protestors at Trump rallies being beaten and a riot breaking out in Portland over Trump's victory. American politics has become polarized to the level that both the sitting Democratic president and the Democratic nominee called the Republican nominee a threat to American democracy itself, and the Republican nominee threatened to have the Democratic nominee imprisoned.

While rising discontent and polarization is critical fuel for third-party movements, an even bigger boost for third-party prospects may relate to the internet and the rise of social media. The internet, of course, emerged in the 1990s, and social media began with the launching of Facebook in 2004. However, the potential of social media for oppositional and outsider candidates became clear during the 2016 presidential election. The continued fragmentation of control over news because of the internet and social media makes it easier for candidates not supported by the major parties to reach their voters. Bernie Sanders reached supporters not on major networks but across a wide range of internet news sites that posted stories about him because, as they discovered, his supporters would click on most stories with his name in the title and then circulate those stories across social media. Donald Trump, a master showman, used not only the current structure of cable programming and internet news sites but also Twitter to attract attention and circumvent gatekeepers that would have likely minimized his impact a decade ago. Besides creating a method for reaching voters that the political establishment cannot control, because of its fragmented nature, these approaches are also dramatically less expensive than running campaign commercials on major television and radio stations.

This approach is not only cheaper. It also creates the possibility of raising significantly more campaign funds. In the pre-internet age, major donors were likely the only avenue for acquiring significant amounts of campaign donations. Over the past few presidential cycles, the Democratic Party and especially the Obama campaigns have learned how to gain large numbers of small donations over the internet (Stromer-Galley 2004). What Bernie Sanders demonstrated is that a candidate who is not supported by a significant portion of the political elite can use this approach to raise significant small donor funding. During the 2016 campaign cycle, Sanders raise $228 million,[1] far more than most other candidates for the Democratic and Republican party nominations.

This change in media and fundraising also removes a critical barrier for third parties. Indeed, there has been a significant amount of information this election cycle that Millennials have become much more open to outsider candidates like Bernie Sanders and to supporting third-party candidates.[2] More significant, I think, is that this group gains its political information in a fundamentally different way than older generations. While older groups are more likely to read traditional news outlets and watch cable new programs, Millennials gain most of their information across social media. This bodes well not only for outsider primary election candidates like Bernie Sanders; it is a clear opening for third parties that did not exist even a decade ago.

The victory by Donald Trump simply increases that probability further, since his presidency will likely continue to increase the tension of a polarized political system as well as deepen divisions within his own party. There is a great deal of uncertainty of how this will all play out in the years following the 2016 election, but the current evidence suggests that the three factors most related to third-party challenge will grow larger. There is every reason to think that polarization will grow more intense, and there is little reason to believe that discontent will decline, both because of the level of polarization and the continued increase of income inequality. At the same time, the fragmentation of the news media combined with the possibility of raising funds without elite

180 Conclusion

donor support has increased the possibility of third parties to take advantage of these changing circumstances.

Politics of Disruption

A final question, then, is how these changes will play themselves out. The time that this book is being written, during the first months of the Trump administration, has a rapidly changing political situation in which there is a great deal of uncertainty. A year ago, few would have predicted Donald Trump to win the Republican nomination much less the presidential election, for example, and few would have expected democratic socialist Bernie Sanders to run a serious challenge for the Democratic nomination fueled by widespread support by young voters and financed by huge numbers of small donations. The specifics of how American politics will change are unclear, and how third parties will respond to shifting circumstances is also not clear. This produces possible outcomes that range from third parties having no impact to the American two-party system breaking up into a multiparty system.

For many scholars, the interest in third parties stems from a support of multiparty democracy. The general framework is that when there are several parties with distinctive ideological stands in government, representation improves. With too few parties, concerns of a large segment of the population can be ignored by the two major parties. With too many parties, it becomes hard in a parliament to maintain the coalition of parties needed to hold a majority of seats, and it creates a greater voice for small and often fringe parties that hold the last few seats needed to maintain that majority. From this framework, power shared across four to six parties, not two, becomes optimal since it would increase the pressure on the largest parties to consider the needs of more citizens as well as force greater compromise across parties.

However, there is little reason as of yet to predict a change this large. In order to predict how the role of third parties might change, one key step is to study the history of these parties in the United States, or more specifically, to examine periods when American politics was highly polarized, media access was easier, and third parties were thriving. Unlike most representative democracies, the United States has never had a multiparty democracy. A brief period around the Civil War aside, when it was temporarily a three-party system that included the Democrats, Whigs, and Republicans, two dominant parties have shared the vast majority of elected positions since mass parties began forming in the Jacksonian era. There have been scatterings of third-party candidates winning congressional seats or positions in state governments, and there have been a few instances of a third party dominating the politics within a single state for a few decades. While single-member district systems like the UK and Australia have tended to have two dominant parties and a group of smaller parties that also win parliamentary seats, this type of party arrangement has not as of yet developed in the United States.

Instead, American third parties have primarily played a disruptive role. The main electoral impact of third parties, when they were strong, was to undermine or at least threaten the electoral prospects of major party candidates. This dynamic has looked like repeated waves. A third party would form and run candidates across many states for a number of election cycles. Then, they would collapse. In several of these cases, notably the Populists, a major party co-opted the positions and rhetoric of the third party and sometimes even joined forces with it. The major party would begin championing the policy positions of the third party, the supporters of the third party would abandon it, and then the organization would either collapse or continue soldiering on as a shell of its previous self.

This process is very much in line with the "sting like a bee" argument presented by Rapoport and Stone (2008). By causing electoral pain for a major party, that party will be more likely to adopt the positions of the third party. This co-optation often translates into policy changes the third-party supports, but at the same time it leads third-party voters to shift their support back to the major party, which effectively causes the third party to die. In this sense, success for a third party is not necessarily measured in the number of elected positions won, and it is certainly not measured by the number of Electoral College votes won, which are at best a symbolic form of political capital. Short of creating some form of a multiparty democracy, success for a third party has been to disrupt normal politics enough to force policy changes.

Strategically, there is one problem with this approach. Major parties and their candidates will adopt virtually any rhetoric or policy stance that increases their chances of winning. They will generally try to co-opt any form of dissent in ways that cost them the least political capital. Career politicians and even incumbent presidents have capitalized on anger against career politicians by running as "Washington outsiders," for example. The same is true for career politicians who had run for reelection by claiming support for term limits. Specifically, even though the goal is usually to force policy change by major parties, the third party has to provide an attack that is not easily responded to. This can mean presenting an ideological framework, a rhetorical style, or a campaigning approach that is different enough that the established parties cannot simply integrate it.

This implies that third-party success in a system of waves of disruption followed by co-optation requires innovation. A key to third-party success is to make this co-optation difficult. In other words, this is not simply an example of a party representing a group or ideology that has been largely ignored by the political establishment. It is a form of electoral guerrilla warfare. Third parties, like insurgent candidates in primary elections, have to challenge the major parties in ways that these parties do not anticipate and, more importantly, have

182 Conclusion

a difficult time responding to. This requires movement in the content and style of rhetoric, and it also requires experimentation in raising resources, building coalitions, and reaching voters.

A question, then, is whether third parties can innovate in a way that reflects this rapidly changing political environment and opens an effective attack on the major parties. There is no clear answer to this question. To the degree that the Libertarian and Green Parties' organizations have been institutionalized and an old guard of third-party activists dominate them, they may be unable to innovate in ways that a rapidly shifting political situation dictates. It is also not clear if new, currently unknown third parties could emerge and capitalize on the current discontent as well as on the excitement and idealism of a freshly founded organization. It may be suggestive, for example, that arguably the most successful challenge to Clinton and Trump in 2016 was not third-party veterans Jill Stein or Gary Johnson but Utah's Evan McMullin, an outsider to both the major party establishment and the third-party movement.

There are also two different ways that the largest third parties after the Civil War emerged. One was by building off of other institutions or social movements. The Greenback Party was built on a coalition of farmer and labor organizations. The Populist and People's Parties were closely connected to the larger Populist movement. The Socialist Party was built off of the more radical organizations of the labor movement. Moving forward, modern third parties need to also build off of existing social structures and organizations. This could be by building the party off of existing organizations, like the Working Families Party has done, but it can also mean using social media or other rapidly developing technology to create a network that echoes many of the structures of a social movement. Indeed, the intensity of Bernie Sanders's supporters and their use of social media to promote their candidate suggests the power of this approach.

The other way third parties emerged after the Civil War was through a major party splitting. In both of these cases, the Republican Party split, and in both cases the Republicans were the governing party. In 1872, the Liberal Republican Party formed in opposition to the reelection bid by Republican president Ulysses Grant. In the end, the Liberal Republicans ran many fusion candidates with the Democratic Party, lost the election, and then collapsed. In 1912, the progressive wing of the Republican Party, led by Teddy Roosevelt, formed the Progressive Party in opposition to President Taft. The Progressives lasted only a few elections, but with the help of other third parties, especially the Socialists, they temporarily undermined Republican domination of American politics and helped usher in critical progressive reforms.

This second type of third party is interesting now, again, because of the uncertainty of coming politics in the Trump era. Donald Trump was actively opposed by large segments of the Republican Party leadership, with rumors that most of the living former presidential nominees and presidents voted against him. More than a few prominent Republican politicians and major donors announced that he would be an unacceptable president, and Trump responded with similar vitriol, often attacking the Republican leadership and even making one of his top advisors Steve Bannon, a leader of a group accused of neo-Nazi ties that openly reject the conservatism of the Republican leadership. While party splitting would have been considered an unheard-of notion a few years ago, within the current political environment, it is unclear how stable the Republican Party is.

Indeed, there had long been signs that severe party divisions as well as third-party activity are currently more likely among conservatives than liberals. As McCarty and his coauthors (McCarty, Poole and Rosenthal 2016) have demonstrated, polarization over the past few decades has been asymmetrical: Republican politicians have moved farther to the right than Democrats have moved to the left. Republicans have also shown greater internal turmoil. There have been repeated calls for the ouster of House Speaker Paul Ryan by the most conservative House Republicans because he had at times compromised with President Obama, and the same group had attacked the previous speaker, John Boehner, for similar reasons. Moreover, as a number of third-party scholars have pointed out, since the 1960s the most important third parties have tended to be on the ideological right, not left. The strongest third party today, for example, is the Libertarians, not the Greens.

Ultimately, then, there are a range of possible changes related to third parties in the upcoming years. The most likely outcome, I argue, is that third parties will develop an increased role in American politics, with the primary effect being not a multiparty or even a "two and a half" party system but a return to a two party system with waves of challenges and electoral disruptions. This is also a rapidly changing environment in which the existing leadership within the main third parties, the Libertarians and Greens, may not be able to remain in power, or in which new third parties run by more innovative groups may usurp the positions of these older third parties.

Finally, I would argue that third-party scholars need to move past the traditional view of third parties that has dominated this area of research since the middle of the twentieth century. The evidence presented here and elsewhere strongly suggests that changes in state election laws did not destroy third parties. It is also hard to explain the various shifts in third-party support over the past century and a half with a theory that American political culture promotes only two parties, and there is no evidence or even a convincing argument behind the notion that the Electoral College undermines third parties. A better answer, I argue, is that third parties nearly disappeared in the middle of the twentieth century because of rising standards of living and progressive reforms, because the major parties became much less polarized and therefore difficult to challenge, and because the changes in mass media and other factors altered campaigning in ways that required third parties to gain resources far out of their reach. These

184 Conclusion

factors, I argue further, were not permanent. While there is no way to predict with any certainty how the American party system will change in the coming years, this environment has improved considerably for third parties. In this regard, it is important to remember that across democracies, including those with SMP, party systems evolve. The UK is no longer a two-party system. The INC no longer dominates Indian politics and is currently the second strongest party. In 2011, the New Democratic Party temporarily went from a smaller party to the second strongest party in Canada, winning far more seats than the Liberals. While the Republicans and Democrats will likely remain the strongest parties in American politics under any circumstances, third parties are likely to begin again playing an important, disruptive role in American politics.

Notes

1 Federal Election Commission, "2016 Presidential Campaign Finance", www.fec.gov/disclosurep/pnational.do. Downloaded November 15, 2016.
2 The Center for Information & Research on Civic Learning and Engagement, Tufts University, "An Estimated 24 Million Young People Voted in 2016 Election", http://civicyouth.org/an-estimated-24-million-young-people-vote-in-2016-election", Downloaded November 19, 2016.

BIBLIOGRAPHY

Abramowitz, Alan. 2009. *The Disappearing Center: Engaged Citizens, Polarization, and American Democracy.* New Haven: Yale University Press.

Abramowitz, Alan I., and Kyle L. Saunders. 1998. "Ideological Realignment in the U.S. Electorate." *Journal of Politics* 60(3): 634–52.

———. 2008. "Is Polarization a Myth?" *Journal of Politics* 70(2): 542–55.

Aldrich, John H. 1995. *Why Parties? The Origin and Transformation of Political Parties in America.* Chicago: Chicago University Press.

Alilunas, Leo. 1940. "The Rise of the 'White Primary' Movement as a Means of Barring the Negro from The Polls." *The Journal of Negro History* 25(2): 161–72.

Andersen, Lisa M. F. 2013. *The Politics of Prohibition: American Governance and the Prohibition Party, 1869–1933.* Cambridge: Cambridge University Press.

Anderson, Christopher William, Leonard Downie, and Michael Schudson. 2016. *The News Media: What Everyone Needs to Know.* New York: Oxford University Press.

Arbour, Brian. 2014. *Candidate-Centered Campaigns: Political Messages, Winning Personalities, and Personal Appeals.* New York: Palgrave Macmillan.

Argersinger, Peter H. 1980. "'A Place on the Ballot': Fusion Politics and Antifusion Laws." *The American Historical Review* 85(2): 287–306.

Bagdikian, Ben H. 2000. *The Media Monopoly.* Vol. 6. Boston: Beacon Press.

Baldassarri, Delia, and Andrew Gelman. 2008. "Partisans without Constraint: Political Polarization and Trends in American Public Opinion." *American Journal of Sociology* 114(2): 408–46.

Baldasty, Gerald J. 1992. *The Commercialization of News in the Nineteenth Century.* Madison: University of Wisconsin Press.

Benoit, Kenneth. 2006. "Duverger's Law and the Study of Electoral Systems." *French Politics* 4: 69–83.

Bibby, John F., and L. Sandy Maisel. 2003. *Two Parties-Or More? The American Party System.* 2nd ed. New York: Westview Press.

Boatright, Robert G. 2014. *Congressional Primary Elections.* New York: Routledge.

Burden, Barry. 2007. "Ballot Regulations and Multiparty Politics in the States." *PS: Political Science and Politics* 40(4): 669–73.

186 Bibliography

Burnham, Walter Dean. 1981. "The System of 1896: An Analysis." In *The Evolution of American Electoral Systems*, edited by Paul Kleppner, Walter Dean Burnham, Ronald P. Formisand, Samuel P. Hays, Richard Jensen and William G. Shade, 147–202. Westport: Greenwood Press.

Campbell, Andrea Louise. 2007. "Parties, Electoral Participation, and Shifting Voting Blocs." In *The Transformation of American Politics: Activist Government and the Rise of Conservatism*, edited by Paul Pierson and Theda Skocpol, 68–102. Princeton: Princeton University Press.

Carey, John M. 2007. "Competing Principals, Political Institutions, and Party Unity in Legislative Voting." *American Journal of Political Science* 51(1): 92–107.

Carson, Jamie L., and Jason M. Roberts. 2005. "Strategic Politicians and U.S. House Elections, 1874–1914." *Journal of Politics* 67(2): 474–96.

Clarke, Peter, and Susan H. Evans. 1983. *Covering Campaigns: Journalism in Congressional Elections*. Stanford: Stanford University Press.

Cofsky, Kevin. 1996. "Pruning the Political Thicket: The Case for Strict Scrutiny of State Ballot Access Laws." *University of Pennsylvania Law Review* 145: 353–421.

Collet, Christian, and Martin P. Wattenberg. 1999. "Strategically Unambitious: Minor Party and Independent Candidates in the 1996 Congressional Elections." In *The State of the Parties: The Changing Role of Contemporary American Parties*, edited by Daniel Shea and John C. Green, 229–48. Lanham: Rowman and Littlefield.

Cox, Gary W. 1997. *Making Votes Count: Strategic Coordination in the World's Electoral Systems*. Cambridge: Cambridge University Press.

Daybell, Donald E. 2000. "Guarding the Treehouse: Are States 'Qualified' to Restrict Ballot Access in Federal Elections?" *Boston University Law Review* 80: 289–339.

Disch, Lisa Jane. 2002. *The Tyranny of the Two-Party System*. New York: Columbia University Press.

Dowling, Conor M., and Steve B. Lem. 2009. "Explaining Major and Third Party Candidate Entry in U. S. Gubernatorial Elections, 1980–2005." *State Politics & Policy Quarterly* 9(1): 1–23.

Downs, Anthony. 1957. *An Economic Theory of Democracy*. New York: Harper.

Dubin, Michael J. 1998. *United States Congressional Elections, 1788–1997*. Jefferson: McFarland.

Duverger, Maurice. 1954. *Political Parties: Their Organization and Activity in the Modern State*. Translated by Barbara and Robert North. New York: John Wiley & Sons.

Epstein, Edward Jay. 1972. *News From Nowhere: Television and the News*. New York: Random House.

Epstein, Leon D. 1967. *Political Parties in Western Democracies*. New York: Praeger.

———. 1986. *Political Parties in the American Mold*. Madison: University of Wisconsin.

Evans, Eldon Cobb. 1917. *A History of the Australian Ballot System in the U.S.* Chicago: University of Chicago Press.

Evseev, Dmitri. 2005. "A Second Look at Third Parties: Correcting the Supreme Court's Understanding of Elections." *Boston University Law Review* 85: 1277–1331.

Farrell, David M. 2011. *Electoral Systems: A Comparative Introduction*. 2nd ed. London: Palgrave Macmillan.

Farrell, David M., and Ian McAllister. 2006. *The Australian Electoral System: Origins, Variations, and Consequences*. Sydney: University of New South Wales Press.

Fetner, Tina, and Brayden G. King. 2014. "Three-Layer Movements, Resources, and the Tea Party's Rapid Mobilization." In *Understanding the Tea Party Movement*, edited by Nella Van Dyke and David S. Meyer, 35–54. New York: Routledge.

Figueiredo, Argelina Cheibub, and Fernando Limongi. 2000. "Presidential Power, Legislative Organization, and Party Behavior in Brazil." *Comparative Politics* 32(1): 151–70.

Fiorina, Morris P. 1981. *Retrospective Voting in American National Elections.* New Haven: Yale University Press.

———. 2005. *Culture War? The Myth of a Polarized America.* New York: Pearson Longman.

Fiorina, Morris P., and Samuel J. Abrams. 2009. *Disconnect: The Breakdown of Representation in American Politics.* Norman: University of Oklahoma Press.

Formisano, Ronald P. 2012. *The Tea Party: A Brief History.* Baltimore: Johns Hopkins University Press.

Freedom House. 2014. *Freedom in the World 2014.* Washington: Freedom House.

Gallagher, Michael. 2005. "Conclusion." In *The Politics of Electoral Systems,* edited by Michael Gallagher and Paul Mitchell, 535–78. Oxford: Oxford University Press.

Gallagher, Michael, and Paul Mitchell. 2005. "Introduction to Electoral Systems." In *The Politics of Electoral Systems,* edited by Michael Gallagher and Paul Mitchell, 3–23. Oxford: Oxford University Press.

Gerston, Larry N., and Terry Christensen. 2015. *Recall!: California's Political Earthquake.* New York: Routledge.

Gillespie, J. David. 1993. *Politics at the Periphery: Third Parties in Two-Party America.* Columbia: University of South Carolina Press.

———. 2012. *Challenges to Duopoly: Why Third Parties Matter in American Two-Party Politics.* Columbia: University of South Carolina.

Graber, Doris A. 1983. *Mass Media in American Politics.* Washington: Congressional Quarterly Press.

Grumm, John G. 1958. "Theories of Electoral Systems." *Midwest Journal of Political Science* 2(4): 357–76.

Hall, Oliver. 2005–2006. "Death by a Thousand Signatures: The Rise of Restrictive Ballot Access Laws and the Decline of Electoral Competition in the United States." *Seattle University Law Review* 29: 407–48.

Haynes, John Earl. 1984. *Dubious Alliance: the Making of Minnesota's DFL Party.* Minneapolis: University of Minnesota Press.

Hein, Clarence J. 1957. "The Adoption of Minnesota's Direct Primary Law." *Minnesota History*: 341–51.

Herrnson, Paul S. 1997. "Two-Party Dominance and Minor Party Forays in American Politics." In *Multiparty Politics in America: People, Passions, and Power,* edited by Paul S. Herrnson and John C. Green, 21–41. Lanham: Rowman & Littlefield.

Hetherington, Marc J. 1999. "The Effect of Political Trust on the Presidential Vote, 1968–96." *American Political Science Review* 93(2): 311–26.

———. 2001. "Resurgent Mass Partisanship: The Role of Elite Polarization." *American Political Science Review* 95(3): 619–31.

———. 2009. "Putting Polarization in Perspective." *British Journal of Political Science* 39(2): 413–48.

Hetherington, Marc J., and Jonathan Weiler. 2009. *Authoritarianism and Polarization in American Politics.* New York: Cambridge University Press.

Hild, Matthew. 2007. *Greenbackers, Knights of Labor, and Populists: Farmer-Labor Insurgency in the Late-Nineteenth-Century South.* Athens: University of Georgia Press.

Hinckley, Barbara. 1980. "The American Voter in Congressional Elections." *American Political Science Review* 74(3): 641–50.

188 Bibliography

Hirano, Shigeo, and James M. Snyder. 2007. "The Decline of Third-Party Voting in the United States." *Journal of Politics* 69(1): 1–16.

———. 2011. "The Direct Primary and Candidate-Centered Voting in U.S. Elections." July. Accessed January 20, 2017. http://scholar.harvard.edu/files/jsnyder/files/directprimariescandidatectr.votinguselect._0.pdf.

Hofstadter, Richard. 1955. *The Age of Reform: From Bryan to F.D.R.* New York: Vintage Books.

Holcombe, Arthur. 1924. *The Political Parties of Today.* New York: Harper.

Jacobson, Gary C. 2005. "Polarized Politics and the 2004 Congressional and Presidential Election." *Political Science Quarterly* 120(2): 199–218.

Jacobson, Gary C., and Jamie L. Carson. 2016. *The Politics of Congressional Elections.* Lanham: Rowman and Littlefield.

Jacobson, Gary C., and Samuel Kernell. 1981. *Strategy and Choice in Congressional Elections.* New Haven: Yale University Press.

Janda, Kenneth. 1980. *Political Parties: A Cross-National Survey.* New York: The Free Press.

Katz, Richard. 2005. "Why are There so Many (or so Few) Electoral Reforms?" In *The Politics of Electoral Systems*, edited by Michael Gallagher and Paul Mitchell, 57–77. Oxford: Oxford University Press.

Key, V. O., Jr. 1949. *Southern Politics in State and Nation.* New York: A.A. Knopf.

———. 1956. *American State Politics: An Introduction.* New York: Knopf.

———. 1964. *Politics, Parties, & Pressure Groups.* New York: Crowell.

Klinghard, Daniel. 2010. *The Nationalization of American Political Parties, 1880–1896.* New York: Cambridge University Press.

Kousser, J. Morgan. 1974. *The Shaping of Southern Politics: Suffrage Restriction and the Establishment of the One-Party South, 1880–1910.* New Haven: Yale University Press.

Küng, Lucy-Shankleman. 2000. *Inside the BBC and CNN: Managing Media Organisations.* New York: Routledge.

Laakso, Markku, and Rein Taagepera. 1979. "'Effective' Number of Parties: A Measure with Application to West Europe." *Comparative Political Studies* 12(1): 3–27.

Lappe, Frances Moore. 2006. *Democracy's Edge: Choosing to Save Our Country by Bringing Democracy to Life.* San Francisco: John Wiley & Sons.

———. 1948. "Legal Obstacles to Minority Party Success." *Yale Law Journal* 57: 1276–91.

Levitsky, Steven, and Lucan A. Way. 2010. *Competitive Authoritarianism: Hybrid Regimes after the Cold War.* New York: Cambridge University Press.

Libby, Ronald. T. 2014. *Purging the Republican Party: Tea Party Campaigns and Elections.* Lanham: Lexington Books.

Lijphart, Arend, and Don Aitkin. 1994. *Electoral Systems and Party Systems: A Study of Twenty-Seven Democracies, 1945–1990.* Oxford: Oxford University Press.

Ludington, Arthur Crosby. 1911. *American Ballot Laws, 1888–1910.* Albany: University of the State of New York.

Mann, Thomas E., and Raymond E. Wolfinger. 1980. "Candidates and Parties in Congressional Elections." *American Political Science Review* 74(3): 617–32.

Martin, Andrew D., and Kevin M. Quinn. 2002. "Dynamic Ideal Point Estimation via Markov Chain Monte Carlo for the U.S. Supreme Court, 1953–1999." *Political Analysis* 10(2): 134–53.

Mayhew, David R. 1974. "Congressional Elections: The Case of the Vanishing Marginals." *Polity* 6(3): 295–317.

McCarty, Nolan, Keith T. Poole, and Howard Rosenthal. 2016. *Polarized America: The Dance of Ideology and Unequal Riches*. 2nd ed. Cambridge: MIT.

Merriam, C. Edward. 1909. *Primary Elections: A Study of the History and Tendencies of Primary Election Legislation*. Chicago: University of Chicago.

Mindich, David T. Z. 1998. *Just the Facts: How "Objectivity" Came to Define American Journalism*. New York: New York University Press.

Nikolenyi, Csaba. 2010. "Party Inflation in India: Why Has a Multiparty Format Prevailed in the National Party System?" In *Duverger's Law of Plurality Voting: The Logic of Party Competition in Canada, India, the United Kingdom and the United States*, edited by Bernard Grofman, Andre Blais and Shaun Bowler, 97–114. New York: Springer.

Parker, David C. W. 2008. *The Power of Money in Congressional Campaigns, 1880–2006*. Norman: University of Oklahoma Press.

Perman, Michael. 2001. *Struggle for Mastery: Disfranchisement in the South, 1888–1908*. Chapel Hill: University of North Carolina Press.

Pomper, Gerald M. 1992. *Passions and Interests: Political Party Concepts of American Democracy*. Lawrence: University Press of Kansas.

Poole, Keith T., and Howard Rosenthal. 1997. *Congress: A Political-Economic History of Roll Call Voting*. Oxford: Oxford University Press.

Putnam, Robert D. 1993. *Making Democracy Work: Civic Traditions in Modern Italy*. Princeton: Princeton University Press.

Rae, Douglas. 1967. *The Political Consequences of Electoral Laws*. New Haven: Yale University Press.

Ranney, Austin. 1975. *Curing the Mischiefs of Faction: Party Reform in America*. Berkeley: University of California Press.

Rapoport, Ronald B., and Walter J. Stone. 2008. *Three's a Crowd: The Dynamic of Third Parties, Ross Perot, & Republican Resurgence*. Ann Arbor: University of Michigan Press.

Ricci, David M. 1984. *The Tragedy of Political Science: Politics, Scholarship and Democracy*. New Haven: Yale University Press.

Riker, William H. 1976. "The Number of Political Parties: A Reexamination of Duverger's Law." *Comparative Politics* 9(1): 93–106.

———. 1982. "The Two-Party System and Duverger's Law: An Essay on the History of Political Science." *American Political Science Review* 76(4): 753–66.

Romance, Joseph. 1998. "Gridlock and Reform at the Close of the Twentieth Century." In *A Republic of Parties? Debating the Two-Party System*, edited by Theodore J. Lowi and Joseph Romance, 31–74. Lanham: Rowman & Littlefield.

Rosenstone, Steven J., Roy L. Behr, and Edward H Lazarus. 1984. *Third Parties in America: Citizen Response to Major Party Failure*. Princeton: Princeton University Press.

Salmore, Stephen A., and Barbara G. Salmore. 1985. *Candidates, Parties, and Campaigns: Electoral Politics in America*. Washington: CQ Press.

Scarrow, Howard A. 1986. "Duverger's Law, Fusion, and the Decline of American "Third" Parties." *The Western Political Quarterly* 39(4): 634–47.

Schattschneider, E. E. 1942. *Party Government*. New York: Holt, Rinehart, and Winston.

Schraufnagel, Scot. 2011. *Third Party Blues: The Truth and Consequences of Two-Party Dominance*. New York: Routledge.

Schraufnagel, Scot, and Kerri Milita. 2010. "Testing the Effects of Ballot Access Reform on Non-Major Party Electoral Fortunes: The Case of Florida's Revision 11." *American Review of Politics* 31: 25–39.

Schwartz, Mildred A. 2006. *Party Movements in the United States and Canada: Strategies of Persistence*. Lanham: Rowman & Littlefield.

190 Bibliography

Skocpol, Theda, and Vanessa Williamson. 2012. *The Tea Party and the Remaking of Republican Conservatism.* New York: Oxford.

Smith, Bradley A. 1999. "Judicial Protection of Ballot-Access Rights: Third-Parties Need Not Apply." *Harvard Journal on Legislation* 28: 167–217.

Stratmann, Thomas. 2005. "Ballot Access Restrictions and Candidate Entry in Elections." *European Journal of Political Economy* 21(1): 59–71.

Stromer-Galley, Jennifer. 2004. *Presidential Campaigning in the Internet Age.* Oxford: Oxford University Press.

Stuart, Guy. 2004. "Databases, Felons, and Voting: Bias and Partisanship of the Florida Felons List in the 2000 Elections." *Political Science Quarterly* 119(3): 453–75.

Summers, Mark W. 2004. *Party Games: Getting, Keeping, and Using Power in Gilded Age Politics.* Chapel Hill: University of North Carolina Press.

Sundquist, James L. 1983. *Dynamics of the Party System: Alignment and Realignment of Political Parties in the United States.* Revised. Washington: Brookings Institute.

Taagepera, Rein. 2001. "Party Size Baselines Imposed by Institutional Constraints: Theory for Simple Electoral Systems." *Journal of Theoretical Politics* 13(4): 331–45.

Taagepera, Rein, and Matthew Soberg Shugart. 1989. *Seats and Votes: The Effects and Determinants of Electoral Systems.* New Haven: Yale University Press.

Tamas, Bernard. 2006. "A Divided Political Elite: Why Congress Banned Multimember Districts in 1842." *New Political Science* 28: 23–44.

Tamas, Bernard, and Matthew Dean Hindman. 2014. "Ballot Access Laws and the Decline of American Third-Parties." *Election Law Journal* 13(2): 260–76.

Tarrow, Sidney. 1998. *Power in Movement: Social Movements and Contentious Politics.* 2nd ed. Cambridge: Cambridge University Press.

Tilly, Charles, and Sidney G. Tarrow. 2015. *Contentious Politics.* 2nd ed. Oxford: Oxford University Press.

Tufte, Edward R. 1975. "Determinants of the Outcomes of Midterm Congressional Elections." *American Political Science Review* 69(3): 812–26.

Van Kessel, Stijn. 2015. *Populist Parties in Europe: Agents of Discontent?* Houndmills, Basingstoke, Hampshire: Palgrave Macmillan.

Walton, Hanes, Sherman C. Puckett, and Donald Richard Deskins. 2012. *African American Electorate: A Statistical History.* Thousand Oaks: CQ Press.

Wand, Jonathan N., Kenneth W. Shotts, Jasjeet S. Sekhon, Walter R. Mebane, Michael C. Herron, and Henry E. Brady. 2001. "The Butterfly Did It: The Aberrant Vote for Buchanan in Palm Beach County, Florida." *American Political Science Review* 95(4): 793–810.

Ware, Alan. 2002. *The American Direct Primary: Party Institutionalization and Transformation in the North.* Cambridge: Cambridge University.

Wattenberg, Martin P. 1991. *The Rise of Candidate-Centered Politics: Presidential Elections of the 1980s.* Cambridge: Harvard University Press.

Williams, Michelle Hale. 2006. *The Impact of Radical Right-Wing Parties in West European Democracies.* New York: Palgrave Macmillan.

Winger, Richard. 1997. "Ballot Format: Must Candidates Be Treated Equally?" *Cleveland State Law Review* 45: 87–100.

———. 1997. "Institutional Obstacles to a Multiparty System." In *Multiparty Politics in America: People, Passions, and Power,* edited by Paul S. Herrnson and John C. Green, 159–71. Lanham: Rowman & Littlefield.

———. 2000. "History of U.S. Ballot Access Law for New and Minor Parties." In *The Encyclopedia of Third Parties in America*, edited by Immanuel Ness and James Ciment, 72–95. Armonk: Sharpe Reference.

———. 2004. "An Analysis of the 2004 Nader Ballot Access: Federal Court Cases." *Fordham Urban Law Journal* 32(3): 101–20.

Yesnowitz, Joshua C. 2008. "American Independent Party." In *Encyclopedia of U.S. Campaigns, Elections, and Electoral Behavior*, edited by Kenneth F. Warren, 30. Los Angeles: Sage.

INDEX

Abramowitz, Alan 132–35
American political culture 21–22, 28–30
Apportionment Act of 1842 40
Argersinger, Peter 78, 83–84
Australia: party resources 159–62; preferential voting and third parties 27, 37, 51–55
Australian ballot 19, 26, 59–60, 78

Ballot access laws 18–19, 26, 57–74; candidates getting onto House ballot 67–69, 71–73; changes in difficulty 62–67; definition 59–60; impact on the vote 73–74; signature and previous vote requirements 60–62
Bharatiya Janata Party (BJP) 45, 47, 49–50
Bibby, John: news media 154; primary elections explanation 98; sore loser laws 20
Bryan, William Jennings 20, 81, 85, 114, 121

California: ballot access laws 62; fusion 79–81, 83–84; recall election of 2003 60
Campaign finance laws 159–60
Canada: strategic voter explanation in Duverger's Law 51–55; third-party resources 159–62; two-party strength since 1945 46–49
Candidate-centered campaigning 148–51, 163
CNN 164
Co-optation 20, 114–27; New Deal explanation 120–26; overview 115–27; sting like a bee explanation 116–20

Democratic-Farmer-Labor Party, see Farmer-Labor Party
Disch, Lisa 77
Disruption, politics of 180–84
Duverger's Law 17, 27, 34–55; comparing third parties in SMP and PR systems 43–44; comparing third parties across SMP systems 46–50; the strategic voter explanation 50–55; mechanical explanation 44–46; and party resources 31–32, 157–63; synopsis 36–39
DW-NOMINATE 131–32, 137–43

Effective number of parties, measurement of 41–43
Election of 1896 *see* Populist Party
Election of 1912 *see* Progressive Party and Socialist Party
Election of 2016 176–80
Electoral College 18, 30
Electoral systems *see* Duverger's Law
Epstein, Leon: candidate-centered campaigns 150; primary elections 98–99

Farmer-Labor Party 79, 109–10, 122, 125, 128n4
Fiorina, Morris 132–33
Florida 2000 election 34–5
Fusion 19, 76–94; attempts to prohibit 82–84; change in use 84–87; definition 19, 77; elections of 1872 and 1896 85, 87; impact 87–92; and third-party decline 77–79; types of fusion 79–82; *see also* major party fusion, mixed party fusion, and third-party fusion

194 Index

Gillespie, J. David: de-legitimization 22; Electoral College 18; labor movement 21–22, 29–30

Greeley, Horace see Liberal Republican Party

Green Party 12n5, 34–35, 182–83; see also Nader, Ralph and Stein, Jill

Greenback Party 12n5, 78, 108–09, 182

Hetherington, Marc 132–33

Hirano, Shigeo see New Deal co-optation of third parties

Idaho ballot access requirements 60

Illinois ballot access requirements 61

Income inequality 134, 136, 173, 175

Independent candidates 4, 12n4

India 46–50, 53–55

Indian National Congress (INC) 47, 49–50

Internet and social media 163–67

Johnson, Gary 177–78

Key, V.O. 99–102, 113n1

Liberal Democratic Party 47–48, 162–63

Liberal Republican Party 81, 85, 87, 93–94, 182

Libertarian Party 12n5, 15, 127n2, 167n3, 177, 182–83; see also Johnson, Gary

Ludington, Author 82–84

Maisel, L. Sandy: news media 154; primary elections explanation 98; sore loser laws 20

Major party fusion 79–81

McCarty, Nolan see income inequality

McMullin, Evan 177, 182

Merriam, Charles: Behavioral Revolution and third-party research 24; primary elections 101–02

Minnesota: ballot access laws 64, 68; primary elections 108–11; see also Farmer-Labor Party

Mississippi ballot access requirements 75n10

Mixed party fusion 81–82

Nader, Ralph 34–5

New Deal, co-optation of third parties 120–26

New York 5; ballot access laws 62, 64, 68, 75n12; fusion 77–78, 85–87, 93

News media 22–23, 154–57

Nixon, Richard 80

Partisan polarization 31, 129–45, 173, 175–76; affects third parties 134–36; impact on third-party activity 137–41; impact on third-party support 141–43; overview 131–34

Pennsylvania: ballot access laws 68; fusion 84

People's Party see Populist Party

Perot, Ross 164, 176–77; see also Reform Party

Polarization see partisan polarization

Political resources 22, 146–67, 174; cyclical nature 147; campaign costs 148; campaign funding 152–54; and Duverger's Law 157–63; see also candidate-centered campaigning, internet and social media, news media, and the strategic politician thesis

Poole, Keith see DW-NOMINATE; see also income inequality

Populist Party 12n5; and cooptation 20, 114, 121; fusion 81, 85, 87–88; in Minnesota and Wisconsin 109–10

Presidential debates 23, 30–31

Previous vote requirements see ballot access laws

Primary elections 19–20, 95–113; explanation 97; impact on third parties 102–08; Minnesota and Wisconsin 108–11; see also Key, V.O.

Progressive Party 12n5, 103–04, 122–24, 143, 182

Progressive Party of Wisconsin 110, 122

Prohibition Party 12n5, 108, 110, 117

Rapoport, Ronald, see sting like a bee explanation

Reform Party 15, 115, 118–19, 127, 127n2

Riker, William: history of Duverger's Law 39; strategic voter thesis and Duverger's Law 49–50

Rosenstone, Stephen: American political culture 21; definition of third-party candidate 12n4; Duverger's Law 17; political resources 22–23

Rosenthal, Howard see DW-NOMINATE; see also income inequality

Sanders, Bernie 3, 9, 11–12, 171, 175; use of social media 165–66, 179

Scarrow, Howard 78, 83

Index

Scottish National Party (SNP) 45, 47
Secret ballot *see* Australian ballot
Signature requirements *see* ballot access laws
Snyder, James see New Deal co-optation of third parties
Social media *see* internet and social media
Socialist Party 79, 12n5, 109–10, 122–24
Sore loser laws 20
South Carolina ballot access laws 61–62
Stein, Jill 178
Sting like a bee explanation 116–20
Stone, Walter, see Sting like a bee explanation
Strategic politician thesis 151–54, 160

Tea Party 95–97, 111–13
Third party, definition 12n4
Third-party fusion 79, 81

Third-party vote, measurement 12n3; comparative 41–43; comparative at district level 51
Trump, Donald 3, 9, 16, 171, 175, 178–79, 182–83

UK: disproportionality of elections 45–46; strategic voter explanation in Duverger's Law 51–53; third-party resources 159–62; two-party strength since 1945 46–49

Ware, Alan 100–02
Winger, Richard 58
Wisconsin: ballot access laws 68; primary elections 108–11
Working Families Party (WFP) 76–78, 82, 93

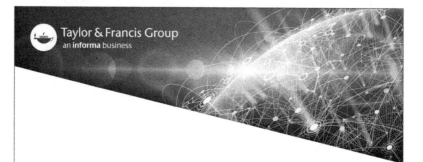

CPSIA information can be obtained
at www.ICGtesting.com
Printed in the USA
BVHW041457101118
532581BV00007B/69/P